Justice and Care

JUSTICE AND CARE

Essential Readings in Feminist Ethics

edited by

Virginia Held

*Hunter College and the Graduate School
of the City University of New York*

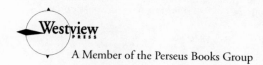

Westview
PRESS

A Member of the Perseus Books Group

Copyright © 1995 by Westview Press, A Member of the Perseus Books Group

Published in 1995 in the United States of America by Westview Press, Inc., 5500 Central Avenue, Boulder, Colorado 80301-2877, and in the United Kingdom by Westview Press, 12 Hid's Copse Road, Cumnor Hill, Oxford OX2 9JJ

Library of Congress Cataloging-in-Publication Data
Justice and care : essential readings in feminist ethics / edited by Virginia Held.
   p. cm.
  Includes bibliographical references.
  ISBN 0-8133-2161-1. — ISBN 0-8133-2162-X (pbk.)
  1. Feminist ethics. 2. Caring. 3. Justice. I. Held, Virginia.
BJ1395.J87 1995
170'.82—dc20

95-2901
CIP

The paper used in this publication meets the requirements of the American National Standard for Permanence of Paper for Printed Library Materials Z39.48-1984.

PERSEUS
POD
ON DEMAND

10   9   8   7   6   5

For my daughter Julia, whose motherly caring and dispensing of justice inspire me, and for my son Philip, who turns ordinary events into occasions of joy and laughter. For their spouses also, who show how marriages can work, and for my grandchildren. Finally, for Robert, who delights his varied audiences and with whom I share the years.

Contents

PART 5   NEW INTEGRATIONS

Credits

Chapter 1   Reprinted with deletions of text and notes from Nel
             Noddings, *Caring: A Feminine Approach to Ethics and
             Moral Education*. Copyright © 1984 by The Regents of the
             University of California.

Chapter 2   Reprinted from Carol Gilligan, "Moral Orientation and
             Moral Development," in*Women and Moral Theory*, edited
             by Eva Feder Kittay and Diana T. Meyers. Copyright © 1987
             by Rowman and Littlefield.

Chapter 3   Reprinted from Annette C. Baier, "The Need for More than
             Justice," in *Science, Morality and Feminist Theory*, edited by
             Marsha Hanen and Kai Nielsen. Copyright © 1987 by the
             University of Calgary Press.

Chapter 4   Reprinted from Marilyn Friedman, "Beyond Caring: The
             De-Moralization of Gender, " in *Science, Morality and
             Feminist Theory*, edited by Marsha Hanen and Kai Nielsen.
             Copyright © 1987 by the University of Calgary Press.

Chapter 5   Reprinted with deletions of the text and notes from
             Claudia Card, "Gender and Moral Luck," in *Identity,
             Character, and Morality: Essays in Moral Psychology*, edited
             by Owen Flanagan and Amélie Oksenberg Rorty.
             Copyright© 1990 by Massachusetts Institute of Technology.

Chapter 6   Reprinted from Joan C. Tronto, "Women and Caring: What
             Can Feminists Learn About Morality from Caring?" in
             Gender/Body/Knowledge, Alison M. Jaggar and Susan
             R. Bordo, eds., copyright © 1989 by Rutgers, the State
             University. Reprinted by permission of Rutgers University
             Press.

Chapter 7   Reprinted with deletions of text and notes from *Black
             Feminist Thought: Knowledge, Consciousness, and*

Chapter 8

Chapter 9

Chapter 10

Introduction

The topics of justice and care have been at the center of what can now be thought of as feminist ethics. Beginning with strong critiques of the nearly exclusive focus on justice, abstract rationality, rights, and individual autonomy in the dominant moral outlooks of recent decades, and recognizing the masculine bias of such a concentration, feminists have explored an alternative focus on care. A focus on justice has sometimes been seen as characteristic of men's ways of thinking about morality and a focus on care as characteristic of women's.

Within philosophy, feminists developed during the 1980s what was most often thought of as a morality of caring. Their views were encouraged by Sara Ruddick's early work analyzing the practice of mothering and supported by the empirical inquiries of Carol Gilligan and other psychologists who claimed that many girls and women tend to interpret moral problems differently from the way boys and men tend to interpret them. For girls and women, caring relationships are often primary; for boys and men, morality is more apt to be seen in terms of individual compliance with rational rules concerning rights. The philosophical attempt to see in caring an alternative ethic rather than merely an empirically present tendency among women was in part a reaction to the overwhelming dominance that the concept of justice, with its associated abstract moral rules, had been accorded in the moral theory taught and discussed in philosophy and fields influenced by it in the previous decade and throughout most of the history of moral theory. Attending to the experience of women, an ethic of care recognizes that caring for children and dependent persons is an important activity involving moral values; it sees persons as interdependent rather than as independent individuals and holds that morality should address issues of caring and empathy and relationships between people rather than only or primarily the rational decisions of solitary moral agents. The first set of readings in this volume shows the early outlines of an ethic of care.

Some feminists, however, have had doubts about substituting an ethic of care for an ethic of justice, since women so clearly need and deserve more justice and fairness than we have received in political life, on the job, at school, and especially at home in the division of labor in the household. Where care is perhaps

most prominent—within the family and in the contexts of health and welfare—
justice is surely needed as well. And perhaps an ethic of care only indicates what
women pressed by patriarchal traditions into doing most of the caregiving tend
to think. As the second set of readings suggests, feminists may do well to be cautious about accepting the values of caring. And doubts can be raised about
whether care can be relevant for political life as well as in the household and
about the cultural and historical limitations of the outlook suggested by an ethic
of care. The third set of readings suggests the relevance of caring to issues of social and political institutions and the importance of care in the distinctive practices of African American communities.

Feminists seeking to develop moral epistemologies more fruitful than the traditional ones have also attended to care as a moral consideration that ought to
inform our processes of moral inquiry. The fourth set of readings illustrates this
approach. In contrast with the view that moral understanding is largely a matter
of knowledge arrived at rationally and impartially, feminist moral theorists have
often seen caring as having an important place in our methods of arriving at
progressively better moral theory and moral practice or reformulated.

The final two essays are published for the first time in this volume. Two leading feminist theorists reconsider justice and care in the light of what has been
learned from previous discussions. They evaluate the arguments and consider
how the values of care and justice can be integrated or reformulated.

As the readings in this collection indicate, feminists have been engaged in
lively and ongoing debates about care and justice. The issues are by no means
resolved, the debate continues, but considerable progress has been made in developing feminist views of morality. A series of questions can be raised about
these central concepts of justice and care: Are they compatible? Are they alternative and incompatible ways of interpreting the same moral situations, and if so,
how can we decide which should guide us? Are care and justice both indispensable for adequate moral understanding? Should care supplement justice, or justice supplement care—is one or the other the more fundamental? Do they appropriately apply to different domains or do both apply to all or most domains?
Can either one be included within the other as a special case, and if so, which is
the more comprehensive?

These are the sorts of questions being raised. There is considerable disagreement on how they should be answered. Not all feminists share the view that
there is something like a separate and different "ethic of care," but many are convinced that there is and that whatever position we hold about justice—for instance, that it can be replaced by care or that it cannot—any adequate morality
must include as a strong component the kinds of moral considerations that have
come to be identified as belonging to a morality of caring.

In recent years the most important discussions have been concerned with
how justice and care can appropriately be combined from a feminist point of
view. How does the framework of justice-equality-rights-obligations mesh with
the network of care-relatedness-trust? To suppose that justice and care should

predominate in different domains—justice in the public sphere and care in the private—seems unsatisfactory, since most feminists reject the traditional public-private distinction itself. Feminists certainly favor regions of privacy, but they recognize that deciding who will have which kinds of privacy is a political issue.

Clearly, justice within the household is needed to protect its members from domestic violence and to ensure that women are not exploited in the provision of care. At the same time, more care is needed in social arrangements and in public policy decisions about a wide variety of matters. Those concerned with health and welfare may be the most obvious, but such matters are by no means the only ones where more of the considerations emphasized by a caring approach are needed. Cultivating more caring, sensitivity, and trust in political life, in legal approaches, and in international affairs should be among our goals.

A satisfactory morality should, if possible, offer guidance for moral concerns in any context. One may have a view that context is highly relevant to any adequate moral evaluation and that different approaches are best for different contexts. One will still look to a general moral approach to indicate which types of contexts to handle in which ways and to recommend how existing contexts ought to be transformed and rearranged. For instance, Western liberal political theories make law and the state central to society and make arrangements for the raising of children and for producing culture peripheral. A feminist morality might reorder these priorities drastically as well as transform arrangements within such contexts as the law or the household.

Another possible way of trying to reconcile justice and care is to think of justice as setting moral minimums beneath which we ought not to fall, or absolute constraints within which we may pursue our different goals, whereas care deals with questions of the good life or of human value over and above the obligatory minimums of justice. Traditional moral theorists, with a few exceptions, often see morality as composed of constraints that limit our pursuits of what we desire. Feminist moral theorists, in contrast, often stress the value of good relationships—whether personal or civil—and of good parenting and emotions conducive to leading admirable lives. And we stress that these are moral values. But as a way of resolving the conceptual conflicts between justice and care, thinking of justice as composed of moral minimums and of care as concerned with the good life above them can be questioned. Justice can be ever more attainable in the sense of gaining an increasingly sensitive understanding of rights, equality, and respect; to think of justice in terms of the necessary constraints of morality may be misleading. And certainly there are minimums of care that must be provided for persons to reach adulthood and to live, though good care will be above these minimums. There are few constraints as nearly absolute as responding to the needs of our children for basic care.

Feminist moral theorists are developing ways of dealing with actual problems through considering the appropriate claims of, at least, care and justice. These readings will show why these approaches are needed, how the debates concerning them have developed, and what some of the prospects are for feminist morality.

PART ONE

Delineations of Care

1

Caring
[1984]

NEL NODDINGS

Ethics and Caring

It is generally agreed that ethics is the philosophical study of morality, but we
also speak of "professional ethics" and "a personal ethic." When we speak in the
second way, we refer to something explicable—a set of rules, an ideal, a constel-
lation of expressions—that guides and justifies our conduct. One can, obviously,
behave ethically without engaging in ethics as a philosophical enterprise, and
one can even put together an ethic of sorts—that is, a description of what it
means to be moral—without seriously questioning what it means to be moral.
Such an ethic, it seems to me, may or may not be a guide to moral behavior. It
depends, in a fundamental way, on an assessment of the answer to the question:
What does it mean to be moral? This question will be central to our investigation. I shall use "ethical" rather than "moral" in most of our discussions but, in
doing so, I am assuming that to behave ethically is to behave under the guidance
of an acceptable and justifiable account of what it means to be moral. To behave
ethically is not to behave in conformity with just any description of morality, and
I shall claim that ethical systems are not equivalent simply because they include
rules concerning the same matters or categories.

In an argument for the possibility of an objective morality (against relativism),
anthropologist Ralph Linton makes two major points that may serve to illumi-
nate the path I am taking. In one argument, he seems to say that ethical relativism is false because it can be shown that all societies lay down rules of some
sort for behavior in certain universal categories. All societies, for example, have
rules governing sexual behavior. But Linton does not seem to recognize that the
content of the rules, and not just their mere existence, is crucial to the discussion of ethicality. He says, for example: ". . . practically all societies recognize

7

adultery as unethical and punish the offenders. The same man who will lend his wife to a friend or brother will be roused to fury if she goes to another man without his permission."[1] But, surely, we would like to know what conception of morality makes adultery "wrong" and the lending of one's wife "right." Just as surely, an ethical system that renders such decisions cannot be equivalent to one that finds adultery acceptable and wife lending unacceptable.

In his second claim, Linton is joined by a substantial number of anthropologists. Stated simply, the claim is that morality is based on common human characteristics and needs and that, hence, an objective morality is possible. That morality is rooted somehow in common human needs, feelings, and cognitions is agreed. But it is not clear to me that we can move easily or swiftly from that agreement to a claim that objective morality is possible. We may be able to describe the moral impulse as it arises in response to particular needs and feelings, and we may be able to describe the relation of thinking and acting in relation to that impulse; but as we tackle these tasks, we may move farther away from a notion of objective morality and closer to the conviction that an irremovable subjective core, a longing for goodness, provides what universality and stability there is in what it means to be moral.

I want to build an ethic on caring, and I shall claim that there is a form of caring natural and accessible to all human beings. Certain feelings, attitudes, and memories will be claimed as universal. But the ethic itself will not embody a set of universalizable moral judgments. Indeed, moral judgment will not be its central concern. It is very common among philosophers to move from the question: What is morality? to the seemingly more manageable question: What is a moral judgment? Fred Feldman, for example, makes this move early on. He suggests:

> Perhaps we can shed some light on the meaning of the noun "morality" by considering the adjective "moral." Proceeding in this way will enable us to deal with a less abstract concept, and we may thereby be more successful. So instead of asking "What is morality?" let us pick one of the most interesting of these uses of the adjective "moral" and ask instead, "What is a moral judgment?"[2]

Now, I am not arguing that this move is completely mistaken or that nothing can be gained through a consideration of moral judgments, but such a move is not the only possibility. We might choose another interesting use of the adjective and ask, instead, about the moral impulse or moral attitude. The choice is important. The long-standing emphasis on the study of moral judgments has led to a serious imbalance in moral discussion. In particular, it is well known that many women—perhaps most women—do not approach moral problems as problems of principle, reasoning, and judgment. . . . If a substantial segment of humankind approaches moral problems through a consideration of the concrete elements of situations and a regard for themselves as caring, then perhaps an attempt should be made to enlighten the study of morality in this alternative mode. Further, such a study has significant implications, beyond ethics, for education. If moral education, in a double sense, is guided only by the study of moral principles and judgments, not only are women made to feel inferior to men in the moral realm but also education itself may suffer from impoverished and one-sided moral guidance.

So building an ethic on caring seems both reasonable and important. One may well ask, at this point, whether an ethic so constructed will be a form of "situation ethics." It is not, certainly, that form of act-utilitarianism commonly labeled "situation ethics."[3] Its emphasis is not on the consequences of our acts, although these are not, of course, irrelevant. But an ethic of caring locates morality primarily in the pre-act consciousness of the one-caring. Yet it is not a form of agapism. There is no command to love nor, indeed, any God to make the commandment. Further, I shall reject the notion of universal love, finding it unattainable in any but the most abstract sense and thus a source of distraction. While much of what will be developed in the ethic of caring may be found, also, in Christian ethics, there will be major and irreconcilable differences. Human love, human caring, will be quite enough on which to found an ethic.

We must look even more closely at that love and caring.

An Ethic of Caring

From Natural to Ethical Caring

David Hume long ago contended that morality is founded upon and rooted in feeling—that the "final sentence" on matters of morality, "that which renders morality an active virtue"—". . . this final sentence depends on some internal sense or feeling, which nature has made universal in the whole species. For what else can have an influence of this nature?"[4]

What is the nature of this feeling that is "universal in the whole species"? I want to suggest that morality as an "active virtue" requires two feelings and not just one. The first is the sentiment of natural caring. There can be no ethical sentiment without the initial, enabling sentiment. In situations where we act on behalf of the other because we want to do so, we are acting in accord with natural caring. A mother's caretaking efforts in behalf of her child are not usually considered ethical but natural. Even maternal animals take care of their offspring, and we do not credit them with ethical behavior.

The second sentiment occurs in response to a remembrance of the first. Nietzsche speaks of love and memory in the context of Christian love and Eros, but what he says may safely be taken out of context to illustrate the point I wish to make here:

> There is something so ambiguous and suggestive about the word love, something
> that speaks to memory and to hope, that even the lowest intelligence and the coldest
> heart still feel something of the glimmer of this word. The cleverest woman and the
> most vulgar man recall the relatively least selfish moments of their whole life, even if
> Eros has taken only a low flight with them.[5]

This memory of our own best moments of caring and being cared for sweeps
over us as a feeling—as an "I must"—in response to the plight of the other and
our conflicting desire to serve our own interests. There is a transfer of feeling
analogous to transfer of learning. In the intellectual domain, when I read a certain kind of mathematical puzzle, I may react by thinking, "That is like the
sailors, monkey, and coconuts problem," and then, "Diophantine equations" or
"modulo arithmetic" or "congruences." Similarly, when I encounter an other and
feel the natural pang conflicted with my own desires—"I must—I do not want
to"—I recognize the feeling and remember what has followed it in my own best
moments. I have a picture of those moments in which I was cared for and in
which I cared, and I may reach toward this memory and guide my conduct by it
if I wish to do so.

Recognizing that ethical caring requires an effort that is not needed in natural
caring does not commit us to a position that elevates ethical caring over natural
caring. Kant has identified the ethical with that which is done out of duty and
not out of love, and that distinction in itself seems right. But an ethic built on
caring strives to maintain the caring attitude and is thus dependent upon, and
not superior to, natural caring. The source of ethical behavior is, then, in twin
sentiments—one that feels directly for the other and one that feels for and with
that best self, who may accept and sustain the initial feeling rather than reject it.

We shall discuss the ethical ideal, that vision of best self, in some depth. When
we commit ourselves to obey the "I must" even at its weakest and most fleeting,
we are under the guidance of this ideal. It is not just any picture. Rather, it is our
best picture of ourselves caring and being cared for. It may even be colored by
acquaintance with one superior to us in caring, but, as I shall describe it, it is
both constrained and attainable. It is limited by what we have already done and
by what we are capable of, and it does not idealize the impossible so that we may
escape into ideal abstraction.

Now, clearly, in pointing to Hume's "active virtue" and to an ethical ideal as the
source of ethical behavior, I seem to be advocating an ethic of virtue. This is certainly true in part. Many philosophers recognize the need for a discussion of
virtue as the energizing factor in moral behavior, even when they have given
their best intellectual effort to a careful explication of their positions on obligation and justification.[6] When we discuss the ethical ideal, we shall be talking
about "virtue," but we shall not let "virtue" dissipate into "the virtues" described
in abstract categories. The holy man living abstemiously on top of the mountain,
praying thrice daily, and denying himself human intercourse may display

"virtues," but they are not the virtues of one-caring. The virtue described by the ethical ideal of one-caring is built up in relation. It reaches out to the other and grows in response to the other.

Since our discussion of virtue will be embedded in an exploration of moral activity we might do well to start by asking whether or under what circumstances we are obliged to respond to the initial "I must." Does it make sense to say that I am obliged to heed that which comes to me as obligation?

Obligation

There are moments for all of us when we care quite naturally. We just do care; no ethical effort is required. "Want" and "ought" are indistinguishable in such cases. I want to do what I or others might judge I ought to do. But can there be a "demand" to care? There can be, surely, no demand for the initial impulse that arises as a feeling, an inner voice saying "I must do something," in response to the need of the cared-for. This impulse arises naturally, at least occasionally, in the absence of pathology. We cannot demand that one have this impulse, but we shrink from one who never has it. One who never feels the pain of another, who never confesses the internal "I must" that is so familiar to most of us, is beyond our normal pattern of understanding. Her case is pathological, and we avoid her.

But even if I feel the initial "I must," I may reject it. I may reject it instantaneously by shifting from "I must do something" to "Something must be done," and removing myself from the set of possible agents through whom the action should be accomplished. I may reject it because I feel that there is nothing I can do. If I do either of these things without reflection upon what I might do in behalf of the cared-for, then I do not care. Caring requires me to respond to the initial impulse with an act of commitment: I commit myself either to overt action on behalf of the cared-for (I pick up my crying infant) or I commit myself to thinking about what I might do. In the latter case, as we have seen, I may or may not act overtly in behalf of the cared-for. I may abstain from action if I believe that anything I might do would tend to work against the best interests of the cared-for. But the test of my caring is not wholly in how things turn out; the primary test lies in an examination of what I considered, how fully I received the other, and whether the free pursuit of his projects is partly a result of the completion of my caring in him.

But am I obliged to embrace the "I must"? In this form, the question is a bit odd, for the "I must" carries obligation with it. It comes to us as obligation. But accepting and affirming the "I must" are different from feeling it, and these responses are what I am pointing to when I ask whether I am obliged to embrace the "I must." The question nags at us; it is a question that has been asked, in a variety of forms, over and over by moralists and moral theorists. Usually, the question arises as part of the broader question of justification. We ask something of the sort: Why must I (or should I) do what suggests itself to reason as "right" or as needing to be done for the sake of some other? We might prefer to supplement "reason" with "and/or feeling." This question is, of course, not the only thorny question in moral theory, but it is one that has plagued theorists who see clearly that there is no way to derive an "I ought" statement from a chain of facts. I may agree readily that "things would be better"—that is, that a certain state of affairs commonly agreed to be desirable might be attained—if a certain chain of events were to take place. But there is still nothing in this intellectual chain that can produce the "I ought." I may choose to remain an observer on the scene.

Now I am suggesting that the "I must" arises directly and prior to consideration of what it is that I might do. The initial feeling is the "I must." When it comes to me indistinguishable from the "I want," I proceed easily as one-caring. But often it comes to me conflicted. It may be barely perceptible and it may be followed almost simultaneously by resistance. When someone asks me to get something for him or merely asks for my attention, the "I must" may be lost in a clamor of resistance. Now a second sentiment is required if I am to behave as one-caring. I care about myself as one-caring and, although I do not care naturally for the person who has asked something of me—at least not at this moment—I feel the genuine moral sentiment, the "I ought," that sensibility to which I have committed myself.

Let me try to make plausible my contention that the moral imperative arises directly.[7] And, of course, I must try to explain how caring and what I am calling the "moral imperative" are related. When my infant cries in the night, I not only feel that I must do something but I want to do something. Because I love this child, because I am bonded to him, I want to remove his pain as I would want to remove my own. The "I must" is not a dutiful imperative but one that accompanies the "I want." If I were tied to a chair, for example, and wanted desperately to get free, I might say as I struggled, "I must do something; I must get out of these bonds." But this "must" is not yet the moral or ethical "ought." It is a "must" born of desire.

The most intimate situations of caring are, thus, natural. I do not feel that taking care of my own child is "moral" but, rather, natural. A woman who allows her own child to die of neglect is often considered sick rather than immoral; that is, we feel that either she or the situation into which she has been thrust must be pathological. Otherwise, the impulse to respond, to nurture the living infant, is overwhelming. We share the impulse with other creatures in the animal kingdom. Whether we want to consider this response as "instinctive" is problematic, because certain patterns of response may be implied by the term and because suspension of reflective consciousness seems also to be implied (and I am not suggesting that we have no choice), but I have no difficulty in considering it as innate. Indeed, I am claiming that the impulse to act in behalf of the present other is itself innate. It lies latent in each of us, awaiting gradual development in a succession of caring relations. I am suggesting that our inclination toward and interest in morality derives from caring. In caring, we accept the natural impulse to act on behalf of the present other. We are engrossed in the other. We have received him and feel his pain or happiness, but we are not compelled by this impulse. We have a choice; we may accept what we feel, or we may reject it. If we have a strong desire to be moral, we will not reject it, and this strong desire to be moral is derived, reflectively, from the more fundamental and natural desire to be and to remain related. To reject the feeling when it arises is either to be in an internal state of imbalance or to contribute willfully to the diminution of the ethical ideal.

But suppose in a particular case that the "I must" does not arise, or that it whispers faintly and disappears, leaving distrust, repugnance, or hate. Why, then, should I behave morally toward the object of my dislike? Why should I not accept feelings other than those characteristic of caring and, thus, achieve an internal state of balance through hate, anger, or malice?

The answer to this is, I think, that the genuine moral sentiment (our second sentiment) arises from an evaluation of the caring relation as good, as better than, superior to, other forms of relatedness. I feel the moral "I must" when I recognize that my response will either enhance or diminish my ethical ideal. It will serve either to increase or decrease the likelihood of genuine caring. My response affects me as one-caring. In a given situation with someone I am not fond of, I may be able to find all sorts of reasons why I should not respond to his need. I may be too busy. He may be undiscerning. The matter may be, on objective analysis, unimportant. But, before I decide, I must turn away from this analytic chain of thought and back to the concrete situation. Here is this person with this perceived need to which is attached this importance. I must put justification aside temporarily. Shall I respond? How do I feel as a duality about the "I" who will not respond?

I am obliged, then, to accept the initial "I must" when it occurs and even to fetch it out of recalcitrant slumber when it fails to awake spontaneously.[8] The source of my obligation is the value I place on the relatedness of caring. This value itself arises as a product of actual caring and being cared-for and my reflection on the goodness of these concrete caring situations.

Now, what sort of "goodness" is it that attaches to the caring relation? It cannot be a fully moral goodness, for we have already described forms of caring that are natural and require no moral effort. But it cannot be a fully nonmoral goodness either, for it would then join a class of goods many of which are widely separated from the moral good. It is, perhaps, properly described as a "premoral good," one that lies in a region with the moral good and shades over into it. We cannot always decide with certainty whether our caring response is natural or ethical. Indeed, the decision to respond ethically as one-caring may cause the lowering of barriers that previously prevented reception of the other, and natural caring may follow.

I have identified the source of our obligation and have said that we are obligated to accept, and even to call forth, the feeling "I must." But what exactly must
I do? Can my obligation be set forth in a list or hierarchy of principles? So far, it
seems that I am obligated to maintain an attitude and, thus, to meet the other as
one-caring and, at the same time, to increase my own virtue as one-caring. If I
am advocating an ethic of virtue, do not all the usual dangers lie in wait:
hypocrisy, self-righteousness, withdrawal from the public domain? We shall discuss these dangers as the idea of an ethical ideal is developed more fully.

Let me say here, however, why it seems preferable to place an ethical ideal
above principle as a guide to moral action. It has been traditional in moral philosophy to insist that moral principles must be, by their very nature as moral
principles, universifiable. If I am obligated to do X under certain conditions,
then under sufficiently similar conditions you also are obligated to do X. But the
principle of universifiability seems to depend, as Nietzsche pointed out, on a
concept of "sameness."[9] In order to accept the principle, we should have to establish that human predicaments exhibit sufficient sameness, and this we cannot do without abstracting away from concrete situations those qualities that
seem to reveal the sameness. In doing this, we often lose the very qualities or
factors that gave rise to the moral question in the situation. That condition
which makes the situation different and thereby induces genuine moral puzzle-
ment cannot be satisfied by the application of principles developed in situations
of sameness.

This does not mean that we cannot receive any guidance from an attempt to
discover principles that seem to be universifiable. We can, under this sort of
plan, arrive at the doctrine of "prima facie duty" described by W. D. Ross.[10] Ross
himself, however, admits that this doctrine yields no real guidance for moral
conduct in concrete situations. It guides us in abstract moral thinking; it tells us,
theoretically, what to do, "all other things being equal." But other things are
rarely if ever equal. A and B, struggling with a moral decision, are two different
persons with different factual histories, different projects and aspirations, and
different ideals. It may indeed be right, morally right, for A to do X and B to do
not-X. We may, that is, connect "right" and "wrong" to faithfulness to the ethical
ideal. This does not cast us into relativism, because the ideal contains at its heart
a component that is universal: Maintenance of the caring relation.

Before turning to a discussion of "right" and "wrong" and their usefulness in
an ethic of caring, we might try to clear up the problem earlier mentioned as a
danger in any ethic of virtue: the temptation to withdraw from the public domain. It is a real danger. Even though we rejected the sort of virtue exhibited by
the hermit-monk on the mountaintop, that rejection may have been one of personal choice. It still remains possible that an ethic of caring is compatible with
the monk's choice, and that such an ethic even induces withdrawal. We are not
going to be able to divide cases clearly. The monk who withdraws only to serve
God is clearly under the guidance of an ethic that differs fundamentally from the

ethic of caring. The source of his ethic is not the source of ours, and he might deny that any form of human relatedness could be a source for moral behavior. But if, when another intrudes upon his privacy, he receives the other as one-caring, we cannot charge him with violating our ethic. Further, as we saw in our discussion of the one-caring, there is a legitimate dread of the proximate stranger—of that person who may ask more than we feel able to give. We saw there that we cannot care for everyone. Caring itself is reduced to mere talk about caring when we attempt to do so. We must acknowledge, then, that an ethic of caring implies a limit on our obligation.

Our obligation is limited and delimited by relation. We are never free, in the human domain, to abandon our preparedness to care; but, practically, if we are meeting those in our inner circles adequately as ones-caring and receiving those linked to our inner circles by formal chains of relation, we shall limit the calls upon our obligation quite naturally. We are not obliged to summon the "I must" if there is no possibility of completion in the other. I am not obliged to care for starving children in Africa, because there is no way for this caring to be completed in the other unless I abandon the caring to which I am obligated. I may still choose to do something in the direction of caring, but I am not obliged to do so. When we discuss our obligation to animals, we shall see that this is even more sharply limited by relation. We cannot refuse obligation in human affairs by merely refusing to enter relation; we are, by virtue of our mutual humanity, already and perpetually in potential relation. Instead, we limit our obligation by examining the possibility of completion. In connection with animals, however, we may find it possible to refuse relation itself on the grounds of a species-specific impossibility of any form of reciprocity in caring.

Now, this is very important, and we should try to say clearly what governs our obligation. On the basis of what has been developed so far, there seem to be two criteria: the existence of or potential for present relation, and the dynamic potential for growth in relation, including the potential for increased reciprocity and, perhaps, mutuality. The first criterion establishes an absolute obligation and the second serves to put our obligations into an order of priority.

If the other toward whom we shall act is capable of responding as cared-for and there are no objective conditions that prevent our receiving this response—if, that is, our caring can be completed in the other—then we must meet that other as one-caring. If we do not care naturally, we must call upon our capacity for ethical caring. When we are in relation or when the other has addressed us, we must respond as one-caring. The imperative in relation is categorical. When relation has not yet been established, or when it may properly be refused (when no formal chain or natural circle is present), the imperative is more like that of the hypothetical: I must if I wish to (or am able to) move into relation.

The second criterion asks us to look at the nature of potential relation and, especially, at the capacity of the cared-for to respond. The potential for response in animals, for example, is nearly static; they cannot respond in mutuality, nor can the nature of their response change substantially. But a child's potential for increased response is enormous. If the possibility of relation is dynamic—if the relation may clearly grow with respect to reciprocity—then the possibility and degree of my obligation also grows. If response is imminent, so also is my obligation. This criterion will help us to distinguish between our obligation to members of the nonhuman animal world and, say, the human fetus. We must keep in mind, however, that the second criterion binds us in proportion to the probability of increased response and to the imminence of that response. Relation itself is fundamental in obligation.

I shall give an example of thinking guided by these criteria, but let us pause for a moment and ask what it is we are trying to accomplish. I am working deliberately toward criteria that will preserve our deepest and most tender human feelings. The caring of mother for child, of human adult for human infant, elicits the tenderest feelings in most of us. Indeed, for many women, this feeling of nurturance lies at the very heart of what we assess as good. A philosophical position that has difficulty distinguishing between our obligation to human infants and, say, pigs is in some difficulty straight off. It violates our most deeply cherished feeling about human goodness. This violation does not, of course, make the position logically wrong, but it suggests that especially strong grounds will be needed to support it. In the absence of such strong grounds—and I shall argue in a later chapter that they are absent—we might prefer to establish a position that captures rather than denies our basic feelings. We might observe that man (in contrast to woman) has continually turned away from his inner self and feeling in pursuit of both science and ethics. With respect to strict science, this turning outward may be defensible; with respect to ethics, it has been disastrous.

 Now, let's consider an example: the problem of abortion. Operating under the guidance of an ethic of caring, we are not likely to find abortion in general either right or wrong. We shall have to inquire into individual cases. An incipient embryo is an information speck—a set of controlling instructions for a future human being. Many of these specks are created and flushed away without their creators' awareness. From the view developed here, the information speck is an information speck; it has no given sanctity. There should be no concern over the waste of "human tissue," since nature herself is wildly prolific, even profligate.[11] The one-caring is concerned not with human tissue but with human consciousness—with pain, delight, hope, fear, entreaty, and response.

 But suppose the information speck is mine, and I am aware of it. This child-to-be is the product of love between a man deeply cared-for and me. Will the child have his eyes or mine? His stature or mine? Our joint love of mathematics or his love of mechanics or my love of language? This is not just an information speck; it is endowed with prior love and current knowledge. It is sacred, but I—humbly, not presumptuously—confer sacredness upon it. I cannot, will not destroy it. It is joined to loved others through formal chains of caring. It is linked to the inner circle in a clearly defined way. I might wish that I were not pregnant, but I cannot destroy this known and potentially loved person-to-be. There is already relation albeit indirect and formal. My decision is an ethical one born of natural caring. But suppose, now, that my beloved child has grown up; it is she who is pregnant and considering abortion. She is not sure of the love between herself and the man. She is miserably worried about her economic and emotional future. I might like to convey sanctity on this information speck; but I am not God—only mother to this suffering cared-for. It is she who is conscious and in pain, and I as one-caring move to relieve the pain. This information speck is an information speck and that is all. There is no formal relation, given the breakdown between husband and wife, and with the embryo, there is no present relation; the possibility of future relation—while not absent, surely—is uncertain. But what of this possibility for growing response? Must we not consider it? We must indeed. As the embryo becomes a fetus and, growing daily, becomes more nearly capable of response as cared-for, our obligation grows from a nagging uncertainty—an "I must if I wish"—to an utter conviction that we must meet this small other as one-caring.

If we try to formalize what has been expressed in the concrete situations described so far, we arrive at a legal approach to abortion very like that of the Supreme Court: abortions should be freely available in the first trimester, subject to medical determination in the second trimester, and banned in the third, when the fetus is viable. A woman under the guidance of our ethic would be likely to recognize the growing possibility of relation; the potential is clearly dynamic. Further, many women recognize the relation as established when the fetus begins to move about. It is not a question of when life begins but of when relation begins.

But what if relation is never established? Suppose the child is born and the mother admits no sense of relatedness. May she commit infanticide? One who asks such questions misinterprets the concept of relatedness that I have been struggling to describe. Since the infant, even the near-natal fetus, is capable of relation—of the sweetest and most unselfconscious reciprocity—one who encounters the infant is obligated to meet it as one-caring. Both parts of this claim are essential; it is not only the child's capability to respond but also the encounter that induces obligation. There must exist the possibility for our caring to be completed in the other. If the mother does not care naturally, then she must summon ethical caring to support her as one-caring. She may not ethically ignore the child's cry to live.

The one-caring, in considering abortion as in all other matters, cares first for the one in immediate pain or peril. She might suggest a brief and direct form of counseling in which a young expectant mother could come to grips with her feelings. If the incipient child has been sanctified by its mother, every effort must be made to help the two to achieve a stable and hopeful life together; if it has not, it should be removed swiftly and mercifully with all loving attention to the woman, the conscious patient. Between these two clear reactions is a possible confused one: the young woman is not sure how she feels. The one-caring

moral
dilemmas

probes gently to see what has been considered, raising questions and retreating when the questions obviously have been considered and are now causing great pain. Is such a view "unprincipled"? If it is, it is boldly so; it is at least connected with the world as it is, at its best and at its worst, and it requires that we—in espousing a "best"—stand ready to actualize that preferred condition. The decision for or against abortion must be made by those directly involved in the concrete situation, but it need not be made alone. The one-caring cannot require everyone to behave as she would in a particular situation. Rather, when she dares to say, "I think you should do X," she adds, also, "Can I help you?" The one under her gaze is under her support and not her judgment.

One under the guidance of an ethic of caring is tempted to retreat to a manageable world. Her public life is limited by her insistence upon meeting the other as one-caring. So long as this is possible, she may reach outward and enlarge her circles of caring. When this reaching out destroys or drastically reduces her actual caring, she retreats and renews her contact with those who address her. If the retreat becomes a flight, an avoidance of the call to care, her ethical ideal is diminished. Similarly, if the retreat is away from human beings and toward other objects of caring—ideas, animals, humanity-at-large, God—her ethical ideal is virtually shattered. This is not a judgment, for we can understand and sympathize with one who makes such a choice. It is more in the nature of a perception: we see clearly what has been lost in the choice.

Our ethic of caring—which we might have called a "feminine ethic"—begins to look a bit mean in contrast to the masculine ethics of universal love or universal justice. But universal love is illusion. Under the illusion, some young people retreat to the church to worship that which they cannot actualize; some write lovely poetry extolling universal love; and some, in terrible disillusion, kill to establish the very principles which should have entreated them not to kill. Thus are lost both principles and persons.

Right and Wrong

How are we to make judgments of right and wrong under this ethic? First, it is important to understand that we are not primarily interested in judging but, rather, in heightening moral perception and sensitivity. But "right" and "wrong" can be useful.

Suppose a mother observes her young child pulling the kitten's tail or picking it up by the ears. She may exclaim, "Oh, no, it is not nice to hurt the kitty," or, "You must not hurt the kitty." Or she may simply say, "Stop. See—you are hurting the kitty," and she may then take the kitten in her own hands and show the child how to handle it. She holds the kitten gently, stroking it, and saying, "See? Ah, ah, kitty, nice kitty. . . ." What the mother is supposing in this interaction is that the realization that his act is hurting the kitten, supplemented by the knowledge of how to avoid inflicting hurt, will suffice to change the child's behavior. If she believes this, she has no need for the statement, "It is wrong to hurt the kitty." She is not threatening sanctions but drawing dual attention to a matter of fact (the hurting) and her own commitment (I will not hurt). Beyond this, she is supposing that her child, well-cared-for himself, does not want to inflict pain.

Now, I am not claiming through use of this illustration that moral statements are mere expressions of approval or disapproval, although they do serve an expressive function. A. J. Ayer, who did make a claim of this sort before modifying his position somewhat, uses an illustration very like the one just given to support an emotivist position.[12] But even if it were possible to take a purely analytic stance with respect to moral theory, as Ayer suggests he has done, that is certainly not what I intend to do. One who labels moral statements as expressions of approval or disapproval, and takes the matter to be finished with that, misses the very heart of morality. He misses both feeling and content. I may, after all, express my approval or disapproval on matters that are not moral. Thus it is clear that when I make a moral judgment I am doing more than simply expressing approval or disapproval. I am both expressing my own commitment to behave in a way compatible with caring and appealing to the hearer to consider what he is doing. I may say first to a child, "Oh! Don't hurt the kitty!" And I may then add, "It is wrong to hurt the kitty." The word is not necessary, strictly speaking, but I may find it useful.

What do I mean by this? I certainly mean to express my own commitment, and I show this best by daily example. But I may mean to say more than this. I may explain to the child that not only do I feel this way but that our family does, that our community does, that our culture does. Here I must be very careful. Our community may say one thing and do quite another. Such contradiction is even more likely at the level of "our culture." But I express myself doubly in words and in acts, and I may search out examples in the larger culture to convince the child that significant others do feel this way. The one-caring is careful to distinguish between acts that violate caring, acts that she herself holds wrong, and those acts that "some people" hold to be wrong. She need not be condescending in this instruction. She is herself so reluctant to universalize beyond the demands of caring that she cannot say, "It is wrong," to everything that is illegal, church-forbidden, or contrary to a prevailing etiquette. But she can raise the question, attempt to justify the alien view, express her own objections, and support the child in his own exploration.

Emotivists are partly right, I think, when they suggest that we might effectively substitute a statement describing the fact or event that triggers our feeling or attitude for statements such as "It is wrong to do *X*." When I say to my child, "It is wrong to hurt the kitty," I mean (if I am not threatening sanctions) to inform him that he is hurting the kitten and, further, that I believe that if he perceives he is doing so, he will stop. I am counting on his gradually developing ability to feel pain in the other to induce a decision to stop. To say, "It is wrong to cause pain needlessly," contributes nothing by way of knowledge and can hardly be thought likely to change the attitude or behavior of one who might ask, "Why is it wrong?" If I say to someone, "You are hurting the cat," and he replies, "I know it—so what? I like hurting cats," I feel "zero at the bone." Saying to him, "It is wrong to hurt cats," adds little unless I intend to threaten sanctions. If I mean to equate "It is wrong to hurt cats" with "There will be a sure and specific punishment for hurting cats," then it would be more honest to say this. One either feels a sort of pain in response to the pain of others, or one does not feel it. If he does feel it, he does not need to be told that causing pain is wrong. If he does not feel it in a particular case, he may remember the feeling—as one remembers the sweetness of love on hearing a certain piece of music—and allow himself to be moved by this remembrance, we must prescribe reeducation or exile. Thus, at the foundation of moral behavior—as we have already pointed out—is feeling or sentiment. But, further, there is commitment to remain open to that feeling, to remember it, and to put one's thinking in its service. It is the particular commitment underlying genuine expressions of moral judgment—as well as the special content—that the emotivist misses.

The one-caring, clearly, applies "right" and "wrong" most confidently to her own decisions. This does not, as we have insisted before, make her a relativist. The caring attitude that lies at the heart of all ethical behavior is universal. As a mother . . . has to decide whether or not to leave her sick child on the basis of a caring evaluation of the conditions and feelings of those involved, so in general the one-caring evaluates her own acts with respect to how faithfully they conform to what is known and felt through the receptivity of caring. But she also uses "right" and "wrong" instructively and respectfully to refer to the judgments of significant others. If she agrees because the matter at hand can be assessed in light of caring, she adds her personal commitment and example; if she has doubts—because the rule appealed to seems irrelevant or ambiguous in the light of caring—she still acknowledges the judgment but adds her own dissent or demurrer. Her eye is on the ethical development of the cared-for and, as she herself withholds judgment until she has heard the "whole story," she wants the cared-for to encounter others, receive them, and reflect on what he has received. Principles and rules are among the beliefs he will receive, and she wants him to consider these in the light of caring.

But is this all we can say about right and wrong? Is there not a firm foundation in morality for our legal judgments? Surely, we must be allowed to say, for example, that stealing is wrong and is, therefore, properly forbidden by law. Because it is so often wrong—and so easily demonstrated to be wrong—under an ethic of caring, we may accede that such a law has its roots partly in morality. We may legally punish one who has stolen, but we may not pass moral judgment on him until we know why he stole. An ethic of caring is likely to be stricter in its judgment, but more supportive and corrective in following up its judgment, than ethics otherwise grounded. For the one-caring, stealing is almost always wrong:

Ms. A talks with her young son. *But, Mother,* the boy pleads, *suppose I want to make you happy and I steal something you want from a big chain store. I haven't hurt anyone, have I? Yes, you have,* responds his mother, and she points to the predicament of the store managers who may be accused of poor stewardship and to the higher prices suffered by their neighbors. *Well, suppose I steal from a rich, rich person? He can replace what I take easily, and . . . Wait,* says Ms. A. *Is someone suffering? Are you stealing to relieve that suffering, and will you make certain that what you steal is used to relieve it? . . . But can't I steal to make some- one happy?* her son persists. Slowly, patiently, Ms. A explains the position of one- caring. *Each one* who comes under our gaze must be met as one-caring. When I want to please X and I turn toward Y as a means for satisfying my desire to please X, I must now meet Y as one-caring. I do not judge him for being rich—for trea- suring what I, perhaps, regard with indifference. I may not cause him pain by taking or destroying what he possesses. *But what if I steal from a bad guy—some- one who stole to get what he has?* Ms. A smiles at her young son, struggling to avoid his ethical responsibility: *Unless he is an immediate threat to you or some- one else, you must meet him, too, as one-caring.*

The lessons in "right" and "wrong" are hard lessons—not swiftly accom- plished by setting up as an objective the learning of some principle. We do not say: It is wrong to steal. Rather, we consider why it was wrong or may be wrong in this case to steal. We do not say: It is wrong to kill. By setting up such a princi- ple, we also imply its exceptions, and then we may too easily act on authorized exceptions. The one-caring wants to consider, and wants her child to consider, the act itself in full context. She will send him into the world skeptical, vulnera- ble, courageous, disobedient, and tenderly receptive. The "world" may not de- pend upon him to obey its rules or fulfill its wishes, but you, the individual he encounters, may depend upon him to meet you as one-caring.

The Problem of Justification

Since I have chided the emotivist for not digging beneath the expressive layer of moral sentiment to the nature of the feeling itself and the commitment to act in accord with the feeling, one might ask whether I should not dig beneath the com- mitment. Why should I be committed to not causing pain? Now, clearly, in one sense, I cannot answer this better than we already have. When the "Why?" refers to motivation, we have seen that the one-caring receives the other and acts in the other's behalf as she would for herself; that is, she acts with a similar motive en- ergy. Further, I have claimed that, when natural caring fails, the motive energy in behalf of the other can be summoned out of caring for the ethical self. We have discussed both natural caring and ethical caring. Ethical caring, as I have de- scribed it, depends not upon rule or principle but upon the development of an ideal self. It does not depend upon just any ideal of self, but the ideal developed in congruence with one's best remembrance of caring and being cared-for.

So far, in recommending the ethical ideal as a guide to ethical conduct, I have suggested that traditional approaches to the problem of justification are mistaken. When the ethical theorist asks, "Why should I behave thus-and-so?" his question is likely to be aimed at justification rather than motivation and at a logic that resides outside the person. He is asking for reasons of the sort we expect to find in logical demonstration. He may expect us to claim that moral judgments can be tested as claims to facts can be tested, or that moral judgments are derived from divine commandment, or that moral truths are intuitively apprehended. Once started on this line of discussion, we may find ourselves arguing abstractly about the status of relativism and absolutism, egoism and altruism, and a host of other positions that, I shall claim, are largely irrelevant to moral conduct. They are matters of considerable intellectual interest, but they are distractions if our primary interest is in ethical conduct.

Moral statements cannot be justified in the way that statements of fact can be justified. They are not truths. They are derived not from facts or principles but from the caring attitude. Indeed, we might say that moral statements come out of the moral view or attitude, which, as I have described it, is the rational attitude built upon natural caring. When we put it this way, we see that there can be no justification for taking the moral viewpoint—that in truth, the moral viewpoint is prior to any notion of justification.

But there is another difficulty in answering the request for justification. Consideration of problems of justification requires us to concentrate on moral judgments, on moral statements. Hence we are led to an exploration of the language and reasoning used to discuss moral conduct and away from an assessment of the concrete events in which we must choose whether and how to behave morally. Indeed, we are often led far beyond what we feel and intuitively judge to be right in a search for some simple and absolute guide to moral goodness.

For an ethic of caring, the problem of justification is not concentrated upon justified action in general. We are not "justified"—we are *obligated*—to do what is required to maintain and enhance caring. We must "justify" not-caring; that is, we must explain why, in the interest of caring for ourselves as ethical selves or in the interest of others for whom we care, we may behave as ones-not-caring toward this particular other. In a related problem, we must justify doing what this other would not have us do to him as part of our genuine effort to care for him. But even in these cases, an ethic of caring does not emphasize justification. As one-caring, I am not seeking justification for my action; I am not standing alone before some tribunal. What I seek is completion in the other—the sense of being cared-for and, I hope, the renewed commitment of the cared-for to turn about and act as one-caring in the circles and chains within which he is defined. Thus, I am not justified but somehow fulfilled and completed in my own life and in the lives of those I have thus influenced.

It sounds all very nice, says my male colleague, but can you claim to be doing "ethics"? After all, ethics is the study of justified action. . . . Ah, yes. But, after "after-all," I am a woman, and I was not party to that definition. Shall we say then that I am talking about "how to meet the other morally"? Is this part of ethics? Is ethics part of this?

Women and Morality: Virtue

Many of us in education are keenly aware of the distortion that results from undue emphasis on moral judgments and justification. Lawrence Kohlberg's theory, for example, is widely held to be a model for moral education, but it is actually only a hierarchical description of moral reasoning.[13] It is well known, further, that the description may not be accurate. In particular, the fact that women seem often to be "stuck" at stage three might call the accuracy of the description into question. But perhaps the description is accurate within the domain of morality conceived as moral justification. If it is, we might well explore the possibility that feminine nonconformity to the Kohlberg model counts against the justification/judgment paradigm and not against women as moral thinkers.

Women, perhaps the majority of women, prefer to discuss moral problems in terms of concrete situations. They approach moral problems not as intellectual problems to be solved by abstract reasoning but as concrete human problems to be lived and to be solved in living. Their approach is founded in caring. Carol Gilligan describes the approach:

> . . . women not only define themselves in a context of human relationship but also judge themselves in terms of their ability to care. Woman's place in man's life cycle has been that of nurturer, caretaker, and helpmate, the weaver of those networks of relationships on which she in turn relies.[14]

Faced with a hypothetical moral dilemma, women often ask for more information. It is not the case, certainly, that women cannot arrange principles hierarchically and derive conclusions logically. It is more likely that they see this process as peripheral to or even irrelevant to moral conduct. They want more information, I think, in order to form a picture. Ideally, they need to talk to the participants, to see their eyes and facial expressions, to size up the whole situation. Moral decisions are, after all, made in situations; they are qualitatively different from the solution of geometry problems. Women, like act-deontologists in general, give reasons for their acts, but the reasons point to feelings, needs, situational conditions, and their sense of personal ideal rather than universal principles and their application.

As we have seen, caring is not in itself a virtue. The genuine ethical commitment to maintain oneself as caring gives rise to the development and exercise of virtues, but these must be assessed in the context of caring situations. It is not, for example, patience itself that is a virtue but patience with respect to some infirmity of a particular cared-for or patience in instructing a concrete cared-for that is virtuous. We must not reify virtues and turn our caring toward them. If we do this, our ethic turns inward and is even less useful than an ethic of principles, which at least remains indirectly in contact with the acts we are assessing. The fulfillment of virtue is both in me and in the other.

A consideration of caring and an ethic built upon it give new meaning to what Kohlberg assesses as "stage three" morality. At this stage, persons behave morally in order to be thought of—or to think of themselves as—"good boys" or "good girls." Clearly, it makes a difference whether one chooses to be good or to be thought of as good. One who chooses to be good may not be "stuck," as Kohlberg suggests, in a stage of moral reasoning. Rather, she may have chosen an alternative route to moral conduct.

It should be clear that my description of an ethic of caring as a feminine ethic does not imply a claim to speak for all women or to exclude men. As we shall see in the next chapter, there is reason to believe that women are somewhat better equipped for caring than men are. This is partly a result of the construction of psychological deep structures in the mother-child relationship. A girl can identify with the one caring for her and thus maintain relation while establishing identity. A boy must, however, find his identity with the absent one—the father—and thus disengage himself from the intimate relation of caring.[15]

There are many women who will deplore my insistence on locating the source of caring in human relations. The longing for something beyond is lovely—alluring—and it persists. It seems to me quite natural that men, many of whom are separated from the intimacy of caring, should create gods and seek security and love in worship. But what ethical need have women for God? I do not mean to suggest that women can brush aside an actually existing God but, if there is such a God, the human role in Its maintenance must be trivial. We can only contemplate the universe in awe and wonder, study it conscientiously, and live in it conservatively. Women, it seems to me, can accept the God of Spinoza and Einstein. What I mean to suggest is that women have no need of a conceptualized God, one wrought in the image of man. All the love and goodness commanded by such a God can be generated from the love and goodness found in the warmest and best human relations.

Let me say a little more here, because I know the position is a hard one for many—even for many I love. In our earlier discussion of Abraham, we saw a fundamental and deeply cut chasm between male and female views. We see this difference illustrated again in the New Testament. In Luke 16, we hear the story of a rich man who ignored the suffering of Lazarus, a beggar. After death, Lazarus finds peace and glory, but the rich man finds eternal torment. He cries to Abraham for mercy:

Father Abraham, have mercy on me, and send Lazarus, that he may dip the tip of his finger in water, and cool my tongue; for I am tormented in this flame.

But Abraham said, Son, remember that thou in thy lifetime receivedst thy good things, and likewise Lazarus evil things: but now he is comforted and thou art tormented.

And beside all this, between us and you there is a great gulf fixed: so that they which would pass from hence to you cannot; neither can they pass to us, that would come from thence.[16]

But what prevents their passage? The judgmental love of the harsh father establishes the chasm. This is not the love of the mother, for even in despair she would cast herself across the chasm to relieve the suffering of her child. If he calls her, she will respond. Even the wickedest, if he calls, she must meet as one-caring. Now, I ask again, what ethical need has woman for God?

In the stories of Abraham, we hear the tragedy induced by the traditional, masculine approach to ethics. When Kierkegaard defends him in an agonized and obsessive search for "something beyond" to which he can repeatedly declare his devotion, he reveals the emptiness at the heart of his own concrete existence. If Abraham is lost, he, Kierkegaard, is lost. He observes: "So either there is a paradox, that the individual as the individual stands in an absolute relation to the absolute/or Abraham is lost."[17]

Woman, as one-caring, pities and fears both Abraham and Kierkegaard. Not only are they lost, but they would take all of us with them into the lonely wilderness of abstraction.

The Toughness of Caring

An ethic built on caring is thought by some to be tenderminded. It does involve construction of an ideal from the fact and memory of tenderness. The ethical sentiment itself requires a prior natural sentiment of caring and a willingness to sustain tenderness. But there is no assumption of innate human goodness and, when we move to the construction of a philosophy of education, we shall find enormous differences between the view developed here and that of those who find the child innately good. I shall not claim that the child is "innately wise and good," or that the aim of life is happiness, or that all will be well with the child if we resist interfering in its intellectual and moral life.[18] We have memories of caring, of tenderness, and these lead us to a vision of what is good—a state that is good-in-itself and a commitment to sustain and enhance that good (the desire and commitment to be moral). But we have other memories as well, and we have other desires. An ethic of caring takes into account these other tendencies and desires; it is precisely because the tendency to treat each other well is so fragile that we must strive so consistently to care.

Far from being romantic, an ethic of caring is practical, made for this earth. Its toughness is disclosed in a variety of features, the most important of which I shall try to describe briefly here.

First, since caring is a relation, an ethic build on it is naturally other-regarding. Since I am defined in relation, I do not sacrifice myself when I move toward the other as one-caring. Caring is, thus, both self-serving and other-serving. Willard Gaylin describes it as necessary to the survival of the species: "If one's frame of reference focuses on the individual, caring seems self-sacrificing. But if the focus is on the group, on the species, it is the ultimate self-serving device— the sine qua non of survival."[19]

Clearly, this is so. But while I am drawn to the other, while I am instinctively called to nurture and protect, I am also the initiator and chooser of my acts. I may act in accordance with that which is good in my deepest nature, or I may seek to avoid it—either by forsaking relation or by trying to transform that which is feeling and action into that which is all propositional talk and principle. If I suppose, for example, that I am somehow alone and totally responsible for either the apprehension or creation of moral principles, I may find myself in some difficulty when it comes to caring for myself. If moral principles govern my conduct with respect to others, if I must always regard the other in order to be moral, how can I properly meet my own needs and desires? How can I, morally, care for myself?

An ethic of caring is a tough ethic. It does not separate self and other in caring, although, of course, it identifies the special contribution of the one-caring and the cared-for in caring. In contrast to some forms of agapism, for example, it has no problem in advocating a deep and steady caring for self. In a discussion of other-regarding forms of agapism, Gene Outka considers the case of a woman tied to a demanding parent. He explores the possibility of her finding justification for leaving in an assessment of the greatest good for all concerned, and he properly recommends that her own interests be included. In discussing the insistence of some agapists on entirely other-regarding justification, he explores the possibility of her breaking away "to become a medical doctor," thereby satisfying the need for multilateral other-interests.[20] The one-caring throws up her hands at such casting about for reasons. She needs no special justification to care for herself for, if she is not supported and cared-for, she may be entirely lost as one-caring. If caring is to be maintained, clearly, the one-caring must be maintained. She must be strong, courageous, and capable of joy.

When we [look] at the one-caring in conflict (e.g., Mr. Jones and his mother), we [see] that he or she can be overwhelmed by cares and burdens. The ethical responsibility of the one-caring is to look clear-eyed on what is happening to her ideal and how well she is meeting it. She sees herself, perhaps, as caring lovingly for her parent. But perhaps he is cantankerous, ungrateful, rude, and even dirty. She sees herself becoming impatient, grouchy, tired, and filled with self-pity. She can stay and live by an honestly diminished ideal—"I am a tired, grouchy, pitiful caretaker of my old father"—or she can free herself to whatever degree she must to remain minimally but actually caring. The ethical self does not live partitioned off from the rest of the person. Thinking guided by caring does not seek to justify a way out by means of a litany of predicted "goods," but it seeks a way to remain one-caring and, if at all possible, to enhance the ethical ideal. In such a quest, there is no way to disregard the self, or to remain impartial, or to adopt the stance of a disinterested observer. Pursuit of the ethical ideal demands impassioned and realistic commitment.

We see still another reason for accepting constraints on our ethical ideals. When we accept honestly our loves, our innate ferocity, our capacity for hate, we may use all this as information in building the safeguards and alarms that must be part of the ideal. We know better what we must work toward, what we must prevent, and the conditions under which we are lost as ones-caring. Instead of hiding from our natural impulses and pretending that we can achieve goodness through lofty abstractions, we accept what is there—all of it—and use what we have already assessed as good to control that which is not-good.

Caring preserves both the group and the individual and, as we have already seen, it limits our obligation so that it may realistically be met. It will not allow us to be distracted by visions of universal love, perfect justice, or a world unified under principle. It does not say, "Thou shalt not kill," and then seek other principles under which killing is, after all, justified. If the other is a clear and immediate danger to me or to my cared-fors, I must stop him, and I might need to kill him. But I cannot kill in the name of principle or justice. I must meet this other—even this evil other—as one-caring so long as caring itself is not endangered by my doing so. I must, for example, oppose capital punishment. I do not begin by saying, "Capital punishment is wrong." Thus I do not fall into the trap of having to supply reasons for its wrongness that will be endlessly disputed at a logical level. I do not say, "Life is sacred," for I cannot name a source of sacredness. I may point to the irrevocability of the decision, but this is not in itself decisive, even for me, because in many cases the decision would be just and I could not regret the demise of the condemned. (I have, after all, confessed my own ferocity; in the heat of emotion, I might have torn him to shreds if I had caught him molesting my child.)

My concern is for the ethical ideal, for my own ethical ideal and for whatever part of it others in my community may share. Ideally, another human being should be able to request, with expectation of positive response, my help and comfort. If I am not blinded by fear, or rage, or hatred, I should reach out as one-caring to the proximate stranger who entreats my help. This is the ideal one-caring creates. I should be able to respond to the condemned man's entreaty, "Help me." We must ask, then, after the effects of capital punishment on jurors, on judges, on jailers, on wardens, on newspersons "covering" the execution, on ministers visiting the condemned, on citizens affirming the sentence, on doctors certifying first that the condemned is well enough to be executed and second that he is dead. What effects have capital punishment on the ethical ideals of the participants? For me, if I had to participate, the ethical ideal would be diminished. Diminished. The ideal itself would be diminished. My act would either be wrong or barely right—right in a depleted sense. I might, indeed, participate ethically—rightly—in an execution but only at the cost of revising my ethical ideal downward. If I do not revise it and still participate, then my act is wrong, and I am a hypocrite and unethical. It is the difference between "I don't believe in killing, but . . ." and "I did not believe in killing cold-bloodedly, but now I see that I must and for these reasons." In the latter case, I may retain my ethicality, but at considerable cost. My ideal must forever carry with it not only what I would be but what I am and have been. There is no unbridgeable chasm between what I am and what I will be. I build the bridge to my future self, and this is why I oppose capital punishment. I do not want to kill if other options are open to me, and I do not want to ask others in the community to do what may diminish their own ethical ideals.

While I must not kill in obedience to law or principle, I may not, either, refuse to kill in obedience to principle. To remain one-caring, I might have to kill. Consider the case of a woman who kills her sleeping husband. Under most circumstances, the one-caring would judge such an act wrong. It violates the very possibility of caring for the husband. But as she hears how the husband abused his wife and children, about the fear with which the woman lived, about the past efforts to solve the problem legally, the one-caring revises her judgment. The jury finds the woman not guilty by reason of an extenuated self-defense. The one-caring finds her ethical, but under the guidance of a sadly diminished ethical ideal. The woman has behaved in the only way she found open to protect herself and her children and, thus, she has behaved in accord with the current vision of herself as one-caring. But what a horrible vision! She is now one-who-has-killed once and who would not kill again, and never again simply one who would not kill. The test of ultimate blame or blamelessness, under an ethic of caring, lies in how the ethical ideal was diminished. Did the agent choose the degraded vision out of greed, cruelty, or personal interest? Or was she driven to it by unscrupulous others who made caring impossible to sustain?

We see that our own ethicality is not entirely "up to us." Like Winston in *Nineteen Eighty-Four,* we are fragile; we depend upon each other even for our own goodness. This recognition casts some doubt on Immanuel Kant's position:

> It is contradictory to say that I make another person's *perfection* my end and consider myself obliged to promote this. For the *perfection* of another man, as a person, consists precisely of *his own* power to adopt his end in accordance with his own concept of duty; and it is self-contradictory to demand that I do (make it my duty to do) what only the other person himself can do.[21]

In one sense, we agree fully with Kant. We cannot define another's perfection; we, as ones-caring, will not even define the principles by which he should live, nor can we prescribe the particular acts he should perform to meet that perfection. But we must be exquisitely sensitive to that ideal of perfection and, in the absence of a repugnance overwhelming to one-caring, we must as ones-caring act to promote that ideal. As parents and educators, we have perhaps no single greater or higher duty than this.

The duty to enhance the ethical ideal, the commitment to caring, invokes a duty to promote skepticism and noninstitutional affiliation. In a deep sense, no institution or nation can be ethical. It cannot meet the other as one-caring or as one trying to care. It can only capture in general terms what particular ones-caring would like to have done in well-described situations. Laws, manifestos, and proclamations are not, on this account, either empty or useless; but they are limited, and they may support immoral as well as moral actions. Only the individual can be truly called to ethical behavior, and the individual can never give way to encapsulated moral guides, although she may safely accept them in ordinary, untroubled times.

Everything depends, then, upon the will to be good, to remain in caring relation to the other. How may we help ourselves and each other to sustain this will?

Notes

1. Ralph Linton, "An Anthropologist's Approach to Ethical Principles," in *Understanding Moral Philosophy*, ed. James Rachels (Encino, Calif.: Dickenson Publishing Company, Inc., 1976), p. 8.

2. Fred Feldman, *Introductory Ethics* (Englewood Cliffs, N.J.: Prentice-Hall, Inc., 1978), p. 2.

3. See, for example, Joseph Fletcher, *Situation Ethics* (Philadelphia: The Westminster Press, 1966).

4. David Hume, "An Enquiry Concerning the Principles of Morals," in *Ethical Theories*, ed. A. I. Melden (Englewood Cliffs, N.J.: Prentice-Hall, Inc., 1967), p. 275.

5. Friedrich Nietzsche, "Mixed Opinions and Maxims," in *The Portable Nietzsche*, ed. Walter Kaufmann (New York: The Viking Press, Inc., 1954), p. 65.

6. See, for example, William F. Frankena, *Ethics* (Englewood Cliffs, N.J.: Prentice-Hall, Inc., 1973), pp. 63–71.

7. The argument here is, I think, compatible with that of Philippa Foot, "Reasons for Action and Desires," in *Virtues and Vices*, ed. Philippa Foot (Berkeley, Los Angeles, London: University of California Press, 1978), pp. 148–156. My argument, however, relies on a basic desire, universal in all human beings, to be in relation—to care and be cared for.

8. The question of "summonability" is a vital one for ethicists who rely on good or altruistic feelings for moral motivation. Note treatment of this problem in Lawrence R. Blum, *Friendship, Altruism, and Morality* (London: Routledge & Kegan Paul, 1980), pp. 20–23 and pp. 194–203. See, also, Henry Sidgwick, *The Methods of Ethics* (Indianapolis: Hackett, 1981), and Philip Mercer, *Sympathy and Ethics* (Oxford: Clarendon Press, 1962).

9. Friedrich Nietzsche, *The Will to Power*, trans. Walter Kaufmann (New York: Random House, 1967), pp. 476, 670. For a contemporary argument against strict application of

universalizability, see Peter Winch, *Ethics and Action* (London: Routledge & Kegan Paul, 1972).

10. W. D. Ross, *The Right and the Good* (Oxford: Clarendon Press, 1930). See also Frankena, *Ethics*.

11. Paul Ramsey raises this concern in *Fabricated Man* (New Haven and London: Yale University Press, 1970).

12. See the discussion in James Rachels, ed., *Understanding Moral Philosophy* (Encino, Calif.: Dickenson Publishing Company, Inc., 1976), pp. 38–39.

13. See Lawrence Kohlberg and R. Kramer, "Continuities and Discontinuities in Childhood and Adult Moral Development," *Human Development* 12 (1969), 93–120. See also Lawrence Kohlberg, "Stages in Moral Development as a Basis for Moral Education," in *Moral Education: Interdisciplinary Approaches,* ed. C. M. Beck, B. S. Crittenden, and E. V. Sullivan (Toronto: Toronto University Press, 1971).

14. Carol Gilligan, "Woman's Place in Man's Life Cycle," *Harvard Educational Review* 49 (1979), 440.

15. See Nancy Chodorow, *The Reproduction of Mothering* (Berkeley, Los Angeles, London: University of California Press, 1978).

16. Luke 16: 24–26.

17. Søren Kierkegaard, *Fear and Trembling,* trans. Walter Lowrie (Princeton: Princeton University Press, 1954), p. 129.

18. For a lovely exposition of this view, see A. S. Neill, *Summerhill* (New York: Hart Publishing Company, 1960).

19. Willard Gaylin, *Caring* (New York: Alfred A. Knopf, 1976), p. 115.

20. Gene Outka, *Agapé: An Ethical Analysis* (New Haven and London: Yale University Press, 1972), pp. 300–305.

21. Immanuel Kant, *The Metaphysics of Morals,* Part II: *The Doctrine of Virtue* (New York: Harper and Row, 1964), pp. 44–45.

2

Moral Orientation and Moral Development [1987]

CAROL GILLIGAN

When one looks at an ambiguous figure like the drawing that can be seen as a young or old woman, or the image of the vase and the faces, one initially sees it in only one way. Yet even after seeing it in both ways, one way often seems more compelling. This phenomenon reflects the laws of perceptual organization that favor certain modes of visual grouping. But it also suggests a tendency to view reality as unequivocal and thus to argue that there is one right or better way of seeing.

The experiments of the Gestalt psychologists on perceptual organization provide a series of demonstrations that the same proximal pattern can be organized in different ways so that, for example, the same figure can be seen as a square or a diamond, depending on its orientation in relation to a surrounding frame. Subsequent studies show that the context influencing which of two possible organizations will be chosen may depend not only on the features of the array presented but also on the perceiver's past experience or expectation. Thus, a bird-watcher and a rabbit-keeper are likely to see the duck-rabbit figure in different ways; yet this difference does not imply that one way is better or a higher form of perceptual organization. It does, however, call attention to the fact that the rabbit-keeper, perceiving the rabbit, may not see the ambiguity of the figure until someone points out that it can also be seen as a duck.

This paper presents a similar phenomenon with respect to moral judgment, describing two moral perspectives that organize thinking in different ways. The analogy to ambiguous figure perception arises from the observation that although

31

people are aware of both perspectives, they tend to adopt one or the other in defining and resolving moral conflict. Since moral judgments organize thinking about choice in difficult situations, the adoption of a single perspective may facilitate clarity of decision. But the wish for clarity may also imply a compelling human need for resolution or closure, especially in the face of decisions that give rise to discomfort or unease. Thus, the search for clarity in seeing may blend with a search for justification, encouraging the position that there is one right or better way to think about moral problems. This question, which has been the subject of intense theological and philosophical debate, becomes of interest to the psychologist not only because of its psychological dimensions—the tendency to focus on one perspective and the wish for justification—but also because one moral perspective currently dominates psychological thinking and is embedded in the most widely used measure for assessing the maturity of moral reasoning.

In describing an alternative standpoint, I will reconstruct the account of moral development around two moral perspectives, grounded in different dimensions of relationship that give rise to moral concern. The justice perspective, often equated with moral reasoning, is recast as one way of seeing moral problems and a care perspective is brought forward as an alternate vision or frame. The distinction between justice and care as alternative perspectives or moral orientations is based empirically on the observation that a shift in the focus of attention from concerns about justice to concerns about care changes the definition of what constitutes a moral problem, and leads the same situation to be seen in different ways. Theoretically, the distinction between justice and care cuts across the familiar divisions between thinking and feeling, egoism and altruism, theoretical and practical reasoning. It calls attention to the fact that all human relationships, public and private, can be characterized *both* in terms of equality and in terms of attachment, and that both inequality and detachment constitute grounds for moral concern. Since everyone is vulnerable both to oppression and to abandonment, two moral visions—one of justice and one of care—recur in human experience. The moral injunctions not to act unfairly toward others, and not to turn away from someone in need, capture these different concerns.

The conception of the moral domain as [comprising] at least two moral orientations raises new questions about observed differences in moral judgment and the disagreements to which they give rise. Key to this revision is the distinction between differences in developmental stage (more or less adequate positions within a single orientation) and differences in orientation (alternative perspectives or frameworks). The findings reported in this paper of an association between moral orientation and gender speak directly to the continuing controversy over sex differences in moral reasoning. In doing so, however, they also offer an empirical explanation for why previous thinking about moral development has been organized largely within the justice framework.

My research on moral orientation derives from an observation made in the course of studying the relationship between moral judgment and action. Two studies, one of college students describing their experiences of moral conflict and choice, and one of pregnant women who were considering abortion, shifted the focus of attention from the ways people reason about hypothetical dilemmas to the ways people construct moral conflicts and choices in their lives. This change in approach made it possible to see what experiences people define in moral terms, and to explore the relationship between the understanding of moral problems and the reasoning strategies used and the actions taken in attempting to resolve them. In this context, I observed that women, especially when speaking about their own experiences of moral conflict and choice, often define moral problems in a way that eludes the categories of moral theory and is at odds with the assumptions that shape psychological thinking about morality and about the self.[1] This discovery, that a different voice often guides the moral judgments and the actions of women, called attention to a major design problem in previous moral judgment research: namely, the use of all-male samples as the empirical basis for theory construction.

The selection of an all-male sample as the basis for generalizations that are applied to both males and females is logically inconsistent. As a research strategy, the decision to begin with a single-sex sample is inherently problematic, since the categories of analysis will tend to be defined on the basis of the initial data gathered and subsequent studies will tend to be restricted to these categories. Piaget's work on the moral judgment of the child illustrates these problems since he defined the evolution of children's consciousness and practice of rules on the basis of his study of boys playing marbles, and then undertook a study of girls to assess the generality of his findings. Observing a series of differences both in the structure of girls' games and "in the actual mentality of little girls," he deemed these differences not of interest because "it was not this contrast which we proposed to study." Girls, Piaget found, "rather complicated our interrogatory in relation to what we know about boys," since the changes in their conception of rules, although following the same sequence observed in boys, did not stand in the same relation to social experience. Nevertheless, he concluded that "in spite of these differences in the structure of the game and apparently in the players' mentality, we find the same process at work as in the evolution of the game of marbles."[2]

Thus, girls were of interest insofar as they were similar to boys and confirmed the generality of Piaget's findings. The differences noted, which included a greater tolerance, a greater tendency toward innovation in solving conflicts, a greater willingness to make exceptions to rules, and a lesser concern with legal elaboration, were not seen as germane to "the psychology of rules," and therefore were regarded as insignificant for the study of children's moral judgment. Given the confusion that currently surrounds the discussion of sex differences in moral judgment, it is important to emphasize that the differences observed by

Piaget did not pertain to girls' understanding of rules *per se* or to the development of the idea of justice in their thinking, but rather to the way girls structured
their games and their approach to conflict resolution—that is, to their use rather
than their understanding of the logic of rules and justice.

Kohlberg, in his research on moral development, did not encounter these
problems since he equated moral development with the development of justice
reasoning and initially used an all-male sample as the basis for theory and test
construction. In response to his critics, Kohlberg has recently modified his
claims, renaming his test a measure of "justice reasoning" rather than of "moral
maturity" and acknowledging the presence of a care perspective in people's
moral thinking.³ But the widespread use of Kohlberg's measure as a measure of
moral development together with his own continuing tendency to equate justice
reasoning with moral judgment leaves the problem of orientation differences
unsolved. More specifically, Kohlberg's efforts to assimilate thinking about care
to the six-stage developmental sequence he derived and refined by analyzing
changes in justice reasoning (relying centrally on his all-male longitudinal sample), underscores the continuing importance of the points raised in this paper
concerning (1) the distinction between differences in developmental stage
within a single orientation and differences in orientation, and (2) the fact that
the moral thinking of girls and women was not examined in establishing either
the meaning or the measurement of moral judgment within contemporary psychology.

An analysis of the language and logic of men's and women's moral reasoning
about a range of hypothetical and real dilemmas underlies the distinction elaborated in this paper between a justice and a care perspective. The empirical association of care reasoning with women suggests that discrepancies observed between moral theory and the moral judgments of girls and women may reflect a
shift in perspective, a change in moral orientation. Like the figure-ground shift
in ambiguous figure perception, justice and care as moral perspectives are not
opposites or mirror-images of one another, with justice uncaring and care unjust. Instead, these perspectives denote different ways of organizing the basic elements of moral judgment: self, others, and the relationship between them.
With the shift in perspective from justice to care, the organizing dimension of relationship changes from inequality/equality to attachment/detachment, reor-
ganizing thoughts, feelings, and language so that words connoting relationship
like "dependence" or "responsibility" or even moral terms such as "fairness" and
"care" take on different meanings. To organize relationships in terms of attachment rather than in terms of equality changes the way human connection is
imagined, so that the images or metaphors of relationship shift from hierarchy
or balance to network or web. In addition, each organizing framework leads to a
different way of imagining the self as a moral agent.

From a justice perspective, the self as moral agent stands as the figure against
a ground of social relationships, judging the conflicting claims of self and others

against a standard of equality or equal respect (the Categorical Imperative, the Golden Rule). From a care perspective, the relationship becomes the figure, defining self and others. Within the context of relationship, the self as a moral agent perceives and responds to the perception of need. The shift in moral perspective is manifest by a change in the moral question from "What is just?" to "How to respond?"

For example, adolescents asked to describe a moral dilemma often speak about peer or family pressure in which case the moral question becomes how to maintain moral principles or standards and resist the influence of one's parents or friends. "I have a right to my religious opinions," one teenager explains, referring to a religious difference with his parents. Yet, he adds, "I respect their views." The same dilemma, however, is also construed by adolescents as a problem of attachment, in which case the moral question becomes: how to respond both to oneself and to one's friends or one's parents, how to maintain or strengthen connection in the face of differences in belief. "I understand their fear of my new religious ideas," one teenager explains, referring to her religious disagreement with her parents, "but they really ought to listen to me and try to understand my beliefs."

One can see these two statements as two versions of essentially the same thing. Both teenagers present self-justifying arguments about religious disagreement; both address the claims of self and of others in a way that honors both. Yet each frames the problem in different terms, and the use of moral language points to different concerns. The first speaker casts the problem in terms of individual rights that must be respected within the relationship. In other words, the figure of the considering is the self looking on the disagreeing selves in relationship, and the aim is to get the other selves to acknowledge the right to disagree. In the case of the second speaker, figure and ground shift. The relationship becomes the figure of the considering, and relationships are seen to require listening and efforts at understanding differences in belief. Rather than the right to disagree, the speaker focuses on caring to hear and to be heard. Attention shifts from the grounds for agreement (rights and respect) to the grounds for understanding (listening and speaking, hearing and being heard). This shift is marked by a change in moral language from the stating of separate claims to rights and respect ("I have a right . . . I respect their views.") to the activities of relationship—the injunction to listen and try to understand ("I understand . . . they ought to listen . . . and try to understand."). The metaphor of moral voice itself carries the terms of the care perspective and reveals how the language chosen for moral theory is not orientation neutral.

The language of the public abortion debate, for example, reveals a justice perspective. Whether the abortion dilemma is cast as a conflict of rights or in terms of respect for human life, the claims of the fetus and of the pregnant woman are balanced or placed in opposition. The morality of abortion decisions thus construed hinges on the scholastic or metaphysical question as to whether the fetus is a life or a person, and whether its claims take precedence over those of the pregnant woman. Framed as a problem of care, the dilemma posed by abortion shifts. The connection between the fetus and the pregnant woman becomes the focus of attention and the question becomes whether it is responsible or irresponsible, caring or careless, to extend or to end this connection. In this construction, the abortion dilemma arises because there is no way not to act, and no way of acting that does not alter the connection between self and others. To ask what actions constitute care or are more caring directs attention to the parameters of connection and the costs of detachment, which become subjects of moral concern.

Finally, two medical students, each reporting a decision not to turn in someone who has violated the school rules against drinking, cast their decision in different terms. One student constructs the decision as an act of mercy, a decision to override justice in light of the fact that the violator has shown "the proper degrees of contrition." In addition, this student raises the question as to whether or not the alcohol policy is just, i.e., whether the school has the right to prohibit drinking. The other student explains the decision not to turn in a proctor who was drinking on the basis that turning him in is not a good way to respond to this problem, since it would dissolve the relationship between them and thus cut off an avenue for help. In addition, this student raises the question as to whether the proctor sees his drinking as a problem.

This example points to an important distinction, between care as understood or construed within a justice framework and care as a framework or a perspective on moral decision. Within a justice construction, care becomes the mercy that tempers justice; or connotes the special obligations or supererogatory duties that arise in personal relationships; or signifies altruism freely chosen—a decision to modulate the strict demands of justice by considering equity or showing forgiveness; or characterizes a choice to sacrifice the claims of the self. All of these interpretations of care leave the basic assumptions of a justice framework intact: the division between the self and others, the logic of reciprocity or equal respect.

As a moral perspective, care is less well elaborated, and there is no ready vocabulary in moral theory to describe its terms. As a framework for moral decision, care is grounded in the assumption that self and other are interdependent, an assumption reflected in a view of action as responsive and, therefore, as arising in relationship rather than the view of action as emanating from within the self and, therefore, "self governed." Seen as responsive, the self is by definition connected to others, responding to perceptions, interpreting events, and governed by the organizing tendencies of human interaction and human language. Within this framework, detachment, whether from self or from others, is morally problematic, since it breeds moral blindness or indifference—a failure to discern or respond to need. The question of what responses constitute care and what responses lead to hurt draws attention to the fact that one's own terms may differ from those of others. Justice in this context becomes understood as respect for people in their own terms.

The medical student's decision not to turn in the proctor for drinking reflects a judgment that turning him in is not the best way to respond to the drinking problem, itself seen as a sign of detachment or lack of concern. Caring for the proctor thus raises the question of what actions are most likely to ameliorate this problem, a decision that leads to the question of what are the proctor's terms.

The shift in organizing perspective here is marked by the fact that the first student does not consider the terms of the other as potentially different but instead assumes one set of terms. Thus the student alone becomes the arbiter of what is *the* proper degree of contrition. The second student, in turn, does not attend to the question of whether the alcohol policy itself is just or fair. Thus each student discusses an aspect of the problem that the other does not mention.

These examples are intended to illustrate two cross-cutting perspectives that do not negate one another but focus attention on different dimensions of the situation, creating a sense of ambiguity around the question of what is the problem to be solved. Systematic research on moral orientation as a dimension of moral judgment and action initially addressed three questions: (1) Do people articulate concerns about justice and concerns about care in discussing a moral dilemma? (2) Do people tend to focus their attention on one set of concerns and minimally represent the other? and (3) Is there an association between moral orientation and gender? Evidence from studies that included a common set of questions about actual experiences of moral conflict and matched samples of males and females provides affirmative answers to all three questions.

When asked to describe a moral conflict they had faced, 55 out of 80 (69 percent) educationally advantaged North American adolescents and adults raised considerations of both justice and care. Two-thirds (54 out of 80) however, focused their attention on one set of concerns, with focus defined as 75 percent or more of the considerations raised pertaining either to justice or to care. Thus the person who presented, say, two care considerations in discussing a moral conflict was more likely to give a third, fourth, and fifth than to balance care and justice concerns—a finding consonant with the assumption that justice and care constitute organizing frameworks for moral decision. The men and the women involved in this study (high school students, college students, medical students, and adult professionals) were equally likely to demonstrate the focus phenomenon (two-thirds of both sexes fell into the outlying focus categories). There were, however, sex differences in the direction of focus. With one exception, all of the men who focused, focused on justice. The women divided, with roughly one third focusing on justice and one third on care.[4]

These findings clarify the different voice phenomenon and its implications for moral theory and for women. First, it is notable that if women were eliminated from the research sample, care focus in moral reasoning would virtually disappear. Although care focus was by no means characteristic of all women, it was almost exclusively a female phenomenon in this sample of educationally advantaged North Americans. Second, the fact that the women were advantaged means that the focus on care cannot readily be attributed to educational deficit or occupational disadvantage—the explanation Kohlberg and others have given for findings of lower levels of justice reasoning in women.[5] Instead, the focus on care in women's moral reasoning draws attention to the limitations of a justice-focused moral theory and highlights the presence of care concerns in the moral thinking of both women and men. In this light, the Care/Justice group composed of one third of the women and one third of the men becomes of particular interest, pointing to the need for further research that attends to the way people organize justice and care in relation to one another—whether, for example, people alternate perspectives, like seeing the rabbit and the duck in the rabbit-duck figure, or integrate the two perspectives in a way that resolves or sustains ambiguity.

Third, if the moral domain is [composed] of at least two moral orientations, the focus phenomenon suggests that people have a tendency to lose sight of one moral perspective in arriving at a moral decision—a liability equally shared by both sexes. The present findings further suggest that men and women tend to lose sight of different perspectives. The most striking result is the virtual absence of care-focus reasoning among the men. Since the men raised concerns about care in discussing moral conflicts and thus presented care concerns as morally relevant, a question is why they did not elaborate these concerns to a greater extent.

In summary, it becomes clear why attention to women's moral thinking led to the identification of a different voice and raised questions about the place of justice and care within a comprehensive moral theory. It also is clear how the selection of an all-male sample for research on moral judgment fosters an equation of morality with justice, providing little data discrepant with this view. In the present study, data discrepant with a justice-focused moral theory comes from a third of the women. Previously, such women were seen as having a problem understanding "morality." Yet these women may also be seen as exposing the problem in a justice-focused moral theory. This may explain the decision of researchers to exclude girls and women at the initial stage of moral judgment research. If one begins with the premise that "all morality consists in respect for rules,"[6] or "virtue is one and its name is justice,"[7] then women are likely to appear problematic within moral theory. If one begins with women's moral judgments, the problem becomes how to construct a theory that encompasses care as a focus of moral attention rather than as a subsidiary moral concern.

The implications of moral orientation for moral theory and for research on moral development are extended by a study designed and conducted by Kay Johnston.[8] Johnston set out to explore the relationship between moral orientation and problem-solving strategies, creating a standard method using fables for assessing spontaneous moral orientation and orientation preference. She asked 60 eleven- and fifteen-year-olds to state and to solve the moral problem posed by the fable. Then she asked: "Is there another way to solve this problem?" Most of the children initially constructed the fable problems either in terms of justice or in terms of care; either they stood back from the situation and appealed to a rule or principle for adjudicating the conflicting claims or they entered the situation in an effort to discover or create a way of responding to all of the needs. About half of the children, slightly more fifteen- than eleven-year-olds, spontaneously switched moral orientation when asked whether there was another way to solve the problem. Others did so following an interviewer's cue as to the form such a switch might take. Finally, the children were asked which of the solutions they described was the best solution. Most of the children answered the question and explained why one way was preferable.

Johnston found gender differences parallel to those previously reported, with boys more often spontaneously using and preferring justice solutions and girls more often spontaneously using and preferring care solutions. In addition, she found differences between the two fables she used, confirming Langdale's finding that moral orientation is associated both with the gender of the reasoner and with the dilemma considered.[9] Finally, the fact that children, at least by the age of eleven, are able to shift moral orientation and can explain the logic of two moral perspectives, each associated with a different problem-solving strategy, heightens the analogy to ambiguous figure perception and further supports the conception of justice and care as organizing frameworks for moral decision.

The demonstration that children know both orientations and can frame and solve moral problems in at least two different ways means that the choice of moral standpoint is an element of moral decision. The role of the self in moral judgment thus includes the choice of moral standpoint, and this decision, whether implicit or explicit, may become linked with self-respect and self-definition. Especially in adolescence, when choice becomes more self-conscious and self-reflective, moral standpoint may become entwined with identity and self-esteem. Johnston's finding that spontaneous moral orientation and preferred orientation are not always the same raises a number of questions as to why and under what conditions a person may adopt a problem-solving strategy that he or she sees as not the best way to solve the problem.

The way people choose to frame or solve a moral problem is clearly not the only way in which they can think about the problem, and is not necessarily the way they deem preferable. Moral judgments thus do not reveal *the* structure of moral thinking, since there are at least two ways in which people can structure moral problems. Johnston's demonstration of orientation-switch poses a serious challenge to the methods that have been used in moral judgment and moral development research, introducing a major interpretive caution. The fact that boys and girls at eleven and fifteen understand and distinguish the logics of justice and care reasoning directs attention to the origins and the development of both ways of thinking. In addition, the tendency for boys and girls to use and prefer different orientations when solving the same problem raises a number of questions about the relationship between these orientations and the factors influencing their representation. The different patterns of orientation use and preference, as well as the different conceptions of justice and of care implied or elaborated in the fable judgments, suggest that moral development cannot be mapped along a single linear stage sequence.

One way of explaining these findings, suggested by Johnston, joins Vygotsky's theory of cognitive development with Chodorow's analysis of sex differences in early childhood experiences of relationship.[10] Vygotsky posits that all of the higher cognitive functions originate as actual relations between individuals. Justice and care as moral ideas and as reasoning strategies thus would originate as relationships with others—an idea consonant with the derivation of justice and care reasoning from experiences of inequality and attachment in early childhood. All children are born into a situation of inequality in that they are less capable than the adults and older children around them and, in this sense, more helpless and less powerful. In addition, no child survives in the absence of some kind of adult attachment—or care, and through this experience of relationship children discover the responsiveness of human connection including their ability to move and affect one another.

Through the experience of inequality, of being in the less powerful position, children learn what it means to depend on the authority and the good will of others. As a result, they tend to strive for equality of greater power, and for freedom. Through the experience of attachment, children discover the ways in which people are able to care for and to hurt one another. The child's vulnerability to oppression and to abandonment thus can be seen to lay the groundwork for the moral visions of justice and care, conceived as ideals of human relationship and defining the ways in which people "should" act toward one another.

Chodorow's work then provides a way of explaining why care concerns tend to be minimally represented by men and why such concerns are less frequently elaborated in moral theory. Chodorow joins the dynamics of gender identity formation (the identification of oneself as male or female) to an analysis of early childhood relationships and examines the effects of maternal child care on the inner structuring of self in relation to others. Further, she differentiates a positional sense of self from a personal sense of self, contrasting a self defined in terms of role or position from a self known through the experience of connection. Her point is that maternal child care fosters the continuation of a relational sense of self in girls, since female gender identity is consonant with feeling connected with one's mother. For boys, gender identity is in tension with mother-child connection, unless that connection is structured in terms of sexual opposition (e.g., as an Oedipal drama). Thus, although boys experience responsiveness or care in relationships, knowledge of care or the need for care, when associated with mothers, pose a threat to masculine identity.[11]

Chodorow's work is limited by her reliance on object relations theory and problematic on that count. Object relations theory ties the formation of the self to the experience of separation, joining separation with individuation and thus counterposing the experience of self to the experience of connection with others. This is the line that Chodorow traces in explicating male development. Within this framework, girls' connections with their mothers can only be seen as problematic. Connection with others or the capacity to feel and think *with* others is, by definition, in tension with self-development when self-development or individuation is linked to separation. Thus, object-relations theory sustains a series of oppositions that have been central in Western thought and moral theory, including the opposition between thought and feelings, self and relationship, reason and compassion, justice and love. Object relations theory also continues the conventional division of psychological labor between women and men. Since the idea of a self, experienced in the context of attachment with others, is theoretically impossible, mothers, described as objects, are viewed as selfless, without a self. This view is essentially problematic for women, divorcing the activity of mothering from desire, knowledge, and agency, and implying that insofar as a mother experiences herself as a subject rather than as an object (a mirror reflecting her child), she is "selfish" and not a good mother. Winnicott's phrase "good-enough mother" represents an effort to temper this judgment.

Thus, psychologists and philosophers, aligning the self and morality with separation and autonomy—the ability to be self-governing—have associated care with self-sacrifice, or with feelings—a view at odds with the current position that care represents a way of knowing and a coherent moral perspective. This position, however, is well represented in literature written by women. For example the short story "A Jury of Her Peers," written by Susan Glaspell in 1917, a time when women ordinarily did not serve on juries, contrasts two ways of knowing that underlie two ways of interpreting and solving a crime.[12] The story centers on a murder; Minnie Foster is suspected of killing her husband.

A neighbor woman and the sheriff's wife accompany the sheriff and the prosecutor to the house of the accused woman. The men, representing the law, seek evidence that will convince a jury to convict the suspect. The women, collecting things to bring Minnie Foster in jail, enter in this way into the lives lived in the house. Taking in rather than taking apart, they begin to assemble observations and impressions, connecting them to past experience and observations until suddenly they compose a familiar pattern, like the log-cabin pattern they recognize in the quilt Minnie Foster was making. "Why do we *know*—what we know this minute?" one woman asks the other, but she also offers the following explanation:

> We live close together, and we live far apart. We all go through the same things—it's all just a different kind of the same thing! If it weren't—why do you and I *understand*.[13]

The activity of quilt-making—collecting odd scraps and piecing them together until they form a pattern—becomes the metaphor for this way of knowing. Discovering a strangled canary buried under pieces of quilting, the women make a series of connections that lead them to understand what happened.

The logic that says you don't kill a man because he has killed a bird, the judgment that finds these acts wildly incommensurate, is counterposed to the logic that sees both events as part of a larger pattern—a pattern of detachment and abandonment that led finally to the strangling. "I *wish* I'd come over here once in a while," Mrs. Hale, the neighbor, exclaims. "That was a crime! Who's going to punish that?" Mrs. Peters, the sheriff's wife, recalls that when she was a girl and a boy killed her cat, "If they hadn't held me back I would have—" and realizes that there had been no one to restrain Minnie Foster. John Foster was known as "a good man . . . He didn't drink, and he kept his word as well as most, I guess, and paid his debts." But he also was "a hard man," Mrs. Hale explains, "like a raw wind that gets to the bone."

Seeing detachment as the crime with murder as its ultimate extension, implicating themselves and also seeing the connection between their own and Minnie Foster's actions, the women solve the crime by attachment—by joining together, like the "knotting" that joins pieces of a quilt. In the decision to remove rather than to reveal the evidence, they separate themselves from a legal system in which they have no voice but also no way of voicing what they have come to understand. In choosing to connect themselves with one another and with Minnie, they separate themselves from the law that would use their understanding and their knowledge as grounds for further separation and killing.

In a law school class where a film-version of this story was shown, the students were divided in their assessment of the moral problem and in their evaluation of the various characters and actions. Some focused on the murder, the strangling of the husband. Some focused on the evidence of abandonment or indifference to others. Responses to a questionnaire showed a bi-modal distribution, indicating two ways of viewing the film. These different perspectives led to different ways of evaluating both the act of murder and the women's decision to remove the evidence. Responses to the film were not aligned with the sex of the viewer in an absolute way, thus dispelling any implication of biological determinism or of a stark division between the way women and men know or judge events. The knowledge gained inductively by the women in the film, however, was also gained more readily by women watching the film, who came in this way to see a logic in the women's actions and to articulate a rationale for their silence.

The analogy to ambiguous figure perception is useful here in several ways. First, it suggests that people can see a situation in more than one way, and even alternate ways of seeing, combining them without reducing them—like designating the rabbit-duck figure as both duck and rabbit. Second, the analogy argues against the tendency to construe justice and care as opposites or mirror-images and also against the implication that these two perspectives are readily integrated or fused. The ambiguous figure directs attention to the way in which a change in perspective can reorganize perception and change understanding, without implying an underlying reality or pure form. What makes seeing both moral perspectives so difficult is precisely that the orientations are not opposites or mirror images or better and worse representations of a single moral truth. The terms of one perspective do not contain the terms of the other. Instead, a shift in orientation denotes a restructuring of moral perception, changing the meaning of moral language and thus the definition of moral conflict and moral action. For example, detachment is considered the hallmark of mature moral thinking within a justice perspective, signifying the ability to judge dispassionately, to weigh evidence in an even-handed manner, balancing the claims of others and self. From a care perspective, detachment is *the* moral problem.

> "I could've come," retorted Mrs. Hale . . . "I wish I had come over to see Minnie Foster sometimes. I can see now . . . If there had been years and years of—nothing, then a bird to sing to you, it would be awful—still—after the bird was still. . . . I know what stillness is."

The difference between agreement and understanding captures the different logics of justice and care reasoning, one seeking grounds for agreement, one seeking grounds for understanding, one assuming separation and thus the need for some external structure of connection, one assuming connection and thus the potential for understanding. These assumptions run deep, generating and reflecting different views of human nature and the human condition. They also point to different vulnerabilities and different sources of error. The potential error in justice reasoning lies in its latent egocentrism, the tendency to confuse one's perspective with an objective standpoint or truth, the temptation to define others in one's own terms by putting oneself in their place. The potential error in care reasoning lies in the tendency to forget that one has terms, creating a tendency to enter into another's perspective and to see oneself as "selfless" by defining oneself in other's terms. These two types of error underlie two common equations that signify distortions or deformations of justice and care: the equation of human with male, unjust in its omission of women; and the equation of care with self-sacrifice, uncaring in its failure to represent the activity and the agency of care.

The equation of human with male was assumed in the Platonic and in the Enlightenment tradition as well as by psychologists who saw all-male samples as "representative" of human experience. The equation of care with self-sacrifice is in some ways more complex. The premise of self-interest assumes a conflict of interest between self and other manifest in the opposition of egoism and altruism. Together, the equations of male with human and of care with self-sacrifice form a circle that has had a powerful hold on moral philosophy and psychology. The conjunction of women and moral theory thus challenges the traditional definition of human and calls for a reconsideration of what is meant by both justice and care.

To trace moral development along two distinct although intersecting dimensions of relationship suggests the possibility of different permutations of justice and care reasoning, different ways these two moral perspectives can be understood and represented in relation to one another. For example, one perspective may overshadow or eclipse the other, so that one is brightly illuminated while the other is dimly remembered, familiar but for the most part forgotten. The way in which one story about relationship obscures another was evident in high school girls' definitions of dependence. These definitions highlighted two meanings—one arising from the opposition between dependence and independence, and one from the opposition of dependence to isolation ("No woman," one student observed, "is an island.") As the word "dependence" connotes the experience of relationship, this shift in the implied opposite of dependence indicates how the valence of relationship changes, when connection with others is experienced as an impediment to autonomy or independence, and when it is experienced as a source of comfort and pleasure, and as a protection against isolation. This essential ambivalence of human connection provides a powerful emotional grounding for two moral perspectives, and also may indicate what is at stake in the effort to reduce morality to a single perspective.

It is easy to understand the ascendance of justice reasoning and of justice-focused moral theories in a society where care is associated with personal vulnerability in the form of economic disadvantage. But another way of thinking about the ascendance of justice reasoning and also about sex differences in moral development is suggested in the novel *Masks*, written by Fumiko Enchi, a Japanese woman.[14] The subject is spirit possession, and the novel dramatizes what it means to be possessed by the spirits of others. Writing about the Rokujo lady in *Tales of Genji*, Enchi's central character notes that

> her soul alternates uncertainly between lyricism and spirit possession, making no philosophical distinction between the self alone and in relation to others, and is unable to achieve the solace of a religious indifference.[15]

The option of transcendence, of a religious indifference or a philosophical detachment, may be less available to women because women are more likely to be possessed by the spirits and the stories of others. The strength of women's moral perceptions lies in the refusal of detachment and depersonalization, and insistence on making connections that can lead to seeing the person killed in war or living in poverty as someone's son or father or brother or sister, or mother, or daughter, or friend. But the liability of women's development is also underscored by Enchi's novel in that women, possessed by the spirits of others, also are more likely to be caught in a chain of false attachments. If women are at the present time the custodians of a story about human attachment and interdependence, not only within the family but also in the world at large, then questions arise as to how this story can be kept alive and how moral theory can sustain this story. In this sense, the relationship between women and moral theory itself becomes one of interdependence.

By rendering a care perspective more coherent and making its terms explicit, moral theory may facilitate women's ability to speak about their experiences and perceptions and may foster the ability of others to listen and to understand. At the same time, the evidence of care focus in women's moral thinking suggests that the study of women's development may provide a natural history of moral development in which care is ascendant, revealing the ways in which creating and sustaining responsive connection with others becomes or remains a central moral concern. The promise in joining women and moral theory lies in the fact that human survival, in the late twentieth century, may depend less on formal agreement than on human connection.

Notes

1. Gilligan, C. (1977). "In a Different Voice: Women's Conceptions of Self and of Morality." *Harvard Educational Review* 47 (1982):481–517; *In a Different Voice: Psychological Theory and Women's Development.* Cambridge, Mass.: Harvard University Press.

2. Piaget, J. (1965). *The Moral Judgment of the Child.* New York: N.Y.: The Free Press Paperback Edition, pp. 76–84.

3. Kohlberg, L. (1984). *The Psychology of Moral Development.* San Francisco, Calif.: Harper & Row Publishers, Inc.

4. Gilligan, C. and J. Attanucci. (1986). *Two Moral Orientations.* Harvard University, unpublished manuscript.

5. See Kohlberg, L. *op. cit.,* also Walker, L. (1984). "Sex Differences in the Development of Moral Reasoning: A Critical Review of the Literature." *Child Development* 55 (3):677–91.

6. Piaget, J., *op. cit.*

7. Kohlberg, L., *op. cit.*

8. Johnston, K. (1985). *Two Moral Orientations—Two Problem-solving Strategies: Adolescents' Solutions to Dilemmas in Fables.* Harvard University, unpublished doctoral dissertation.

9. Langdale, C. (1983). *Moral Orientation and Moral Development: The Analysis of Care and Justice Reasoning Across Different Dilemmas in Females and Males from Childhood through Adulthood.* Harvard University, unpublished doctoral dissertation.

10. Johnston, K., *op. cit.;* Vygotsky, L. (1978). *Mind in Society.* Cambridge, Mass.: Harvard University Press; Chodorow, N. (1974). "Family Structure and Feminine Personality" in *Women, Culture and Society,* L. M. Rosaldo and L. Lamphere, eds., Stanford, Calif.: Stanford

University Press; see also Chodorow, N. (1978). *The Reproduction of Mothering: Psychoanalysis and the Sociology of Gender,* Berkeley, Calif.: University of California Press.

11. Chodorow, N., *op. cit.*
12. Glaspell, S. (1927). *A Jury of Her Peers,* London: E. Benn.
13. *Ibid.*
14. Fumiko, E. (1983). *Masks.* New York: Random House.
15. Ibid. p. 54.

3

The Need for More
than Justice [1987]

ANNETTE C. BAIER

In recent decades in North American social and moral philosophy, alongside the development and discussion of widely influential theories of justice, taken as Rawls takes it as the 'first virtue of social institutions,'[1] there has been a counter-movement gathering strength, one coming from some interesting sources. For some of the most outspoken of the diverse group who have in a variety of ways been challenging the assumed supremacy of justice among the moral and social virtues are members of those sections of society whom one might have expected to be especially aware of the supreme importance of justice, namely blacks and women. Those who have only recently won recognition of their equal rights, who have only recently seen the correction or partial correction of longstanding racist and sexist injustices to their race and sex, are among the philosophers now suggesting that justice is only one virtue among many, and one that may need the presence of the others in order to deliver its own undenied value. Among these philosophers of the philosophical counterculture, as it were—but an increasingly large counterculture—include Alasdair MacIntyre,[2] Michael Stocker,[3] Lawrence Blum,[4] Michael Slote,[5] Laurence Thomas,[6] Claudia Card,[7] Alison Jaggar,[8] Susan Wolf[9] and a whole group of men and women, myself included, who have been influenced by the writings of Harvard educational psychologist Carol Gilligan, whose book *In a Different Voice* (Harvard 1982; hereafter D. V.) caused a considerable stir both in the popular press and, more slowly, in the philosophical journals.[10]

Let me say quite clearly at this early point that there is little disagreement that justice is *a* social value of very great importance, and injustice an evil. Nor would those who have worked on theories of justice want to deny that other things matter besides justice. Rawls, for example, incorporates the value of freedom into his account of justice, so that denial of basic freedoms counts as injustice. Rawls also leaves room for a wider theory of the right, of which the theory of justice is just a part. Still, he does claim that justice is the 'first' virtue of social institutions, and it is only that claim about priority that I think has been challenged. It is easy to exaggerate the differences of view that exist, and I want to avoid that. The differences are as much in emphasis as in substance, or we can say that they are differences in tone of voice. But these differences do tend to make a difference in approaches to a wide range of topics not just in moral theory but in areas like medical ethics, where the discussion used to be conducted in terms of patients' rights, of informed consent, and so on, but now tends to get conducted in an enlarged moral vocabulary, which draws on what Gilligan calls the ethics of *care* as well as that of *justice*.

For 'care' is the new buzz-word. It is not, as Shakespeare's Portia demanded, mercy that is to season justice, but a less authoritarian humanitarian supplement, a felt concern for the good of others and for community with them. The 'cold jealous virtue of justice' (Hume) is found to be too cold, and it is 'warmer' more communitarian virtues and social ideals that are being called in to supplement it. One might say that liberty and equality are being found inadequate without fraternity, except that 'fraternity' will be quite the wrong word, if as Gilligan initially suggested, it is *women* who perceive this value most easily. ('Sorority' will do no better, since it is too exclusive, and English has no gender-neuter word for the mutual concern of siblings.) She has since modified this claim, allowing that there are two perspectives on moral and social issues that we all tend to alternate between, and which are not always easy to combine, one of them what she called the justice perspective, the other the care perspective. It is increasingly obvious that there are many male philosophical spokespersons for the care perspective (Laurence Thomas, Lawrence Blum, Michael Stocker) so that it cannot be the prerogative of women. Nevertheless Gilligan still wants to claim that women are most unlikely to take *only* the justice perspective, as some men are claimed to, at least until some mid-life crisis jolts them into 'bifocal' moral vision (see D. V., ch. 6).

Gilligan in her book did not offer any explanatory theory of why there should be any difference between female and male moral outlook, but she did tend to link the naturalness to women of the care perspective with their role as primary care-takers of young children, that is with their parental and specifically maternal role. She avoided the question of whether it is their biological or their social parental role that is relevant, and some of those who dislike her book are worried precisely by this uncertainty. Some find it retrograde to hail as a special sort of moral wisdom an outlook that may be the product of the socially enforced restriction of women to domestic roles (and the reservation of such roles for them alone). For that might seem to play into the hands of those who still favor such restriction. (Marxists, presumably, will not find it so surprising that moral truths might depend for their initial clear voicing on the social oppression, and memory of it, of those who voice the truths.) Gilligan did in the first chapter of D. V. cite the theory of Nancy Chodorow (as presented in *The Reproduction of Mothering* [Berkeley 1978]) which traces what appears as gender differences in personality to early social development, in particular to the effects of the child's primary caretaker being or not being of the same gender as the child. Later, both in 'The Conquistador and the Dark Continent: Reflections on the Nature of Love' (*Daedalus* [Summer 1984]), and 'The Origins of Morality in Early Childhood' [in J. Kagan and S. Lamb, eds., *The Emergence of Morality in Early Childhood*, (Chicago: University of Chicago Press, 1987)], she develops this explanation. She postulates two evils that any infant may become aware of, the evil of detachment or isolation from others whose love one needs, and the evil of relative powerlessness and weakness. Two dimensions of moral development are thereby set—one aimed at achieving satisfying community with others, the other aimed at autonomy or equality of power. The relative predominance of one over the other development will depend both upon the relative salience of the two evils in early childhood, and on early and later reinforcement or discouragement in attempts made to guard against these two evils. This provides the germs of a theory about *why*, given current customs of childrearing, it should be mainly women who are not content with only the moral outlook that she calls the justice perspective, necessary though that was and is seen by them to have been to their hard won liberation from sexist oppression. They, like the blacks, used the language of rights and justice to change their own social position, but nevertheless see limitations in that language, according to Gilligan's findings as a moral psychologist. She reports their discontent with the individualist more or less Kantian moral framework that dominates Western moral theory and which influenced moral psychologists such as Lawrence Kohlberg,[11] to whose conception of moral maturity she seeks an alternative. Since the target of Gilligan's criticism is the dominant Kantian tradition, and since that has been the target also of moral philosophers as diverse in their own views as Bernard Williams,[12] Alasdair MacIntyre, Philippa Foot,[13] Susan Wolf, Claudia Card, her book is of interest as much for its attempt to articulate an alternative to the Kantian justice perspective as for its implicit raising of the question of male bias in Western moral theory, especially liberal-democratic theory. For whether the supposed blind spots of that outlook are due to male bias, or to non-parental bias, or to early traumas of powerlessness or to early resignation to 'detachment' from others, we need first to be persuaded that they *are* blind spots before we will have any interest in their cause and cure. Is justice blind to important social values, or at least only one-eyed? What is it that comes into view from the 'care perspective' that is not seen from the 'justice perspective'?

Gilligan's position here is most easily described by contrasting it with that of Kohlberg, against which she developed it. Kohlberg, influenced by Piaget and the Kantian philosophical tradition as developed by John Rawls, developed a theory about typical moral development which saw it to progress from a pre-conventional level, where what is seen to matter is pleasing or not offending parental authority-figures, through a conventional level in which the child tries to fit in with a group, such as a school community, and conform to its standards and rules, to a post-conventional critical level, in which such conventional rules are subjected to tests, and where those tests are of a Utilitarian, or, eventually, a Kantian sort—namely ones that require respect for each person's individual rational will, or autonomy, and conformity to any implicit social contract such wills are deemed to have made, or to any hypothetical ones they would make if thinking clearly. What was found when Kohlberg's questionnaires (mostly by verbal response to verbally sketched moral dilemmas) were applied to female as well as male subjects, Gilligan reports, is that the girls and women not only scored generally lower than the boys and men, but tended to *revert* to the lower stage of the conventional level even after briefly (usually in adolescence) attaining the post-conventional level. Piaget's finding that girls were deficient in 'the legal sense' was confirmed.

These results led Gilligan to wonder if there might not be a quite different pattern of development to be discerned, at least in female subjects. She therefore conducted interviews designed to elicit not just how far advanced the subjects were towards an appreciation of the nature and importance of Kantian autonomy, but also to find out what the subjects themselves saw as progress or lack of it, what conceptions of moral maturity they came to possess by the time they were adults. She found that although the Kohlberg version of moral maturity as respect for fellow persons, and for their rights as equals (rights including that of free association), did seem shared by many young men, the women tended to speak in a different voice about morality itself and about moral maturity. To quote Gilligan, 'Since the reality of interconnexion is experienced by women as given rather than freely contracted, they arrive at an understanding of life that reflects the limits of autonomy and control. As a result, women's development delineates the path not only to a less violent life but also to a maturity realized by interdependence and taking care' (D. V., 172). She writes that there is evidence that 'women perceive and construe social reality differently from men, and that these differences center around experiences of attachment and separation . . . because women's sense of integrity appears to be intertwined with an ethics of care, so that to see themselves as women is to see themselves in a relationship of connexion, the major changes in women's lives would seem to involve changes in the understanding and activities of care' (D. V., 171). She contrasts this progressive understanding of care, from merely pleasing others to helping and nurturing, with the sort of progression that is involved in Kohlberg's stages, a progression in the understanding, not of mutual care, but of mutual *respect,* where this has its Kantian overtones of distance, even of some fear for the respected, and where personal autonomy and *in*dependence, rather than more satisfactory interdependence, are the paramount values.

This contrast, one cannot but feel, is one which Gilligan might have used the Marxist language of alienation to make. For the main complaint about the Kantian version of a society with its first virtue justice, construed as respect for equal rights to formal goods such as having contracts kept, due process, equal opportunity including opportunity to participate in political activities leading to policy and law-making, to basic liberties of speech, free association and assembly, religious worship, is that none of these goods do much to ensure that the people who have and mutually respect such rights will have any other relationships to one another than the minimal relationship needed to keep such a 'civil society' going. They may well be lonely, driven to suicide, apathetic about their work and about participation in political processes, find their lives meaningless and have no wish to leave offspring to face the same meaningless existence. Their rights, and respect for rights, are quite compatible with very great misery, and misery whose causes are not just individual misfortunes and psychic sickness, but social and moral impoverishment.

What Gilligan's older male subjects complain of is precisely this sort of alienation from some dimly glimpsed better possibility for human beings, some richer sort of network of relationships. As one of Gilligan's male subjects put it, 'People have real emotional needs to be attached to something, and equality does not give you attachment. Equality fractures society and places on every person the burden of standing on his own two feet' (D. V., 167). It is not just the difficulty of self-reliance which is complained of, but its socially 'fracturing' effect. Whereas the younger men, in their college years, had seen morality as a matter of reciprocal non-interference, this older man begins to see it as reciprocal attachment. 'Morality is . . . essential . . . for creating the kind of environment, interaction between people, that is a prerequisite to the fulfillment of individual goals. If you want other people not to interfere with your pursuit of whatever you are into, you have to play the game,' says the spokesman for traditional liberalism (D. V., 98). But if what one is 'into' is interconnexion, interdependence rather than an individual autonomy that may involve 'detachment,' such a version of morality will come to seem inadequate. And Gilligan stresses that the interconnexion that her mature women subjects, and some men, wanted to sustain was not merely freely chosen interconnexion, nor interconnexion between equals, but also the sort of interconnexion that can obtain between a child and her unchosen mother and father, or between a child and her unchosen older and younger siblings, or indeed between most workers and their unchosen fellow workers, or most citizens and their unchosen fellow citizens.

A model of a decent community different from the liberal one is involved in the version of moral maturity that Gilligan voices. It has in many ways more in common with the older religion-linked versions of morality and a good society

than with the modern Western liberal ideal. That perhaps is why some find it so
dangerous and retrograde. Yet it seems clear that it also has much in common
with what we can call Hegelian versions of moral maturity and of social health
and malaise, both with Marxist versions and with so-called right-Hegelian views.

Let me try to summarize the main differences, as I see them, between on the
one hand Gilligan's version of moral maturity and the sort of social structures
that would encourage, express and protect it, and on the other the orthodoxy
she sees herself to be challenging. I shall from now on be giving my own interpretation of the significance of her challenges, not merely reporting them.[14] The
most obvious point is the challenge to the individualism of the Western tradition, to the fairly entrenched belief in the possibility and desirability of each person pursuing his own good in his own way, constrained only by a minimal formal common good namely a working legal apparatus that enforces contracts
and protects individuals from undue interference by others. Gilligan reminds us
that noninterference can, especially for the relatively powerless, such as the very
young, amount to neglect, and even between equals can be isolating and alien-
ating. On her less individualist version of individuality, it becomes defined by responses to dependency and to patterns of interconnexion, both chosen and
unchosen. It is not something a person *has*, and which she then chooses relationships to suit, but something that develops out of a series of dependencies
and interdependencies, and responses to them. This conception of individuality
is not flatly at odds with, say, Rawls's Kantian one, but there is at least a difference of tone of voice between speaking as Rawls does of each of us having our
own rational life plan, which a just society's moral traffic rules will allow us to
follow, and which may or may not include close association with other persons,
and speaking as Gilligan does of a satisfactory life as involving 'progress of affiliative relationship' (D. V., 170) where 'the concept of identity expands to include
the experience of interconnexion' (D. V., 173). Rawls can allow that progress to
Gilligan-style moral maturity may be *a* rational life plan, but not a moral constraint on every life-pattern. The trouble is that it will not do just to say 'let this
version of morality be an optional extra. Let us agree on the essential minimum,
that is on justice and rights, and let whoever wants to go further and cultivate
this more demanding ideal of responsibility and care.' For, first, it cannot be satisfactorily cultivated without closer cooperation from others than respect for
rights and justice will ensure, and, second, the encouragement of some to cultivate it while others do not could easily lead to exploitation of those who do. It
obviously *has* suited some in most societies well enough that others take on the
responsibilities of care (for the sick, the helpless, the young) leaving them free to
pursue their own less altruistic goods. Volunteer forces of those who accept an
ethic of care, operating within a society where the power is exercised and the institutions designed, redesigned, or maintained by those who accept a less communal ethic of minimally constrained self-advancement, will not be the solution. The liberal individualists may be able to 'tolerate' the more communally

minded, if they keep the liberals' rules, but it is not so clear that the more com-munally minded can be content with just those rules, nor be content to be toler-ated and possibly exploited.

For the moral tradition which developed the concept of rights, autonomy and justice is the same tradition that provided 'justifications' of the oppression of those whom the primary right-holders depended on to do the sort of work they themselves preferred not to do. The domestic work was left to women and slaves, and the liberal morality for right-holders was surreptitiously supple-mented by a different set of demands made on domestic workers. As long as women could be got to assume responsibility for the care of home and children, and to train their children to continue the sexist system, the liberal morality could continue to be the official morality, by turning its eyes away from the con-tribution made by those it excluded. The long-unnoticed moral proletariat were the domestic workers, mostly female. Rights have usually been for the privi-leged. Talking about laws, and the rights those laws recognize and protect, does not in itself ensure that the group of legislators and rights-holders will not be re-stricted to some elite. Bills of rights have usually been proclamations of the rights of some in-group, barons, land-owners, males, whites, non-foreigners. The 'justice perspective,' and the legal sense that goes with it, are shadowed by their patriarchal past. What did Kant, the great prophet of autonomy, say in his moral theory about women? He said they were incapable of legislation, not fit to vote, that they needed the guidance of more 'rational' males.[15] Autonomy was not for them, only for first-class, really rational, persons. It is ironic that Gilligan's original findings in a way confirm Kant's views—it seems that autonomy really may not be for women. Many of them reject that ideal (D. V., 48), and have been found not as good at making rules as are men. But where Kant concludes—'so much the worse for women,' we can conclude—'so much the worse for the male fixation on the special skill of drafting legislation, for the bureaucratic mentality of rule worship, and for the male exaggeration of the importance of indepen-dence over mutual interdependence.'

It is however also true that the moral theories that made the concept of a per-son's rights central were not just the instruments for excluding some persons, but also the instruments used by those who demanded that more and more per-sons be included in the favored group. Abolitionists, reformers, women, used the language of rights to assert their claims to inclusion in the group of full members of a community. The tradition of liberal moral theory has in fact devel-oped so as to include the women it had for so long excluded, to include the poor as well as rich, blacks and whites, and so on. Women like Mary Wollstonecraft used the male moral theories to good purpose. So we should not be wholly un-grateful for those male moral theories, for all their objectionable earlier content. They were undoubtedly patriarchal, but they also contained the seeds of the challenge, or antidote, to this patriarchal poison.

But when we transcend the values of the Kantians, we should not forget the facts of history—that those values were the values of the oppressors of women. The Christian church, whose version of the moral law Aquinas codified, in his very legalistic moral theory, still insists on the maleness of the God it worships, and jealously reserves for males all the most powerful positions in its hierarchy. Its patriarchical prejudice is open and avowed. In the secular moral theories of men, the sexist patriarchal prejudice is today often less open, not as blatant as it is in Aquinas, in the later natural law tradition, and in Kant and Hegel, but is often still there. No moral theorist today would say that women are unfit to vote, to make laws, or to rule a nation without powerful male advisors (as most queens had), but the old doctrines die hard. In one of the best male theories we have, John Rawls's theory, a key role is played by the idea of the 'head of a household.' It is heads of households who are to deliberate behind a 'veil of ignorance' of historical details, and of details of their own special situation, to arrive at the 'just' constitution for a society. Now of course Rawls does not think or say that these 'heads' are fathers rather than mothers. But if we have really given up the age-old myth of women needing, as Grotius put it, to be under the 'eye' of a more 'rational' male protector and master, then how do families come to have any one 'head,' except by the death or desertion of one parent? They will either be two-headed, or headless. Traces of the old patriarchal poison still remain in even the best contemporary moral theorizing. Few may actually say that women's place is in the home, but there is much muttering, when unemployment figures rise, about how the relatively recent flood of women into the work force complicates the problem, as if it would be a good thing if women just went back home whenever unemployment rises, to leave the available jobs for the men. We still do not really have a wide acceptance of the equal right of women to employment outside the home. Nor do we have wide acceptance of the equal duty of men to perform those domestic tasks which in no way depend on special female anatomy, namely cooking, cleaning, and the care of weaned children. All sorts of stories (maybe true stories), about children's need for one 'primary' parent, who must be the mother if the mother breast feeds the child, shore up the unequal division of domestic responsibility between mothers and fathers, wives and husbands. If we are really to transvalue the values of our patriarchal past, we need to rethink all of those assumptions, really test those psychological theories. And how will men ever develop an understanding of the 'ethics of care' if they continue to be shielded or kept from that experience of caring for a dependent child, which complements the experience we all have had of being cared for as dependent children? These experiences form the natural background for the development of moral maturity as Gilligan's women saw it.

Exploitation aside, why would women, once liberated, not be content to have their version of morality merely tolerated? Why should they not see themselves as voluntarily, for their own reasons, taking on *more* than the liberal rules demand, while having no quarrel with the content of those rules themselves, nor with their remaining the only ones that are expected to be generally obeyed? To see why, we need to move on to three more differences between the Kantian liberals (usually contractarians) and their critics. These concern the relative weight put on relationships between equals, and the relative weight put on freedom of choice, and on the authority of intellect over emotions. It is a typical feature of the dominant moral theories and traditions, since Kant, or perhaps since Hobbes, that relationships between equals or those who are deemed equal in some important sense, have been the relations that morality is concerned primarily to regulate. Relationships between those who are clearly unequal in power, such as parents and children, earlier and later generations in relation to one another, states and citizens, doctors and patients, the well and the ill, large states and small states, have had to be shunted to the bottom of the agenda, and then dealt with by some sort of 'promotion' of the weaker so that an appearance of virtual equality is achieved. Citizens collectively become equal to states, children are treated as adults-to-be, the ill and dying are treated as continuers of their earlier more potent selves, so that their 'rights' could be seen as the rights of equals. This pretence of an equality that is in fact absent may often lead to desirable protection of the weaker, or more dependent. But it somewhat masks the question of what our moral relationships *are* to those who are our superiors or our inferiors in power. A more realistic acceptance of the fact that we begin as helpless children, that at almost every point of our lives we deal with both the more and the less helpless, that equality of power and interdependency, between two persons or groups, is rare and hard to recognize when it does occur, might lead us to a more direct approach to questions concerning the design of institutions structuring these relationships between unequals (families, schools, hospitals, armies) and of the morality of our dealings with the more and the less powerful. One reason why those who agree with the Gilligan version of what morality is about will not want to agree that the liberals' rules are a good minimal set, the only ones we need pressure *everyone* to obey, is that these rules do little to protect the young or the dying or the starving or any of the relatively powerless against neglect, or to ensure an education that will form persons to be *capable* of conforming to an ethics of care and responsibility. Put badly, and in a way Gilligan certainly has not put it, the liberal morality, if unsupplemented, may *unfit* people to be anything other than what its justifying theories suppose them to be, ones who have no interest in each others' interests. Yet some must take an interest in the next generation's interests. Women's traditional work, of caring for the less powerful, especially for the young, is obviously socially vital. One cannot regard any version of morality that does not ensure that it gets well done as an adequate 'minimal morality,' any more than we could so regard one that left any concern for more distant future generations an optional extra. A moral theory, it can plausibly be claimed, cannot regard concern for new and future persons as an optional charity left for those with a taste for it. If the morality the theory endorses is to sustain itself, it must provide for its own continuers, not just take out a loan on a carefully encouraged maternal instinct or on the enthusiasm of a self-selected group of environmentalists, who make it their business or hobby to be concerned with what we are doing to mother earth.

The recognition of the importance for all parties of relations between those who are and cannot but be unequal, both of these relations in themselves and for their effect on personality formation and so on other relationships, goes along with a recognition of the plain fact that not all morally important relationships can or should be freely chosen. So far I have discussed three reasons women have not to be content to pursue their own values within the framework of the liberal morality. The first was its dubious record. The second was its inattention to relations of inequality or its pretence of equality. The third reason is its exaggeration of the scope of choice, or its inattention to unchosen relations. Showing up the partial myth of equality among actual members of a community, and of the undesirability of trying to pretend that we are treating all of them as equals, tends to go along with an exposure of the companion myth that moral obligations arise from freely *chosen* associations between such equals. Vulnerable future generations do not choose their dependence on earlier generations. The unequal infant does not choose its place in a family or nation, nor is it treated as free to do as it likes until some association is freely entered into. Nor do its parents always choose their parental role, or freely assume their parental responsibilities any more than we choose our power to affect the conditions in which later generations will live. Gilligan's attention to the version of morality and moral maturity found in women, many of whom had faced choice of whether or not to have an abortion, and who had at some point become mothers, is attention to the perceived inadequacy of the language of rights to help in such choices or to guide them in their parental role. It would not be much of an exaggeration to call the Gilligan 'different voice' the voice of the potential parents. The emphasis on care goes with a recognition of the often unchosen nature of the responsibilities of those who give care, both of children who care for their aged or infirm parents, and of parents who care for the children they in fact have. Contract soon ceases to seem the paradigm source of moral obligation once we attend to parental responsibility, and justice as a virtue of social institutions will come to seem at best only first equal with the virtue, whatever its name, that ensures that each new generation is made appropriately welcome and prepared for their adult lives.

This all constitutes a belated reminder to Western moral theorists of a fact they have always known, that as Adam Ferguson, and David Hume before him emphasized, we are born into families, and the first society we belong to, one that fits or misfits us for later ones, is the small society of parents (or some sort of child-attendants) and children, exhibiting as it may both relationships of near equality and of inequality in power. This simple reminder, with the fairly considerable implications it can have for the plausibility of contractarian moral theory, is at the same time a reminder of the role of human emotions as much as human reason and will in moral development as it actually comes about. The fourth feature of the Gilligan challenge to liberal orthodoxy is a challenge to its typical *rationalism,* or intellectualism, to its assumption that we need not worry what passions persons have, as long as their rational wills can control them. This Kantian picture of a controlling reason dictating to possibly unruly passions also tends to seem less useful when we are led to consider what sort of person we need to fill the role of parent, or indeed want in any close relationship. It might be important for father figures to have rational control over their violent urges to beat to death the children whose screams enrage them, but more than control of such nasty passions seems needed in the mother or primary parent, or parent-substitute, by most psychological theories. They need to love their children, not just to control their irritation. So the emphasis in Kantian theories on rational control of emotions, rather than on cultivating desirable forms of emotion, is challenged by Gilligan, along with the challenge to the assumption of the centrality of autonomy, or relations between equals, and of freely chosen relations.

The same set of challenges to 'orthodox' liberal moral theory has come not just from Gilligan and other women, who are reminding other moral theorists of the role of the family as a social institution and as an influence on the other relationships people want to or are capable of sustaining, but also, as I noted at the start, from an otherwise fairly diverse group of men, ranging from those influenced by both Hegelian and Christian traditions (MacIntyre) to all varieties of other backgrounds. From this group I want to draw attention to the work of one philosopher in particular, namely Laurence Thomas, the author of a fairly remarkable article[16] in which he finds sexism to be a more intractable social evil than racism. In a series of articles and a book,[17] Thomas makes a strong case for the importance of supplementing a concern for justice and respect for rights with an emphasis on equally needed virtues, and on virtues seen as appropriate *emotional* as well as rational capacities. Like Gilligan (and unlike MacIntyre) Thomas gives a lot of attention to the childhood beginnings of moral and social capacities, to the role of parental love in making that possible, and to the emotional as well as the cognitive development we have reason to think both possible and desirable in human persons.

It is clear, I think, that the best moral theory has to be a cooperative product of women and men, has to harmonize justice and care. The morality it theorizes about is after all for all persons, for men and for women, and will need their combined insights. As Gilligan said (D. V., 174), what we need now is a 'marriage' of the old male and the newly articulated female insights. If she is right about the special moral aptitudes of women, it will most likely be the women who propose the marriage, since they are the ones with more natural empathy, with the better diplomatic skills, the ones more likely to shoulder responsibility and take moral initiative, and the ones who find it easiest to empathize and care about how the other party feels. Then, once there is this union of male and female moral wisdom, we maybe can teach each other the moral skills each gender currently lacks, so that the gender difference in moral outlook that Gilligan found will slowly become less marked.

Notes

1. John Rawls, *A Theory of Justice* (Cambridge: Harvard University Press 1970).

2. Alasdair MacIntyre, *After Virtue* (Notre Dame: Notre Dame University Press 1981).

3. Michael Stocker, 'The Schizophrenia of Modern Ethical Theories,' *Journal of Philosophy* 73, 14, 453–66, and 'Agent and Other: Against Ethical Universalism,' *Australasian Journal of Philosophy* 54, 206–20.

4. Lawrence Blum, *Friendship, Altruism and Morality* (London: Routledge & Kegan Paul 1980).

5. Michael Slote, *Goods and Virtues* (Oxford: Oxford University Press 1983).

6. Laurence Thomas, 'Love and Morality,' in *Epistemology and Sociobiology,* James Fetzer, ed. (1985); and 'Justice, Happiness and Self Knowledge,' *Canadian Journal of Philosophy* (March 1986). Also 'Beliefs and the Motivation to Be Just,' *American Philosophical Quarterly* 22 (4), 347–52.

7. Claudia Card, 'Mercy,' *Philosophical Review* 81, 1, and 'Gender and Moral Luck,' in *Identity, Character, and Morality,* ed. Owen Flanagan and Amélie O. Rorty, [Cambridge: MIT Press 1990].

8. Alison Jaggar, *Feminist Politics and Human Nature* (London: Rowman and Allenheld 1983).

9. Susan Wolf, 'Moral Saints,' *Journal of Philosophy* 79 (August 1982), 419–39.

10. For a helpful survey article see Owen Flanagan and Kathryn Jackson, 'Justice Care & Gender: The Kohlberg-Gilligan Debate Revisited,' *Ethics* 97, 3 (April 1987).

11. Lawrence Kohlberg, *Essays in Moral Development,* vols. I & II (New York: Harper and Row 1981, 1984).

12. Bernard Williams, *Ethics and the Limits of Philosophy* (Cambridge: Cambridge University Press 1985).

13. Philippa Foot, *Virtues and Vices* (Berkeley: University of California Press 1978).

14. I have previously written about the significance of her findings for moral philosophy in 'What Do Women Want in a Moral Theory?' *Nous* 19 (March 1985), 'Trust and Antitrust,' *Ethics* 96 (1986), and in 'Hume the Women's Moral Theorist?' in *Women and Moral Theory,* E. Kittay and D. Meyers, ed., [Totowa, N.J.: Rowman and Littlefield 1987].

15. Immanuel Kant, *Metaphysics of Morals,* sec. 46.

16. Laurence Thomas, 'Sexism and Racism: Some Conceptual Differences,' *Ethics* 90 (1980), 239–50; republished in *Philosophy, Sex and Language,* Vetterling-Braggin, ed. (Totowa, NJ: Littlefield Adams 1980).

17. See articles listed in note 6, above. [Laurence Thomas, *Living Morally: A Psychology of Moral Character* (Philadelphia: Temple University Press 1989).]

PART TWO

Doubts and Reservations

4

Beyond Caring:
The De-Moralization
of Gender [1987]

MARILYN FRIEDMAN

Carol Gilligan heard a 'distinct moral language' in the voices of women who were subjects in her studies of moral reasoning.[1] Though herself a developmental psychologist, Gilligan has put her mark on contemporary feminist moral philosophy by daring to claim the competence of this voice and the worth of its message. Her book *In a Different Voice*, which one theorist has aptly described as a best-seller,[2] explored the concern with care and relationships which Gilligan discerned in the moral reasoning of women and contrasted it with the orientation toward justice and rights which she found to typify the moral reasoning of men.

According to Gilligan, the standard (or 'male') moral voice articulated in moral psychology derives moral judgments about particular cases from abstract, universalized moral rules and principles which are substantively concerned with justice and rights. For justice reasoners: the major moral imperative enjoins respect for the rights of others (100); the concept of duty is limited to reciprocal noninterference (147); the motivating vision is one of the equal worth of self and other (63); and one important underlying presupposition is a highly individuated conception of persons.

By contrast, the other (or 'female') moral voice which Gilligan heard in her studies eschews abstract rules and principles. This moral voice derives moral judgments from the contextual detail of situations grasped as specific and unique (100). The substantive concern for this moral voice is care and responsibility, particularly as these arise in the context of interpersonal relationships (19). Moral judgments, for care reasoners, are tied to feelings of empathy and compassion (69); the major moral imperatives center around caring, not hurting others, and avoiding selfishness (90); and the motivating vision of this ethic is 'that everyone will be responded to and included, that no one will be left alone or hurt' (63).

While these two voices are not necessarily contradictory in all respects, they seem, at the very least, to be different in their orientation. Gilligan's writings about the differences have stimulated extensive feminist reconsideration of various ethical themes.[3] In this paper, I use Gilligan's work as a springboard for extending certain of those themes in new directions. My discussion has three parts. In the first part, I will address the unresolved question of whether or not a gender difference in moral reasoning is empirically confirmed. I will propose that even if actual statistical differences in the moral reasoning of women and men cannot be confirmed, there is nevertheless a real difference in the moral norms and values culturally associated with each gender. The genders are 'moralized' in distinctive ways. Moral norms about appropriate conduct, characteristic virtues and typical vices are incorporated into our conceptions of femininity and masculinity, female and male. The result is a dichotomy which exemplifies what may be called a 'division of moral labor'[4] between the genders.

In the second part of the paper, I will explore a different reason why actual women and men may not show a divergence of reasoning along the care-justice dichotomy, namely, that the notions of care and justice overlap more than Gilligan, among others, has realized. I will suggest, in particular, that morally adequate care involves considerations of justice. Thus, the concerns captured by these two moral categories do not define necessarily distinct moral perspectives, in practice.

Third, and finally, I propose that, even if care and justice do not define distinct moral perspectives, nevertheless, these concepts do point to other important differences in moral orientation. One such difference has to do with the nature of relationship to other selves, and the underlying form of moral commitment which is the central focus of that relationship and of the resulting moral thought. In short, the so-called 'care' perspective emphasizes responsiveness to particular persons, in their uniqueness, and commitment to them as such. By contrast, the so-called 'justice' perspective emphasizes adherence to moral rules, values and principles, and an abstractive treatment of individuals, based on the selected categories which they instantiate.

Let us turn first to the issue of gender difference.

I. The Gender Difference Controversy

Gilligan has advanced at least two different positions about the care and the justice perspectives. One is that the care perspective is distinct from the moral perspective which is centered on justice and rights. Following Gilligan,[5] I will call this the 'different voice' hypothesis about moral reasoning. Gilligan's other hypothesis is that the care perspective is typically, or characteristically, a *woman's* moral voice, while the justice perspective is typically, or characteristically, a *man's* moral voice. Let's call this the 'gender difference' hypothesis about moral reasoning.

The truth of Gilligan's gender difference hypothesis has been questioned by a number of critics who cite what seems to be disconfirming empirical evidence.[6] This evidence includes studies by the psychologist Norma Haan, who has discerned two distinct moral voices among her research subjects, but has found them to be utilized to approximately the same extent by both females and males.[7]

In an attempt to dismiss the research-based objections to her gender differences hypothesis, Gilligan now asserts that her aim was not to disclose a statistical gender difference in moral reasoning, but rather simply to disclose and interpret the differences in the two perspectives.[8] Psychologist John Broughton has argued that if the gender difference is not maintained, then Gilligan's whole explanatory framework is undermined.[9] However, Broughton is wrong. The different voice hypothesis has a significance for moral psychology and moral philosophy which would survive the demise of the gender difference hypothesis. At least part of its significance lies in revealing the lopsided obsession of contemporary theories of morality, in both disciplines, with universal and impartial conceptions of justice and rights and the relative disregard of *particular*, interpersonal relationships based on partiality and affective ties.[10] (However, the different voice hypothesis is itself also suspect if it is made to depend on a dissociation of justice from care, a position which I shall challenge in Part II of this paper.)

But *what about* that supposed empirical disconfirmation of the gender difference hypothesis? Researchers who otherwise accept the disconfirming evidence have nevertheless noticed that many women readers of Gilligan's book find it to 'resonate . . . thoroughly with their own experience.'[11] Gilligan notes that it was precisely one of her purposes to expose the gap between women's experience and the findings of psychological research,[12] and, we may suppose, to critique the latter in light of the former.

These unsystematic, anecdotal observations that females and males do differ in ways examined by Gilligan's research should lead us either: (1) to question, and examine carefully, the methods of that empirical research which does not reveal such differences; or (2) to suspect that a gender difference exists but in some form which is not, strictly speaking, a matter of statistical differences in the moral reasoning of women and men. Gilligan has herself expressed the first of these alternatives. I would like to explore the second possibility.

Suppose that there were a gender difference of a sort, but one which was not a simple matter of differences among the form or substance of women's and men's moral reasonings. A plausible account might take this form. Among the white middle classes of such western industrial societies as Canada and the United

States, women and men are associated with different moral norms and values at the level of the stereotypes, symbols, and myths which contribute to the social construction of gender. One might say that morality is 'gendered' and that the genders are 'moralized.' Our very conceptions of femininity and masculinity, female and male, incorporate norms about appropriate behavior, characteristic virtues, and typical vices.

Morality, I suggest, is fragmented into a 'division of moral labor' along the lines of gender, the rationale for which is rooted in historic developments pertaining to family, state, and economy. The tasks of governing, regulating social order, and managing other 'public' institutions have been monopolized by men as their privileged domain, and the tasks of sustaining privatized personal relationships have been imposed on, or left to, women.[13] The genders have thus been conceived in terms of special and distinctive moral projects. Justice and rights have structured male moral norms, values, and virtues, while care and responsiveness have defined female moral norms, values, and virtues. The division of moral labor has had the dual function both of preparing us each for our respective socially defined domains and of rendering us incompetent to manage the affairs of the realm from which we have been excluded. That justice is symbolized in our culture by the figure of a woman is a remarkable irony; her blindfold hides more than the scales she holds.

To say that the genders are moralized is to say that specific moral ideals, values, virtues, and practices are culturally conceived as the special projects or domains of specific genders. These conceptions would determine which commitments and behaviors were to be considered normal, appropriate, and expected of each gender, which commitments and behaviors were to be considered remarkable or heroic, and which commitments and behaviors were to be considered deviant, improper, outrageous, and intolerable. Men who fail to respond to the cry of a baby, fail to express tender emotions, or fail to show compassion in the face of the grief and sorrow of others, are likely to be tolerated, perhaps even benignly, while women who act similarly can expect to be reproached for their selfish indifference. However, women are seldom required to devote themselves to service to their country or to struggles for human rights. Women are seldom expected to display any of the special virtues associated with national or political life. At the same time, women still carry the burden of an excessively restrictive and oppressive sexual ethic; sexual aggressiveness and promiscuity are vices for which women in all social groups are roundly condemned, even while many of their male counterparts win tributes for such 'virility.'

Social science provides ample literature to show that gender differences are alive and well at the level of popular perception. Both men and women, on average, still conceive women and men in a moralized fashion. For example, expectations and perceptions of women's greater empathy and altruism are expressed by both women and men.[14] The gender stereotypes of women center around qualities which some authors call 'communal.' These include: a concern for the welfare of others; the predominance of caring and nurturant traits; and, to a lesser extent, interpersonal sensitivity, emotional expressiveness, and a gentle personal style.[15]

By contrast, men are stereotyped according to what are referred to as 'agentic' norms.[16] These norms center primarily around assertive and controlling tendencies. The paradigmatic behaviors are self-assertion, including forceful dominance, and independence from other people. Also encompassed by these norms are patterns of self-confidence, personal efficacy, and a direct, adventurous personal style.

If reality failed to accord with myth and symbol, if actual women and men did not fit the traits and dispositions expected of them, this might not necessarily undermine the myths and symbols, since perception could be selective and disconfirming experience reduced to the status of 'occasional exceptions' and 'abnormal, deviant cases.' 'Reality' would be misperceived in the image of cultural myth, as reinforced by the homogenizing tendencies of mass media and mass culture, and the popular imagination would have little foothold for the recognition that women and men were not as they were mythically conceived to be.

If I am right, then Gilligan has discerned the *symbolically* female moral voice, and has disentangled it from the *symbolically* male moral voice. The moralization of gender is more a matter of how we *think* we reason than of how we actually reason, more a matter of the moral concerns we *attribute* to women and men than of true statistical differences between women's and men's moral reasoning. Gilligan's findings resonate with the experiences of many people because those experiences are shaped, in part, by cultural myths and stereotypes of gender which even feminist theorizing may not dispel. Thus, both women and men in our culture *expect* women and men to exhibit this moral dichotomy, and, on my hypothesis, it is this expectation which has shaped both Gilligan's observations and the plausibility which we attribute to them. Or, to put it somewhat differently, *whatever* moral matters men concern themselves with are categorized, estimably, as matters of 'justice and rights,' whereas the moral concerns of women are assigned to the devalued categories of 'care and personal relationships.'

It is important to ask why, if these beliefs are so vividly held, they might, nevertheless, still not produce a reality in conformity with them.[17] How could those critics who challenge Gilligan's gender hypothesis be right to suggest that women and men show no significant differences in moral reasoning, if women and men are culturally educated, trained, pressured, expected, and perceived to be so radically different?[18]

Philosophy is not, by itself, capable of answering this question adequately. My admittedly *partial* answer to it depends upon showing that the care/justice dichotomy is rationally implausible and that the two concepts are conceptually compatible. This conceptual compatibility creates the empirical possibility that the two moral concerns will be intermingled in practice. That they are actually intermingled in the moral reasonings of real women and men is, of course, not determined simply by their conceptual compatibility, but requires as well the wisdom and insight of those women and men who comprehend the relevance of both concepts to their experiences.[19] Philosophy does not account for the actual emergence of wisdom. That the genders do not, in reality, divide along those moral lines is made *possible*, though not inevitable, by the conceptual limitations of both a concept of care dissociated from considerations of justice and a concept of justice dissociated from considerations of care. Support for this partial explanation requires a reconceptualization of care and justice—the topic of the next part of my discussion.

II. Surpassing the Care/Justice Dichotomy

I have suggested that if women and men do not show statistical differences in moral reasoning along the lines of a care/justice dichotomy, this should not be thought surprising since the concepts of care and justice are mutually compatible. People who treat each other justly can also care about each other. Conversely, personal relationships are arenas in which people have rights to certain forms of treatment, and in which fairness can be reflected in ongoing interpersonal mutuality. It is this latter insight—the relevance of justice to close personal relationships—which I will emphasize here.

Justice, at the most general level, is a matter of giving people their due, of treating them appropriately. Justice is relevant to personal relationships and to care precisely to the extent that considerations of justice itself determine appropriate ways to treat friends or intimates. Justice as it bears on relationships among friends or family, or on other close personal ties, might not involve duties which are universalizable, in the sense of being owed to all persons simply in virtue of shared moral personhood. But this does not entail the irrelevance of justice among friends or intimates.

Moral thinking has not always dissociated the domain of justice from that of close personal relationships. The earliest Greek code of justice placed friendship at the forefront of conditions for the realization of justice, and construed the rules of justice as being coextensive with the limits of friendship. The reader will recall that one of the first definitions of justice which Plato sought to contest, in the *Republic*, is that of 'helping one's friends and harming one's enemies.'[20] Although the ancient Greek model of justice among friends reserved that moral privilege for free-born Greek males, the conception is, nevertheless, instructive for its readiness to link the notion of justice to relationships based on affection and loyalty. This provides an important contrast to modern notions of justice which are often deliberately constructed so as to avoid presumptions of mutual concern on the parts of those to whom the conception is to apply.

As is well known, John Rawls, for one, requires that the parties to the original position in which justice is to be negotiated be mutually disinterested.[21] Each party is assumed, first and foremost, to be concerned for the advancement of her own interests, and to care about the interests of others only to the extent that her own interests require it. This postulate of mutual disinterestedness is intended by Rawls to ensure that the principles of justice do not depend on what he calls 'strong assumptions,' such as 'extensive ties of natural sentiment.'[22] Rawls is seeking principles of justice which apply to everyone in all their social interrelationships, *whether or not* characterized by affection and a concern for each other's well-being. While such an account promises to disclose duties of justice owed to all other parties to the social contract, it may fail to uncover *special* duties of justice which arise in close personal relationships the foundation of which is affection or kinship, rather than contract. The methodological device of assuming mutual disinterest might blind us to the role of justice among mutually interested and/or intimate parties.

Gilligan herself has suggested that mature reasoning about care incorporates considerations of justice and rights. But Gilligan's conception of what this means is highly limited. It appears to involve simply the recognition 'that self and other are equal,' a notion which serves to override the problematic tendency of the ethic of care to become *self-sacrificing* care in women's practices. However, important as it may be, this notion hardly does justice to justice.

There are several ways in which justice pertains to close personal relationships. The first two ways which I will mention are largely appropriate only among friends, relatives, or intimates who are of comparable development in their realization of moral personhood, for example, who are both mature responsible adults. The third sort of relevance of justice to close relationships, which I will discuss shortly, pertains to families, in which adults often interrelate with children—a more challenging domain for the application of justice. But first the easier task.

One sort of role for justice in close relationships among people of comparable moral personhood may be discerned by considering that a personal relationship is a miniature social system, which provides valued mutual intimacy, support, and concern for those who are involved. The maintenance of a relationship requires effort by the participants. One intimate may bear a much greater burden for sustaining a relationship than the other participant(s) and may derive less support, concern, and so forth than she deserves for her efforts. Justice sets a constraint on such relationships by calling for an appropriate sharing, among the participants, of the benefits and burdens which constitute their relationship.

Marilyn Frye, for example, has discussed what amounts to a pattern of *violation* of this requirement of justice in heterosexual relationships. She has argued that women of all races, social classes, and societies can be defined as a coherent group in terms of a distinctive function which is culturally assigned to them.

This function is, in Frye's words, 'the service of men and men's interests as men define them.'[23] This service work includes personal service (satisfaction of routine bodily needs, such as hunger, and other mundane tasks), sexual and reproductive service, and ego service. Says Frye, '. . . at every race/class level and even across race/class lines men do not serve women as women serve men.'[24] Frye is, of course, generalizing over society and culture, and the sweep of her generalization encompasses both ongoing close personal relationships as well as other relationships which are not close or are not carried on beyond specific transactions, for example, that of prostitute to client. By excluding those latter cases for the time being, and applying Frye's analysis to familial and other close ties between women and men, we may discern the sort of one-sided relational exploitation, often masquerading in the guise of love or care, which constitutes this first sort of injustice.

Justice is relevant to close personal relationships among comparable moral persons in a second way as well. The trust and intimacy which characterize special relationships create special vulnerabilities to harm. Commonly recognized harms, such as physical injury and sexual assault, become more feasible; and special relationships, in corrupt, abusive, or degenerate forms, make possible certain uncommon emotional harms not even possible in impersonal relationships. When someone is harmed in a personal relationship, she is owed a rectification of some sort, a righting of the wrong which has been done her. The notion of justice emerges, once again, as a relevant moral notion.

Thus, in a close relationship among persons of comparable moral personhood, care may degenerate into the injustices of exploitation, or oppression. Many such problems have been given wide public scrutiny recently as a result of feminist analysis of various aspects of family life and sexual relationships. Woman-battering, acquaintance rape, and sexual harassment are but a few of the many recently publicized injustices of 'personal' life. The notion of distributive or corrective injustice seems almost too mild to capture these indignities, involving, as they do, violation of bodily integrity and an assumption of the right to assault and injure. But to call these harms injustices is certainly not to rule out impassioned moral criticism in other terms as well.

The two requirements of justice which I have just discussed exemplify the standard distinction between distributive and corrective justice. They illustrate the role of justice in personal relationships regarded in abstraction from a social context. Personal relationships may also be regarded in the context of their various institutional settings, such as marriage and family. Here justice emerges again as a relevant ideal, its role being to define appropriate institutions to structure interactions among family members, other household cohabitants, and intimates in general. The family, for example,[25] is a miniature society, exhibiting all the major facets of large-scale social life: decision-making affecting the whole unit; executive action; judgments of guilt and innocence; reward and punishment; allocation of responsibilities and privileges, of burdens and benefits; and monumental influences on the life-chances of both its maturing and its matured members. Any of these features *alone* would invoke the relevance of justice; together, they make the case overwhelming.

Women's historically paradigmatic role of mothering has provided a multitude of insights which can be reconstructed as insights about the importance of justice in family relationships, especially those relationships involving remarkable disparities in maturity, capability, and power.[26] In these familial relationships, one party grows into moral personhood over time gradually acquiring the capacity to be a responsible moral agent. Considerations of justice pertain to the mothering of children in numerous ways. For one thing, there may be siblings to deal with, whose demands and conflicts create the context for parental arbitration and the need for a fair allotment of responsibilities and privileges. Then there are decisions to be made, involving the well-being of all persons in the family unit, whose immature members become increasingly capable over time of participating in such administrative affairs. Of special importance in the practice of raising children are the duties to nurture and to promote growth and maturation. These duties may be seen as counterparts to the welfare rights viewed by many as a matter of social justice.[27] Motherhood continually presents its practitioners with moral problems best seen in terms of a complex framework which integrates justice with care, even though the politico-legal discourse of justice has not shaped its domestic expression.[28]

I have been discussing the relevance of justice to close personal relationships. A few words about my companion thesis—the relevance of care to the public domain—is also in order.[29] In its more noble manifestation, care in the public realm would show itself, perhaps, in foreign aid, welfare programs, famine or disaster relief, or other social programs designed to relieve suffering and attend to human needs. If untempered by justice in the public domain, care degenerates precipitously. The infamous 'boss' of Chicago's old-time Democratic machine, Mayor Richard J. Daley, was legendary for his nepotism and political partisanship; he cared extravagantly for his relatives, friends, and political cronies.[30]

In recounting the moral reasoning of one of her research subjects, Gilligan once wrote that the 'justice' perspective fails 'to take into account the reality of relationships' (147). What she meant is that the 'justice' perspective emphasizes a self's various rights to noninterference by others. Gilligan worried that if this is all that a concern for justice involved, then such a perspective would disregard the moral value of positive interaction, connection, and commitment among persons.

However, Gilligan's interpretation of justice is far too limited. For one thing, it fails to recognize positive rights, such as welfare rights, which may be endorsed from a 'justice' perspective. But beyond this minor point, a more important problem is Gilligan's failure to acknowledge the potential for *violence and harm* in human interrelationships and human community.[31] The concept of justice, in general, arises out of relational conditions in which most human beings have the capacity, and many have the inclination, to treat each other badly.

Thus, notions of distributive justice are impelled by the realization that people who together [constitute] a social system may not share fairly in the benefits and burdens of their social cooperation. Conceptions of rectificatory, or corrective, justice are founded on the concern that when harms are done, action should be taken either to restore those harmed as fully as possible to their previous state, or to prevent further similar harm, or both. And the specific rights which people are variously thought to have are just so many manifestations of our interest in identifying ways in which people deserve protection against harm by others. The complex reality of social life encompasses the human potential for helping, caring for, and nurturing others *as well as* the potential for harming, exploiting, and oppressing others. Thus, Gilligan is wrong to think that the justice perspective completely neglects 'the reality of relationships.' Rather, it arises from a more complex, and more realistic, estimate of the nature of human interrelationship.

In light of these reflections, it seems wise both to reconsider the seeming dichotomy of care and justice, and to question the moral adequacy of either orientation dissociated from the other. Our aim would be to advance 'beyond caring,' that is, beyond *mere* caring dissociated from a concern for justice. In addition, we would do well to progress beyond gender stereotypes which assign distinct and different moral roles to women and men. Our ultimate goal should be a non-gendered, non-dichotomized, moral framework in which all moral concerns could be expressed. We might, with intentional irony, call this project, 'demoralizing the genders.'

III. Commitments to Particular Persons

Even though care and justice do not define mutually exclusive moral frameworks, it is still too early to dispose of the 'different voice hypothesis.' I believe that there is something to be said for the thesis that there are different moral orientations, even if the concepts of care and justice do not capture the relevant differences and even if the differences do not correlate statistically with gender differences.

My suggestion is that one important distinction has to do with the nature and focus of what may be called 'primary moral commitments.' Let us begin with the observation that, from the so-called 'care standpoint,' responsiveness to other persons in their wholeness and their particularity is of singular importance. This idea, in turn, points toward a notion of moral commitment which takes *particular persons* as its primary focus.[32] A form of moral commitment which contrasts with this is one which involves a focus on general and abstract rules, values, or principles. It is no mere coincidence, I believe, that Gilligan found the so-called 'justice' perspective to feature an emphasis on *rules* (e.g., p. 73).

In Part II of this paper, I argued that the concepts of justice and care are mutually compatible and, to at least some extent, mutually dependent. Based on my analysis, the 'justice perspective' might be said to rest, at bottom, on the assumption that the best way to *care* for persons is to respect their rights, and to accord them their due, both in distribution of the burdens and benefits of social cooperation, and in the rectification of wrongs done. But to uphold these principles, it is not necessary to respond with emotion, feeling, passion, or compassion to other persons. Upholding justice does not require the full range of mutual responsiveness which is possible between persons.

By contrast, the so-called 'ethic of care' stresses an ongoing responsiveness. This ethic is, after all, the stereotypic moral norm for women in the domestic role of sustaining a family in the face of the harsh realities of a competitive marketplace and an indifferent polis. The domestic realm has been idealized as the realm in which people, as specific individuals, were to have been nurtured, cherished, and succored. The 'care' perspective discussed by Gilligan is a limited one; it is not really about care in all its complexity, for, as I have argued, that notion *includes* just treatment. But it *is* about the nature of relationships to particular persons grasped as such. The key issue is the sensitivity and responsiveness to another person's emotional states, individuating differences, specific uniqueness, and whole particularity. The 'care' orientation focuses on whole persons and de-emphasizes adherence to moral rules.

Thus, the important conception which I am extracting from the so-called 'care' perspective is that of commitment to particular persons. What is the nature of this form of moral commitment? Commitment to a specific person, such as a lover, child, or friend, takes as its primary focus the needs, wants, attitudes, judgments, behavior, and overall way of being of that particular person. It is specific to that individual and is not generalizable to others. We show a commitment to someone whenever we attend to her needs, enjoy her successes, defer to her judgment, and find inspiration in her values and goals, simply because they are *hers.* If it is *who she is,* and not her actions or traits subsumed under general rules, which matters as one's motivating guide, then one's responsiveness to her reflects a person-oriented, rather than a rule-based, moral commitment.

Thus, the different perspectives which Gilligan called 'care' and 'justice' do point toward substantive differences in human interrelationship and commitment. Both orientations take account of relationships in some way; both may legitimately incorporate a concern for justice and for care, and both aim to avoid harm to others and (at the highest stages) to the self. But from the standpoint of 'care,' self and other are conceptualized in their *particularity* rather than as instances for the application of generalized moral notions. This difference ramifies into what appears to be a major difference in the organization and focus of moral thought.

This analysis requires a subtle expansion. Like care and justice, commitments to particular persons and commitments to values, rules, and principles are not mutually exclusive within the entire panorama of one person's moral concerns. Doubtless, they are intermingled in most people's moral outlooks. Pat likes and admires Mary because of Mary's resilience in the face of tragedy, her intelligent courage, and her good-humored audacity. Pat thereby shows a commitment *in general* to resilience, courage, and good-humored audacity as traits of human personality.

However, in Mary, these traits coalesce in a unique manner: perhaps no one will stand by a friend in deep trouble quite so steadfastly as Mary; perhaps no one petitions the university president as effectively as Mary. The traits which Pat likes, in general, converge to make *Mary*, in Pat's eyes, an especially admirable human individual, a sort of moral exemplar. In virtue of Pat's loyalty to her, Mary may come to play a role in Pat's life which exceeds, in its weightiness, the sum total of the values which pat sees in Mary's virtues, taken individually and in abstraction from any particular human personality.

Pat is someone with commitments both to moral abstractions and to particular persons. Pat is, in short, like most of us. When we reason morally, we can take up a stance which makes either of these forms of commitment the focal point of our attention. The choice of which stance to adopt at a given time is probably, like other moral alternatives, most poignant and difficult in situations of moral ambiguity or uncertainty when we don't know how to proceed. In such situations, one can turn *either* to the guidance of principled commitments to values, forms of conduct, or human virtues, *or* one can turn to the guidance which inheres in the example set by a trusted friend or associate—the example of how *she* interprets those same moral ambiguities, or how *she* resolves those same moral uncertainties.

Of course, the commitment to a particular person is evident in more situations than simply those of moral irresolution. But the experience of moral irresolution may make clearer the different sorts of moral commitment which structure our thinking. Following cherished values will lead one out of one's moral uncertainties in a very different way than following someone else's example.

Thus, the insight that each person needs some others in her life who recognize, respect, and cherish her particularity in its richness and wholeness is the distinctive motivating vision of the 'care' perspective.[33] The sort of respect for persons which grows out of this vision is not the abstract respect which is owed to all persons in virtue of their common humanity, but a respect for individual worth, merit, need, or, even, idiosyncracy. It is a form of respect which involves admiration and cherishing, when the distinctive qualities are valued intrinsically, and which, at the least, involves toleration when the distinctive qualities are not valued intrinsically.

Indeed, there is an apparent irony in the notion of personhood which underlies some philosophers' conceptions of the universalized moral duties owed to all persons. The rational nature which Kant, for example, takes to give each person dignity and to make each of absolute value, and, therefore, irreplaceable,[34] is no more than an abstract rational nature in virtue of which we are all alike. But if we are all alike in this respect, it is hard to understand why we would be irreplaceable. Our common rational nature would seem to make us indistinguishable and, therefore, mutually interchangeable. Specific identity would be a matter of indifference, so far as our absolute value is concerned. Yet it would seem that only in *virtue* of our distinctive particularity could we each be truly irreplaceable.

Of course, our particularity does not *exclude* a common nature, conceptualized at a level of suitable generality. We still deserve equal respect in virtue of our common humanity. But we are also *more* than abstractly and equivalently human. It is this 'more' to which we commit ourselves when we care for others in their particularity.

Thus, as I interpret it, there is at least one important difference in moral reasoning brought to our attention by Gilligan's 'care' and 'justice' frameworks. This difference hinges on the primary form of moral commitment which structures moral thought and the resulting nature of the response to other persons. For so-called 'care' reasoners, recognition of, and commitment to, persons in their particularity is an overriding moral concern.[35]

Unlike the concepts of justice and care, which admit of a mutual integration, it is less clear that these two distinct forms of moral commitment can jointly [compose] the focus of one's moral attention, in any single case. Nor can we respond to all other persons equally well in either way. The only integration possible here may be to seek the more intimate, responsive, committed relationships with people who are known closely, or known in contexts in which differential needs are important and can be known with some reliability, and to settle for rule-based equal respect toward that vast number of others whom one cannot know in any particularity.

At any rate, to tie together the varied threads of this discussion, we may conclude that nothing intrinsic to gender demands a division of moral norms which assigns particularized, personalized commitments to women and universalized, rule-based commitments to men. We need nothing less than to 'de-moralize' the genders, advance beyond the dissociation of justice from care, and enlarge the symbolic access of each gender to all available conceptual and social resources for the sustenance and enrichment of our collective moral life.[36]

Notes

1. *In a Different Voice* (Cambridge, MA: Harvard University Press 1982), 73. More recently, the following works by Gilligan on related issues have also appeared: 'Do the Social Sciences Have an Adequate Theory of Moral Development?' in Norma Haan, Robert N. Bellah, Paul Rabinow and William M. Sullivan, eds., *Social Science as Moral Inquiry* (New York: Columbia University Press 1983), 33–51; 'Reply,' *Signs* 11 (1986), 324–33; and 'Remapping the Moral Domain: New Images of the Self in Relationship,' in Thomas C. Heller, Morton Sosna and David E. Wellberry, eds., *Reconstructing Individualism* (Stanford, CA: Stanford University Press 1986) 237–52. Throughout this paper, all page references inserted in the text are to *In a Different Voice*.

2. Frigga Haug, 'Morals Also Have Two Genders,' trans. Rodney Livingstone, *New Left Review* 143 (1984), 55.

3. These sources include: Owen J. Flanagan, Jr. and Jonathan E. Adler, 'Impartiality and Particularity,' *Social Research* 50 (1983); 576–96; Nel Noddings, *Caring* (Berkeley: University of California Press 1984); Claudia Card, 'Virtues and Moral Luck' (unpublished paper presented at American Philosophical Association, Western Division Meetings, Chicago, IL, April 1985, and at the Conference on Virtue Theory, University of San Diego, San Diego, CA, February 1986); Marilyn Friedman, *Care and Context in Moral Reasoning*, MOSAIC Monograph #1 (Bath, England: University of Bath 1985), reprinted in Carol Harding, ed., *Moral Dilemmas* (Chicago: Precedent 1986), 25–42, and in Diana T. Meyers and Eva Feder Kittay, eds., *Women and Moral Theory* (Totowa, NJ: Rowman and Littlefield 1987), 190–204; all the papers in Meyers and Kittay; Linda K. Kerber, 'Some Cautionary Words for Historians,' *Signs* 11 (1986), 304–10; Catherine G. Greeno and Eleanor E. Maccoby, 'How Different is the "Different Voice,"' *Signs* 11 (1986) 310–16; Zella Luria, 'A Methodological Critique,' *Signs* 11 (1986), 316–21; Carol B. Stack, 'The Culture of Gender: Women and Men of Color,' *Signs* 11 (1986), 321–4; Owen Flanagan and Kathryn Jackson, 'Justice, Care, and Gender: The Kohlberg-Gilligan Debate Revisited,' *Ethics* 97 (1987), 622–37. An analysis of this issue from an ambiguously feminist standpoint is to be found in: John M. Broughton, 'Women's Rationality and Men's Virtues,' *Social Research* 50 (1983), 597–642. For a helpful review of some of these issues, cf. Jean Grimshaw, *Philosophy and Feminist Thinking* (Minneapolis: University of Minnesota Press 1986), esp. chs. 7 and 8.

4. This term is used by Virginia Held to refer, in general, to the division of moral labor among the multitude of professions, activities, and practices in culture and society, though not specifically to gender roles. Cf. *Rights and Goods* (New York: The Free Press 1984), ch. 3. Held is aware that gender roles are part of the division of moral labor but she mentions this topic only in passing, p. 29.

5. Gilligan, 'Reply,' 326.

6. Research on the 'gender difference' hypothesis is very mixed. The studies which appear to show gender differences in moral reasoning for one or more age levels include: Norma Haan, M. Brewster-Smith and Jeanne Block, 'Moral Reasoning of Young Adults: Political-social Behavior, Family Background, and Personality Correlates,' *Journal of Personality and Social Psychology* 10 (1968), 183–201; James Fishkin, Kenneth Keniston and Catharine MacKinnon, 'Moral Reasoning and Political Ideology,' *Journal of Personality and Social Psychology* 27 (1973), 109–19; Norma Haan, 'Hypothetical and Actual Moral Reasoning in a Situation of Civil Disobedience,' *Journal of Personality and Social Psychology* 32 (1975), 255–70; Constance Holstein, 'Development of Moral Judgment: A Longitudinal Study of Males and Females,' *Child Development* 47 (1976), 51–61 (showing gender differences in middle adulthood but not for other age categories; see references below); Sharry Langdale, 'Moral Orientations and Moral Development: The Analysis of Care and Justice Reasoning across Different Dilemmas in Females and Males from Childhood through Adulthood' (Ed. D. diss., Harvard Graduate School of Education, 1983); Kay Johnston, 'Two Moral Orientations—Two Problem-solving Strategies: Adolescents' Solutions to Dilemmas in Fables' (Ed. D. diss., Harvard Graduate School of Education 1985). The last two sources are cited by Gilligan, 'Reply,' p. 330.

Among the studies which show no gender differences in moral reasoning at one or more age levels are: E. Turiel, 'A Comparative Analysis of Moral Knowledge and Moral Judgment in Males and Females,' *Journal of Personality* 44 (1976), 195–208; C. B. Holstein,

'Irreversible Stepwise Sequence in the Development of Moral Judgment: A Longitudinal Study of Males and Females' (showing no differences in childhood or adolescence but showing differentiation in middle adulthood; see reference above); N. Haan, et al., 'Family Moral Patterns,' *Child Development* 47 (1976), 1204–6; M. Berkowitz, et al., 'The Relation of Moral Judgment Stage Disparity to Developmental Effects of Peer Dialogues,' *Merrill-Palmer Quarterly* 26 (1980), 341–57; and Mary Brabeck, 'Moral Judgment: Theory and Research on Differences between Males and Females,' *Developmental Review* 3 (1983), 274–91.

Lawrence J. Walker surveyed all the research to date and claimed that rather than showing a gender-based difference in moral reasoning, it showed differences based on occupation and education: 'Sex Differences in the Development of Moral Reasoning,' *Child Development* 55 (1984), 677–91. This 'meta-analysis' has itself recently been disputed: Norma Haan, 'With Regard to Walker (1984) on Sex "Differences" in Moral Reasoning' (University of California, Berkeley, Institute of Human Development mimeograph 1985); Diana Baumrind, 'Sex Differences in Moral Reasoning: Response to Walker's (1984) Conclusion That There Are None,' *Child Development* [57 (1986), 511–521]. The last two sources are cited by Gilligan, 'Reply,' p. 330.

7. Norma Haan, 'Two Moralities in Action Contexts,' *Journal of Personality and Social Psychology* 36 (1978), 286–305. Also cf. Norma Haan, 'Moral Reasoning in a Hypothetical and an Actual Situation of Civil Disobedience,' *Journal of Personality and Social Psychology* 32 (1975), 255–70; and Gertrud Nunner-Winkler, 'Two Moralities? A Critical Discussion of an Ethic of Care and Responsibility versus an Ethic of Rights and Justice,' in William M. Kurtines and Jacob L. Gewirtz, *Morality, Moral Behavior, and Moral Development* (New York: John Wiley & Sons 1984), 348–61.

8. Gilligan, 'Reply,' 326.

9. Broughton, 'Women's Rationality and Men's Virtues,' 636.

10. Gilligan's work arose largely as a critical reaction to the studies of moral reasoning carried on by Lawrence Kohlberg and his research associates. For the reaction by those scholars to Gilligan's work and their assessment of its importance to moral psychology, see Lawrence Kohlberg, 'A Reply to Owen Flanagan and Some Comments on the Puka-Goodpaster Exchange,' *Ethics* 92 (1982), 513–28; and Lawrence Kohlberg, Charles Levine and Alexandra Hewer, *Moral Stages: A Current Reformulation and Response to Critics* (Basel: Karger 1983), 20–7, 121–50.

In philosophy, themes related to Gilligan's concerns have been raised by, among others: Michael Stocker, 'The Schizophrenia of Modern Ethical Theories,' *Journal of Philosophy* 63 (1976) 453–66; Bernard Williams, 'Persons, Character and Morality,' in Amelie O. Rorty, ed., *The Identities of Persons* (Berkeley: University of California 1976), reprinted in Bernard Williams, *Moral Luck* (New York: Cambridge University Press 1982), 1–19; Lawrence Blum, *Friendship, Altruism and Morality* (London: Routledge & Kegan Paul 1980); Alasdair MacIntyre, *After Virtue* (Notre Dame, IN: University of Notre Dame 1981), esp. ch. 15; Michael Stocker, 'Values and Purposes: The Limits of Teleology and the Ends of Friendship,' *Journal of Philosophy* 78 (1981), 747–65; Owen Flanagan, 'Virtue, Sex and Gender: Some Philosophical Reflections on the Moral Psychology Debate,' *Ethics* 92 (1982), 499–512; Michael Slote, 'Morality Not a System of Imperatives,' *American Philosophical Quarterly* 19 (1982), 331–40; and Christina Hoff Sommers, 'Filial Morality,' *Journal of Philosophy* 83 (1986), 439–56.

11. Greeno and Maccoby, 'How Different Is the "Different" Voice?' 314–15.

12. Gilligan, 'Reply,' 325.

13. For a discussion of this historical development, cf. Linda Nicholson, 'Women, Morality and History,' *Social Research* 50 (1983), 514–36; and her *Gender and History* (New York: Columbia University Press 1986) esp. chs. 3 and 4.

14. Cf. Nancy Eisenberg and Roger Lennon, 'Sex Differences in Empathy and Related Capacities,' *Psychological Bulletin* 94 (1983), 100–31.

15. Cf. Alice H. Eagly, 'Sex Differences and Social Roles' (unpublished paper presented at Experimental Social Psychology, Tempe, AZ, October 1986), esp. p. 7. Also cf: Alice H. Eagly and Valerie J. Steffen, 'Gender Stereotypes Stem from the Distribution of Women and Men into Social Roles,' *Journal of Personality and Social Psychology* 46 (1984), 735–54.

16. The stereotypes of men are not obviously connected with justice and rights, but they are connected with the excessive individualism which Gilligan takes to underlie the justice orientation. Cf. Eagly, 'Sex Differences and Social Roles,' 8.

17. Eagly argues both that people do show a tendency to conform to shared and known expectations, on the parts of others, about their behavior, and that a division of labor which leads people to develop different skills also contributes to differential development; 'Sex Differences and Social Roles,' *passim*. It follows from Eagly's view that if the genders are stereotypically 'moralized,' they would then be likely to develop so as to conform to those different expectations.

18. Eagly and Steffen have found that stereotypic beliefs that women are more 'communal' and less 'agentic' than men, and that men are more 'agentic' and less 'communal' than women, are based more deeply on occupational role stereotypes than on gender stereotypes; 'Gender Stereotypes Stem from the Distribution of Women and Men into Social Roles,' *passim*. In this respect, Eagly and Steffen force us to question whether the gender categorization which pervades Gilligan's analysis really captures the fundamental differentiation among persons. I do not address this question in this paper.

19. In correspondence, Marcia Baron has suggested that a factor accounting for the actual emergence of 'mixed' perspectives on the parts of women and men may have to do with the instability of the distinction between public and private realms to which the justice/care dichotomy corresponds. Men have always been recognized to participate in both realms and, in practice, many women have participated, out of choice or necessity, in such segments of the public world as that of paid labor. The result is a blurring of the experiential segregation which otherwise might have served to reinforce distinct moral orientations.

20. Book I, 322–35. A thorough discussion of the Greek conception of justice in the context of friendship can be found in Horst Hutter, *Politics as Friendship* (Waterloo, ON: Wilfrid Laurier University Press 1978).

21. Rawls, *Theory of Justice*, 13 and elsewhere.

22. Ibid., 129.

23. *The Politics of Reality* (Trumansburg, NY: The Crossing Press 1983), 9.

24. Ibid., 10.

25. For an important discussion of the relevance of justice to the family, cf. Susan Moller Okin, 'Justice and Gender,' *Philosophy and Public Affairs* 16 (1987), 42–72.

26. For insightful discussions of the distinctive modes of thought to which mothering gives rise, cf. Sara Ruddick, 'Maternal Thinking,' *Feminist Studies* 6 (1980), 342–67; and her 'Preservative Love and Military Destruction: Some Reflections on Mothering and Peace,' in Joyce Trebilcot, ed., *Mothering: Essays in Feminist Theory* (Totowa, NJ: Rowman &

Allanheld 1983), 231–62; also Virginia Held, 'The Obligations of Mothers and Fathers,' in Trebilcot, ed., 7–20.

27. This point was suggested to me by L. W. Sumner.

28. John Broughton also discusses the concern for justice and rights which appears in women's moral reasoning as well as the concern for care and relationships featured in men's moral reasoning: 'Women's Rationality and Men's Virtues,' esp. 603–22. For a historical discussion of male theorists who have failed to hear the concern for justice in women's voices, cf. Carole Pateman, '"The Disorder of Women": Women, Love, and the Sense of Justice,' *Ethics* 91 (1980), 20–34.

29. This discussion owes a debt to Francesca M. Cancian's warning that we should not narrow our conception of love to the recognized ways in which women love, which researchers find to center around the expression of feelings and verbal disclosure. Such a conception ignores forms of love which are stereotyped as characteristically male, including instrumental help and the sharing of activities. Cf. 'The Feminization of Love,' *Signs* 11 (1986), 692–709.

30. Cf. Mike Royko, *Boss: Richard J. Daley of Chicago* (New York: New American Library 1971).

31. Claudia Card has critiqued Gilligan's work for ignoring, in particular, the dismaying harms to which women have historically been subjected in heterosexual relationships, including, but by no means limited to, marriage ('Virtues and Moral Luck,' 15–17).

32. Discussion in Part III of my paper draws upon the insights of Claudia Card, 'Virtues and Moral Luck' and Seyla Benhabib, 'The Generalized and the Concrete Other: Visions of the Autonomous Self,' in Meyers and Kittay, eds., *Women and Moral Theory*, 154–77.

33. This part of my discussion owes a debt to Claudia Card.

34. Cf. Immanuel Kant, *Groundwork of the Metaphysics of Morals*, trans. Lewis White Beck (Indianapolis: Bobbs-Merrill 1959), 46–7, 53–4.

35. For a helpful discussion on this topic, cf. Margaret Walker, 'Moral Particularism,' unpublished manuscript presented at the Pacific Division Meetings of the American Philosophical Association, March 1987.

36. I am grateful to Larry May, L. W. Sumner, Marcia Baron, and Christopher Morris for helpful comments on previous drafts of this paper. Earlier versions were presented to the Society for Women in Philosophy, Midwestern Division (USA), Madison, WI, October 1986; Society for Value Inquiry, Chicago, IL, April 1987; Seminar on Contemporary Social and Political Thought, University of Chicago, May 1987; Third International Interdisciplinary Congress on Women, Dublin, Ireland, July 1987; and Annual Conference of MOSAIC (Moral and Social Action Interdisciplinary Colloquium), Brighton, England, July 1987.

5

Gender and Moral Luck
[1990]

CLAUDIA CARD

Pasts we inherit affect who we become.[1] As gendered beings in a society with a history of patriarchy, women and men inherit different pasts and consequently different social expectations, lines of communication, opportunities, and barriers. When these things influence character development, they make gender part of our "moral luck."[2] By "luck" I mean factors, good or bad, beyond the control of the affected agent: matters of chance and predictable results of social practice.[3]

I am interested in how gender-related moral luck illuminates biases in ethical theory. My special interest is character development under oppressive practices. In the present essay I question a view of women and care that proceeds as though women have no real damage to overcome, as though women's values and virtues need only to be appreciated and allowed to develop as they are, or at most, need to be supplemented by those more characteristically attributed to men. I then examine a more historically oriented view of women and ethics preserving, without glorifying women's moral sensibilities, the idea that attention to women's lives can deepen and correct modern Western ethical thinking.

A number of feminist scholars are sympathetic to the idea, popularly associated with the work of Carol Gilligan, that an ethic of care is more characteristic of women or is more apt to be implicit in the experience and ideals of women and that an ethic of justice or rights, or abstract action-guiding principle, is more implicit in the experience of men.[4] If some such hypothesis were true, we might expect a bias in ethical theory toward justice or rights, or at least toward abstract action-guiding principles, given the history of sexism. Such a bias appears evident in the contractarianism and utilitarianism of modern Western ethics. Yet these theories have not always been dominant. A more modest hypothesis—less exciting, perhaps less romantic—also found in Carol Gilligan's work but often not distinguished from the "justice and care" hypothesis, is that *the responsibilities of different kinds of relationships* yield different ethical preoccupations, methods, priorities, even concepts.[5] Different kinds of relationships have been differently distributed among women and men in patriarchal society: a larger share of the responsibilities of certain personal and informal relationships to women, a larger share of the responsibilities of formal and impersonal relationships defined by social institutions to men. It is plausible that a result has been the creation of a significant difference in ethical orientation.[6] Putting it this way opens better to philosophical inquiry the questions of how good these relationships have been, what their virtues and vices are, their major values, their roles in a good life, in a good society. It allows us, for example, to explore the place of fairness in friendship and to note its absence as a flaw.[7]

The hypothesis in terms of *relationships* puts us into a better position than the justice and care hypothesis to identify moral damage resulting from and perpetuating sex oppression. We need to be sensitive to the possibility, easily disguised by the honorific language of "justice" and "care," that what often pass for virtues for both sexes are vices (see Houston 1987). Histories of oppression require us to read between the lines of what we say. The privileged are liable to arrogance with its blindness to others' perspectives. The oppressed are liable to low self-esteem, ingratiation, and affiliation with abusers ("female masochism"), as well as to a tendency to dissemble, a fear of being conspicuous, and chameleonism—taking on the colors of our environment as protection against assault. Histories of exploitation lead us to identify with service, to find our value in our utility or ability to please. Moral damage among both privileged and oppressed tends to be unselfconscious, mutually reinforcing, and stubborn. Where our identities are at stake, oppression is hard to face. Beneficiaries face guilt issues and are liable to defensiveness. The oppressed face damage to an already precarious self-esteem in admitting impotence.

It may also be our moral luck to develop special insights, even under oppressive institutions. I do not have in mind the *experience* of resisting oppressors. Temptations to romanticize resistance are sobered by the thought that so doing seems to glorify oppression (see Ringelheim 1985). Yet a priori, it seems plausible that divisions of responsibility divide opportunities for kinds of moral insight by unevenly distributing the decision-making experience that develops it. However, two cautions are in order. First, oppressive divisions of responsibility may encourage delusion more readily than insight. This suggests that insight is hard won. Second, the hypothesis that insights in the areas of *justice* and *care* might be unevenly distributed appears to assume uncritically that these are such different areas that insights in each are separable from insights in the other, assumptions that may be oversimple (Friedman 1987a, Stocker 1986, Flanagan and Jackson 1987). Both cautions are themes in the present chapter.

The remainder of this chapter has two main tasks. First, I sketch a tension between the two kinds of feminist critique represented by Carol Gilligan and Mary

Wollstonecraft, the former flattering both sexes, the latter flattering neither, and both focusing on maternal and adult heterosexual relationships.[8] I argue that correcting misperceptions of women identified by a care perspective, such as Carol Gilligan's, is not enough to vindicate women's characters, nor, therefore, to lend much support to the hypothesis that women's values and aspirations can deepen and correct defects in modern ethical theory.[9] My second task is to explore what more is needed to make that "corrective hypothesis" more plausible. To do so, I examine the sense of responsibility attaching to informal, often personal relationships, contrasting it with that of formal and impersonal ones, and attaching to it independently of a contrast between justice and care. I argue that taking only formal and impersonal relationships as paradigms of obligation and responsibility has produced arbitrarily biased and probably superficial theory. This idea, suggested also in recent work of Annette Baier (1986, see also Flanagan and Jackson 1987), is not that *justice* is superficial. I do not find justice superficial. The idea is rather that the ethical significance of basic informal and personal relationships is at least as much of the first order as that of basic social institutions. To the extent that the personal and informal underlie and circumscribe formal institutions, they are *more* basic. I argue throughout that a focus on formality is not the only bias in modern ethical theory but that fairness has also been systematically ignored in personal and informal relationships, especially where women are involved.

I. Women and Care

Sigmund Freud (1961) criticized women as deficient in the sense of justice. As Carol Gilligan (1982, 18) observes, the behavior underlying this common criticism of women by men is also often cited under different descriptions as evidence of women's "special goodness"—caring, sensitivity, responsiveness to others' needs, and appreciation of the concrete particular. Both the criticism and the praise are part of the tradition of modern Western moral philosophy. "The very thought of seeing women administer justice raises a laugh," said Arthur Schopenhauer. He thought women "far less capable than men of understanding and sticking to universal principles," yet also that "they surpass men in the virtues of *philanthropy* and *lovingkindness* [*Menschenliebe*], for the origin of this is . . . intuitive" (1965, 151). On women and principles he followed Immanuel Kant, who exclaimed, "I hardly believe the fair sex is capable of principles," and speculated instead, "Providence has put in their breast kind and benevolent sensations, a fine feeling for propriety, and a complaisant soul" (1960b, 81). The contradiction is acute in Immanuel Kant, whose views on women and on morality seem to imply that good women lack moral character.[10]

I refer loosely to the above views from the academic canon as "the patriarchal view." Women criticize this view from different angles. Some, like Carol Gilligan, defend the moral responses attributed to women as "different but also valuable," arguing that theories by which women appear deficient are faulty. I call this "the rosy view" because it presents a fairly romantic picture of the insights of women and men. Everyone comes out looking good though not perfect; the insights of each sex, basically sound, need to be supplemented by those of the other. Other critics, like Mary Wollstonecraft (1982), reject so-called "women's goodness" as a euphemism for vices that make it easier for women to be controlled by men. Mary Wollstonecraft argued that women under sexist institutions become morally deformed, neither loving nor just. Noticing similarities between the vices of women and those of the relatively powerless men in military service, she disagreed with her contemporaries, Jean-Jacques Rousseau and Immanuel Kant, on the gender relatedness of virtues. Her view was that *duties* might vary but *virtues* are the same for everyone. She ridiculed the idea that powerless, abused, uneducated women have a special kind of goodness. I call this view, generously, "the skeptical view," for it suggests skepticism about the likelihood that the per- spectives of oppressed women yield special moral insights. The correlative idea, that oppressors' perspectives are no wiser, is not developed by Mary Woll- stonecraft, who was writing in 1792 to an audience of men without benefit of a supporting women's community. It is implicit in her approach, however. On this view, the problem with "women's ethics" and "men's ethics" is not that they are incomplete or underdeveloped but that they are warped from the start.

However mutually incompatible they appear, the protests of both Carol Gilligan and Mary Wollstonecraft initially seem right. I have wanted to find more truth in the rosy view. Yet the skeptical view refuses to let go of me. If the two views are to be reconciled, it seems to me utterly crucial not to deny the truths of the skeptical view.

An observation documented in Carol Gilligan's recent essays is that nearly everyone interviewed seemed readily able to adopt both the care and justice perspectives but, as with incompatible gestalts, not simultaneously, and that most found one perspective more comfortable than the other (Gilligan et al. 1988). To me, these observations suggest the presence of something *other* than justice and care—such as an oppressive relationship—skewing both perspec- tives. For how can we judge ethical conflicts between considerations of justice and care if we cannot hold them in mind without a priori subordinating consid- erations of one sort to those of the other?[11] By looking at cases, Marilyn Friedman (1987a) has convincingly argued that neither a priori ranking is plau- sible.

In friendship both fairness and caring are valuable. Although friendship does not usually center on formulating rules and applying them to cases, it typically does involve, as Marilyn Friedman (1987a) has pointed out, a division of respon- sibilities in a more or less extensive mutual support system. A good friendship is fair about such divisions. Such fairness may even be a requirement of caring.

Fairness in friendship also requires responsiveness to personal deserts or wor-thiness.[12] If anything, to be a good friend one needs a *better* sense of fairness than to be a good citizen or soldier, an idea that makes good sense of Aristotle's report that people say that "when [we] are friends [we] have no need of justice, while when [we] are just [we] need friendship as well, and the truest form of jus-tice is thought to be a friendly quality" (1925, 1155a). If "justice" here is meant to suggest enforcement, the idea seems sound. Responsiveness where enforce-ment is not forthcoming is a greater test of one's fairness than where there is possible recourse to sanctions. If the idea is that the values of justice are superfi-cial, however, it seems confused. For what makes sense of friends not needing justice is that they have the relevant values so well internalized.

This interpretation suggests that it is *not* a mistake to evaluate the conduct of personal relationships by values associated with justice, such as fairness. Nevertheless, errors turn up in the patriarchal view of women and ethics, as Carol Gilligan has pointed out. Women's motives and intentions are often mis-perceived, misrepresented, oversimplified. The question arises whether righting these errors reveals virtues and values wrongly overlooked in patriarchal ethics.

In Lawrence Kohlberg's moral stages (Kohlberg 1981), for example, women may appear more concerned with approval, more conventional, when what they are actually doing is exhibiting a concern for maintaining relationships. In main-taining relationships, we respect points of view different from our own and at-tempt to empathize with them. Sigmund Freud found women to have "weak ego-boundaries," poor self-definition, problems with separation and autonomy, and a weaker sense of justice, at least a weaker "legal sense," and concluded that women were thereby deficient in moral reasoning. Carol Gilligan (1982, 43–45) responded that if women have a problem with separation, *men* have a problem with *connection*. She also responded that women judged deficient in justice may be resolving conflicts of interest by favoring inclusiveness over ranking or bal-ancing claims. She illustrated the difference with the endearing story of "the pi-rate who lives next door."[13]

And yet despite the genuineness of such misperceptions and oversimplifica-tions, disturbing facts remain. Women's political options in misogynist environ-ments complicate the assessment of women's moral responses. Institutionalized dependence on men for protection against male assault, for employment, pro-motion, and validation, have given women reasons to seek "approval," usually *male* approval. This approval is granted for conventional affiliations with men, respect for their views, empathy with them, etc. Just as there is no need to sup-pose that women value approval or conventionality *for its own sake* or that we confuse "right" with "conventional" (or "approved"), there is no need to assume on the basis of women's empathy that women value these connections for their own sake. Many women are prudent. many are convinced that this exchange is what heterosexual love is about, since, after all, convention requires women to affiliate with masculine protectors out of "love." How many attachments are the product of what Adrienne Rich (1980) called "compulsory heterosexuality," the result of orientations molded at an age when our powers of assessment are morally undeveloped?

Speculation that many women are basically prudent about heterosexual relationships may strike some as ungenerous to women. However, where women are not respected, prudence is necessary. It is less generous to assume our readiness to be basically moved by attachment to those who do not respect us. If the distribution of power in society's basic structure is a clue to its members' level of respect for others, as is argued by John Rawls (1971, secs. 67, 82), a pervasive gender-related imbalance of power is evidence of widespread social disrespect for women. If so, what is at stake in evaluating heterosexual relationships is not simply the uses of power by those with more of it but also what it means that they have more of it. In such a context, reciprocity of respect might be extraordinary.

The variety of motives from which women may affiliate raises ethical questions that both the rosy view and the patriarchal view tend to bury. Male "disapproval" commonly reaches the pitch of harassment. What are some ethically honorable ways of avoiding, resisting, and stopping harassment? Entering into heterosexual relationships to purchase "protection" may be not only risky but also unfair to other women in further entrenching women's need for protection rather than combatting that need. Women are often surprised to hear that *they* are *unfair* if they reject sexual advances from men and similarly, when they bring accusations of rape, that expecting anything else was *not fair* under the circumstances. For patriarchy lacks a history of giving women *honorable* ways of invoking fairness to reject sexual overtures from men, especially from men from whom they cannot, or for various reasons do not wish to, sever connections altogether. Similar problems exist for the issues of self-definition and autonomy. Given women's inferior political position together with the lifelong message that a woman "alone" is "asking for it," who could be surprised that "studies show" women seeking to create and maintain affiliations? Again, cautions are in order: we need to look at why women affiliate and with whom. Women don't embrace just any affiliation. Many are terrified of lesbian connections and disdainful of interracial connections, for example. We who are women are taught that identifying ourselves in relation to certain men as sister, mother, wife, lover, etc., can reduce threats of assault. It does not follow that such a reduction amounts to *safety* or that women are under the illusion that it does. Nor does it follow that we do not know well where we leave off and men begin. We learn our places early.

Reciprocity is associated in modern ethics primarily with justice. Yet lack of reciprocity is probably a major cause of the breakup of friendships among peers. If, as Carol Gilligan noted early in her work (1982, 17), *at midlife* men come to see the value of intimacy, which women have seen all along, what does that say about the quality of heterosexual intimacy *prior to midlife,* and about the judgment of those who valued such relationships? Perhaps, as Phillippa Foot said of the villain's courage (1978c, 14–18), women's caring here is not functioning as a virtue. It is also doubtful that paradigms of relationship in which women's choices are less than free represent women's values fairly or well.

Women's connectedness is not always a good thing. When our *primary* relationships lack reciprocity of valuing, we risk losing (or failing to develop) self-esteem. Valuing others independently of their utility is at the core of both respect and love, and being so valued is important to self-esteem. In respect we appreciate others as like ourselves in certain fundamental ways; in love we also cherish their particularities. Identifying and valuing ourselves in terms of relationships to others who likewise identify and value themselves in relation to us can leave us with enriched self-esteem. But when our primary attachments are to those who define and value themselves by what they take to be their own achievements while they define and value us in terms of our relationships to them, we are encouraged at best to assimilate, not really to affiliate. We risk becoming extensions, tools. Our caring does not have the same meaning that it has when it is valued because it comes from us. It is not the same source of self-esteem.

Failure to appreciate the value of others independently of utility has not been the failure of only those with the lion's share of power. In military boot camps males of a variety of ages and political strata learn misogynist attitudes toward females in general.[14] Fear of the same phenomena seems to underlie Mary Wollstonecraft's opposition to boys' boarding schools, although she doesn't comment on military misogyny. When those who lack respect also come into the lion's share of power, affiliative relationships with them are not only impoverished but dangerous for those on the short end.

Recent work on women's conception of the self as rooted in relationships with others has led to speculations about men and violence. On the basis of fantasy studies, Carol Gilligan has suggested that violence in men's fantasies is rooted in men's fear of intimacy (Gilligan 1982, 39–45; Gilligan et al. 1988, chap. 12). She reported that in the studies in which subjects constructed stories in response to pictures, women tended to find safety in intimacy and danger in isolation while men tended to find danger in intimacy and safety in independence. We should be skeptical, however, about the conclusion that women find safety in intimacy. The conclusion about men's fears may clarify why, if it is amplified and made more specific.

Many relationships women construct are informal, even personal, but not intimate. Like the nets that women test subjects supplied in response to a picture of trapeze artists, women's relationships with women are often for safety and protection—they are *networks* of connections, not sexual unions. Thus they are not the same as the relationships men seem to fear. The fantasies of both sexes may be compatible with *both* sexes fearing intimacy, each for different reasons. Fear of isolation is compatible with fear of intimacy; fear of isolation may be stronger for women. Women's networks are often cushions against the violence of intimate relationships. Where men do not construct such networks, perhaps they do not have a similar need. When men fear heterosexual intimacy, they usually have the power to avoid it.

If we examine fantasies for clues to our senses of danger, what do women's infamous rape fantasies tell us? Women are reluctant to articulate them, and not always because they reinforce stereotypes of female masochism. Rape fantasies are not only of attack *by* rapists but also of responsive attack *on* rapists, killing rapists, maiming them, etc. Intimacy has not cured the violence in women's lives. It has given the violent greater access to their victims. Rape is one of the most underreported crimes because it is committed more readily by acquaintances and intimates than by strangers (Amir 1971). Battery of women by intimates is a serious issue in misogynist environments.[15] Men's fears of rejection and entrapment by women in this context are not altogether misplaced. Men's fantasy violence may betray an appreciation of the implications of misogyny. Perhaps what men fear is *women's* historically well-grounded *fears of men*, which predictably issue in the tangle of women's clinging to men for acceptability and protection (against other men) and at the same time in their withdrawing sexually, engaging in manipulation, daily resentful hostilities, and eventual fantasies of widowhood.

Women's failure to value separation and autonomy is a genuine problem. But the problem is political, not simply psychological. Women are systematically penalized for not being available on demand to children, relatives, spouses, male lovers. A good example of women's moral luck may be that as a result of our political inability to end bad relationships, we have not learned to discriminate well between good ones and bad ones but have learned instead to assume responsibility for maintaining whatever relationships "fate" seems to throw our way. The great danger, as well as the great strength, of the method of inclusion is its presumption that there should be a way to satisfy everyone. Women are afraid to say no. But separation can be preferable to inclusion.

Inclusion brings us again to the sense of justice. Why contrast the search for inclusive solutions with justice or with *fairness?* Fairness is not only a matter of ranking, taking turns, or balancing claims—ways of distributing power among competing parties—but also a matter of recognizing who deserves what from whom, and deserts tend to bring the affects of sympathy and antipathy into the picture. Sometimes everyone deserves to be included. Although inclusion is an alternative to balancing claims, it is not necessarily an alternative to justice. The *difference principle* in John Rawls's theory of justice as fairness could favor inclusion over competition or taking turns. This principle directs that basic social institutions be so arranged that those least advantaged are as well-off as possible

(Rawls 1971, secs. 11–12). If a more inclusive solution were more to the advantage of those least well-off, the difference principle would favor it. If methods of inclusion are *among* the methods of justice, women's reputation for a weak sense of justice may be undeserved in proportion to the accuracy of Carol Gilligan's observations. Where inclusion is unjust, it is unclear what can be said to recommend it.

Although women probably have more sense of justice than Freud thought, the truth that women are liable to misperception does not yet sustain the view that women's reasonings reveal virtues and values that can deepen and correct the ethics of those more privileged. Often our reasonings reveal survival strategies and, less flatteringly, vices complementary to those of the privileged. Still, I find the corrective potentialities of the data of women's lives to be genuine. To show how, I want to look at those data as giving us a domain of basic informal and personal relationships.

II. Women's Luck and Modern Ethical Theory

Women's care often takes the form of responsiveness to the needs of others. Thus in her 1982 writing Carol Gilligan naturally moved from "an ethic of care" to "an ethic of responsibility," understanding responsibility as a capacity for responsiveness. The Kohlbergian tradition from which she began took over the Rawlsian view that the business of justice is to distribute rights. Hence her easy move from "justice perspectives" to "rights perspectives." However, two different views are conflated by these equations, one of which is more plausible, if less sweeping or dramatic, than the other. The thesis that women develop an ethic of care and men an ethic of justice is not logically tied to the thesis that women develop an ethic of responsibility and men an ethic of rights. The "responsibility and rights" thesis, or something like it, is more promising than the "justice and care" thesis.

Justice is not exhausted by rights. Justice is a far older concept. Nor does caring exhaust the responsibilities of women's relationships. By "an ethic of responsibility" what was more specifically meant was the ethics of informal and personal relationships; by "an ethic of rights," the ethics of formal or impersonal relationships. Both involve responsibilities, however, just as both involve relationship—different kinds of responsibilities and different kinds of relationships. That we can hear a "different moral voice" in the ethics of informal and personal relationships is plausible, even if it is not always the voice of "care" or the voice from which it diverges, that of "justice."

Modern moral philosophy has been preoccupied with power and control—its uses, its distribution, its forms (Hoagland 1988).[16] Attachment, in the sense that suggests emotion or feeling, has been downplayed, underrated, dismissed. In her more recent essays (Gilligan et al. 1988) Carol Gilligan emphasizes that power and attachment are two ways of defining relationships, two ways of defining responsibilities. She no longer contrasts rights with responsibilities or presents only women as focused on relationships but sees women and men as often focused on different relationships and different responsibilities.

Contractarian and utilitarian ethics are preoccupied with control. They take formal and impersonal relationships as paradigms. Both kinds of theory reflect administrative practical wisdom. Ideal observers and veils of ignorance give versions of the perspective of an administrator (who may be a member of a board rather than a lone administrator). The data for these theories are drawn first of all from the public worlds of law and commerce, as are the concepts used in their analysis: *right* (or duty) and *good* (or interest). "Right" is rooted in law, the world of rights. "Good," in the relevant sense, suggests commerce, the world of goods. Ethics as normative theorizing about impersonal relationships is epitomized by John Rawls's theory of justice, by the current fascination with the prisoner's dilemma, and by consequentialist paradoxes concerning nuclear deterrence.

Responsibility in administration is a matter of supervision, management, accountability, and answerability. One who is responsible for something answers for it, takes whatever credit or blame is due. Those whose responsibilities go unfulfilled are expected to explain to others. This credit-and-blame sense of responsibility is the sense that figures in Nietzsche's obsession with the genealogy of morality as control. It is not at all what Carol Gilligan meant in attributing to women an ethic of responsibility. She had in mind responsiveness to needs, to situations. This is more congruent with the idea of *taking* responsibility *for* someone or something—committing oneself to look after its maintenance or well-being, preserve its value, even to make it good.[17] Here the focus is on well-being, not on control. When the focus is on well-being, responsiveness to needs comes to the fore. The administrative point of view is not noted for its responsiveness to needs.

The administrative point of view does not yield a theory of friendship. Philosophers in the last third of this century have begun remedying the relative lack of attention to friendship in modern ethics (Telfer 1970/1971, Stocker 1976a, Blum 1980, Raymond 1986). Friendship belongs to the larger area of personal relationships and informal practices—sexual intimacy, kinship, and a variety of networks loosely dubbed "friendships." As Annette Baier notes, historically, men have been able to take for granted a background of informal and personal relationships with women for the reproduction of populations and institutions, women have had less choice than men about participating in these relationships, and men have had material stakes in not scrutinizing such relationships morally (Baier 1986). It can be added that men also have stakes in not scrutinizing many informal relationships with one another underlying and circumscribing the formal ones on which attention is typically focused in their discussions of moral issues. If, as Annette Baier observes (1986), it has often been women's luck to have to make the best of involuntarily assumed personal relationships and to have to create networks of informal relationships in a world that denied women a voice in law, men also have recourse to networks and relationships of varying degrees of informality—the Ku Klux Klan, gentlemen's agreements—when they want to *circumvent* the law.[18]

We need theories of the ethics of informal and personal relationships at least as well developed as administrative ethics. Informal relationships tend to *underlie* formal ones, circumscribe them, come into play when formal ones break down. On the view developed by John Rawls, obligations (or, we might say, responsibilities) require for their analyses references to criteria formulated specifically for evaluating public institutions. Perhaps *personal and informal* responsibilities require for their analyses references to criteria formulated *specifically for evaluating personal relationships and informal practices.*

What are "informal" and "personal" relationships? The informal and the personal are not the same. An informal agreement need not be personal. An interpersonal relationship is *personal* when it matters to the parties who the other parties are and when this mattering is important to the nature of the relationship.[19] "Personal" suggests closeness, intimacy. The personal introduces issues of attachment and antipathy. Informal relationships are characterized by responsibilities that can facilitate relationships of attachment.

A relationship is *formal* to the extent that it is well-defined, limited, in ways that are publicly understood and publicly sanctioned. Formality facilitates control where there would otherwise be a lack of trust or simply an inability to predict and plan. Formality is not the same as legality; both legal and nonlegal relationships have varying degrees of formality. Spousehood, for example, is a formally defined status in law, but the obligations of spouses to one another tend to be highly informal. Those of outsiders to spouses, on the other hand, become more formal in consequence of marriage.

Within limits, formality and personality are matters of degree. *Very* formal relationships, however, involve rights, which one either has or lacks. Friendship is personal and relatively informal. We may have formal relationships, such as contracts, with friends. But that can also create problems for friendship. Personal relationships tend toward informality. The relationships of clients and patients to physicians and other caretakers become more formal as clients and patients insist upon rights, which creates tensions for those who find it desirable that such relationships retain personal aspects. The relationship of judge to defendant, on the other hand, is (supposed to be) impersonal, not merely formal.[20]

Relationships defined by what John Rawls calls "the basic structure of society" are institutional. Institutions define responsibilities, or obligations, closely correlated with rights; the relationships are thus formal. They are also impersonal;

persons are repeatedly presented as competing for positions defined by basic institutions. The perspective from which such responsibilities are ultimately analyzed and evaluated—the "Original Position"—is thoroughly impersonal (Rawls 1971, chap. 3).

The ethics of basic *institutions* is the subject of Rawls's theory of justice. Basic informal and personal relationships, however, are *like* basic institutions in possessing the three major features he identifies to support his view of those institutions as basic to the structure of society. Basic informal and personal relationships should therefore also be recognized as belonging to the basic structure of society. Goodness here is at least as important as justice in basic institutions.

The points of similarity are as follows. First, personal relationships are at least as important to our "starting places" in life as the institutions constituting the basic structure. Second, self-esteem, especially the conviction that one's life is worth living, is contingent not only on basic rights but also on informal practices and primary personal relationships. Third, personal relationships and informal practices create special responsibilities (but ones that are not closely correlated with rights), just as impersonal relationships and formal institutions create special responsibilities (which are closely correlated with rights). If such considerations support the moral importance of basic institutions, they support that of basic informal and personal relationships as well.

Consider starting places. The importance of justice as the first virtue of basic institutions rests heavily, in Rawls's theory, on the fact these institutions determine our starting places in life. People born into different social positions have different expectations because these institutions work together in such a way as to favor certain starting points over others, and these inequalities, which tend to be deep, are not justifiable by appeal to merit or desert (Rawls 1971, p. 7). This is surely true. However, the profundity and pervasiveness of the effects of our personal and informal starting places is at least equal to those of our formal starting places. Our personal relationships with parents are a starting point. Parents who handle such relationships badly may leave us seriously disadvantaged for life. We have no more choice over these starting relationships than over participation in society's class structure or its basic economic institutions. Nor are they deserved or justifiable by appeal to merit. If involuntariness of participation and profundity of the effects upon health and well-being ground the ethical significance of social institutions, they can likewise ground that of basic informal and primary personal relationships. Yet the latter are not defined by rights. They do not give us a "rights perspective," although they do give us a "responsibility perspective." Treating the monogamous family as an institution defined by rights does not adequately recognize the morality of family relationships.

Second, consider the effect of such relationships on self-esteem. The basis of self-esteem in a just society, according to Rawls (1971, 544), is a certain publicly affirmed distribution of basic rights and liberties. However, self-esteem is also contingent upon primary personal relationships, upon the sense we develop of ourselves in such relationships, our sense of ourselves as capable of faithfulness, understanding, warmth, empathy, as having the qualities we should want in a personal affiliate, not only the qualities that it is rational to want in a "fellow citizen." Our sense of these things can be destroyed, warped, or undeveloped if our starting affiliations in life are impoverished, and it can be undermined later by abusive primary affiliations. If the connection with self-esteem explains part of the ethical importance of justice in institutions, it also explains part of the ethical importance of the responsibilities of informal personal relationships.

Third, like the relationships defined by basic rights, informal personal relationships involve special responsibilities. They seem even to involve responsibility in a *different sense* from that of formal relationships: responsibilities that are *not duties* closely correlated with *rights*. Immanuel Kant attempted to capture such responsibilities with the concept of "imperfect duties" (Kant 1948, chap. 2) and later "ethical duties" in contrast with "juridical duties" (Kant 1964b, 7–28). Intuitionists have also tried to cover them with the concept of duty (Ross 1930, chap. 2). To utilitarians, such responsibilities have seemed no more ethically fundamental than responsibilities correlated with rights, which also are not fundamental from the standpoint of utility (Mill 1957, chap. 5; Brandt 1984). What all of them have missed is the moral *relationship* between persons—literally, the *obligation* in its original sense of a *bond*—that grounds responsibilities.

The concept of obligation has paradigmatic use in two different contexts, as has been pointed out by Richard Brandt (1964): the context of promises or agreements and the context of accepting benefactions. The latter seems fundamental insofar as willingness to accept another's word manifests goodwill that does not itself rest on respect for contracts or promises. Such goodwill is, or can be, a benefaction. Promises and agreements ground duties correlated with rights, while accepting benefactions grounds responsibilities in relationships that are often highly informal. We commonly refer to both the responsibilities of carrying out duties and the responsibilities of informal and personal relationships as "obligations." But they differ from each other in *specificity* and in the *roles* they play in social relationships.

Formal obligations, like Immanual Kant's "perfect duties," are to do some particular thing, often by a specified time and for or to some particular person. They are correlated with a right to that performance on the part of those to whom one is obligated. They are relatively well defined and often publicly sanctioned. They are the kind of obligation associated with the possible use of force or coercion, with a justification for limiting another's freedom. By contrast, as with "imperfect duties," when accepting a benefaction places us under obligation, there is often no specific thing we are obligated to do and no specific person to or for whom we are obligated to do it. There is consequently no correlated right to a specific performance on the part of the benefactor. We are typically responsible for determining what needs to be done (and when and how much), which requires initiative, imagination, and creativity. The most sympathetic way to interpret Carol Gilligan's method of inclusiveness is to see it as taking on a certain responsibility in this sense, the responsibility of *making it good* that everyone is included, of finding, creating, a *good* way to do that, thereby maintaining informal connections with everyone.

The different roles of the two kinds of obligation are suggested by differences in the consequences of fulfilling or failing to fulfill them. In fulfilling formal obligations, we *discharge* them, as in paying a debt. Discharging the obligation brings the relationship to a close, terminates that formal connection. Failing to fulfill responsibilities that are correlated with rights does not relieve us of the responsibility; it often makes us liable to penalties as substitutes for what we failed to do (sometimes in addition to making up what we failed to do). By contrast, with obligations incurred to a benefactor, we often think in terms of *living up to* them rather than of discharging them. Living up to them tends to *affirm* the relationship rather than to bring it to a close; the ties are extended, deepened. Putting pressure on those who are informally obligated to us can undermine the relationship on which the obligation depends. Failing to live up to an informal obligation likewise undermines the relationship in virtue of which the obligation existed. Formal obligations can thus facilitate goodwill between parties who are not intimate and perhaps have no wish to be, while informal ones can facilitate personal relationships.

Deontological ethics, especially contractarian, takes relatively formal, impersonal relationships as paradigmatic for moral theory, applying their metaphors and concepts to other relationships as well. This can yield farfetched results, as in Immanuel Kant's notion that ethical duties arise from a kind of contract with one's (bifurcated) self (Kant 1964b, pt. 1, secs. 1–4). Modern teleologies, on the other hand, drop the idea of obligation as a *relationship* in favor of a looser idea of "obligation" as what one morally ought to do. Utilitarianism thus assimilates obligations constitutive of personal and informal relationships to the theory of impersonal moral choice focusing on abstract action-guiding principles, albeit without taking rights as a fundamental concept.

The promising idea I find in the hypothesis that "women's ethics" can deepen and correct modern Western ethical theory is that the informal and personal relationships salient in women's lives raise issues of the ethics of attachment that are not reducible to the issues of control that have preoccupied contractualist and utilitarian theorists. Informal, personal relationships are as basic as any relationships in our lives. Acknowledging this does not imply that women have more or better knowledge of the ethics of such relationships. What women more clearly have had is more than our share of the responsibility for maintaining these kinds of relationships and less than our share of the responsibilities of participating in and defining formal institutions.

III. Conclusions

I have argued that attachment to individuals is not sufficient to yield caring as a virtue. However, without the values of attachment, there can be no satisfactory ethics of personal relationships. Utilitarian and contractualist theories recognize at best general benevolence, impersonal goodwill toward others, and a kind of general faith in others' ability to reciprocate such goodwill. But they do not recognize as ethically significant the caring partial to individuals. Carol Gilligan observed in her discussion of the fantasy study that "women . . . try to change the rules in order to preserve relationships," while "men, in abiding by these rules, depict relationships as easily replaced" (1982, 44). The sense of relationships as not replaceable recalls Immanuel Kant's insistence that individuals have a value for which nothing can satisfactorily take the place (Kant 1948, chap. 2). Kant was thinking of human dignity, attributed to everyone alike. What is irreplaceable here is what is distinctive, what sets individuals apart from others, not something they have in common.

An ethic of attachment is not necessarily an ethic of care, any more than an ethic of principle—such as utilitarianism—is necessarily one of justice. To sustain the view that the capacity for love, like the sense of justice, is part of character, we need an understanding of this capacity comparable in sophistication to Immanuel Kant's understanding of the capacity for acting on principle. Not every passionate attachment to persons is valuable, any more than every passionate espousal of principles is. The nature and basis of the attachment matters. Immanuel Kant missed the differences in attachment to persons in his dismissal of "pathological love." Yet he appreciated the differences in acting on principle. In a little-known passage in the same essay in which good women are presented as morally characterless, he wrote, "Among men there are but few who behave according to principles—which is extremely good, as it can so easily happen that one errs in these principles, and then the resulting disadvantage extends all the further, the more universal the principle and the more resolute the person who has set it before himself" (Kant 1960b, 74). This danger did not deter him from searching for a devotion to principle having moral worth. Nor need present-day theorists be deterred by the danger of ill-founded personal attachments from recognizing the ethical value of others.

IV. Postscript

I have cautioned against minimizing women's bad moral luck in a society with a history of sex oppression. I end with examples of moral damage that a rosy view of women and care may disguise and that a sound ethic of personal and informal relationships should reveal.

When people are affiliated with "protectors," their affirmations of those affiliations may have little to do with love, though the language of love be the language of their discourse. Women's caretaking is often unpaid or underpaid labor performed from a variety of motives. More likely mistaken for a caring virtue is women's misplaced gratitude to men who take less than full advantage of their power to abuse or who offer women the privilege of service in exchange for "protection." Women have assumed caretaking responsibilities as a debt of gratitude for such "benefactions."[21]

Misplaced gratitude is a kind of moral damage women have suffered. There are others. Feminist thinkers are understandably reluctant to address publicly women's reputation for lying, cunning, deceit, and manipulation. (Arthur Schopenhauer did not have this problem.) But *are* these vices, one may ask, if they are needed for defense? They are surely not virtues, even if they are justified from the point of view of justice. Those who tell just the right lies to the right people on the right occasions may have a useful and needed skill. But it does not promote or manifest human good, even if needed for survival under oppressive conditions. Human good may be unrealizable under such conditions. Lying blocks the trust of friendship: though you are confident I lie only when justified, if you believe I am *often* justified, how can you know when to rely on me (Rich 1979b)?

I have supported a view of the moral luck of the sexes more specific and less romantic than the view that justice and care are gender-related. If informal practices and personal relationships are more salient in women's lives (and not only in women's discourse), women's characters may have a certain depth and complexity because of it. This does not imply that women are better; complexity is not virtue. Perhaps there *are* gender-related virtues, however, and perhaps they are best understood by the moral luck of the sexes. I have not argued that this idea is incoherent. My investigations suggest that some of our *vices* are gender-related because of a history of sex oppression. If so, we might expect to find, as Mary Wollstonecraft did, similar vices in relation to other forms of oppression— oppression by class and by race, for example—and perhaps more complex vices where oppression is compounded.

Then why use the language of *gender*-relatedness, one may ask, rather than that of *oppression*-relatedness? The answers are that gender is not incidental and that oppression is not everything. Those oppressed do not just happen to be female, brown-skinned, workers, or all of these. Social practices have made such aspects of our identities the bearers of fortune. Nor is all the fortune bad. Terms like "gender-related" enable us to call attention to these facts in order to clarify the myths and truths surrounding the moral luck of individuals.

Notes

1. This essay has benefited from critical readings by Victoria Davion, Owen Flanagan, Nel Noddings, participants in a University of Wisconsin Women and Legal Theory Conference, and Joan Ringelheim's colleagues in a New York City women's discussion group; from the encouragement of Amélie Rorty for more than a decade; and from discussions with audiences at the Philosophy Department of the University of Wisconsin at Madison, the APA Central Division Meetings, and a University of San Diego conference on virtues. Part of the work on it was supported by a sabbatical from the University of Wisconsin at Madison.

2. My interest is in what Bernard Williams called *constitutive* moral luck, which enters into one's character. He contrasts this with *incident* moral luck (on which he focuses in the essay introducing the concept "moral luck"), which affects the morality of particular acts (Williams 1981b).

3. In Card, unpublished c, I address the compatibility of luck with moral responsibility. In this essay I do not treat moral luck as a problematic concept but plunge into what we can learn from recognizable examples.

4. Carol Gilligan reports that nearly all those tested could readily adopt both justice and care orientations, although not simultaneously, but that two thirds of each sex preferred one, and of these, almost all the men preferred the justice orientation, while half the women with a preference preferred the care orientation. Thus the care orientation might easily be overlooked in a study excluding women (Gilligan et al. 1988). Although she focuses on orientations rather than on their distribution, her recent essays describing testing across racial and class groups confirm her impressions about gender distribution. She sees a need for the care ethic where violence threatens but does not claim its superiority in all contexts.

Nel Noddings (1984) has defended a care-based ethic *against* a justice-based one, arguing that abstract action-guiding principles have at best a subordinate role in care-based ethics.

Sara Ruddick (1989) develops the idea of "maternal thinking" from ideals *implicit* in the practice of mothering and argues for their extension to international politics. Like Nel Noddings, she is not optimistic about the value of abstract action-guiding principles in general.

5. Focus on *differences in contexts and relationships* is more characteristic of the writings on women and care by Virginia Held (1984, 1987a, 1987b), Annette Baier (1985a, 1986, 1987a, 1987b), and Sarah Hoagland (1988).

6. If oppression were at the root of the differences in moral preoccupation attributed to the sexes, such differences should have a more complex distribution. Benefits of sex privilege can be diluted or counteracted and burdens of sex oppression overwhelmed by racial or class oppression, and women can have race and class privilege.

7. Marilyn Friedman (1987a), also concerned about underrating justice, urges similar shifts and likewise explores interconnections of justice and care.

8. I do not take up here, since I discuss in Card 1989, the lesbian care ethics developed by Sarah Hoagland (1988), which works from different paradigms, those of adult lesbians engaged in creating social alternatives to patriarchy.

9. I do not argue that women's development fares worse than that of men. My interest is more in women's characters than in such comparisons.

10. On the same page he says, "Women will avoid the wicked not because it is unright but, because it is ugly." Traits he calls women's virtues he called "merely adoptive virtues" in the preceding chapter, contrasting them with genuine virtues. That he never reconsidered shows in his anthropology lectures published late in his life (Kant 1974, part 2, B).

11. For extended critique of the "gestalt view," see Flanagan and Jackson 1987.

12. On justice and personal desert, see Feinberg 1970b and Card 1972.

13. The story, which I first heard from her at a conference in 1984, is this: "Two four-year olds—a boy and a girl—were playing together and wanted to play different games. . . . The girl said, "Let's play next-door neighbors.' 'I want to play pirates,' the boy replied. 'Okay said the girl, 'then you can be the pirate that lives next door."' Gilligan et al. write here of "comparing the inclusive solution of combining the games with the fair solution of taking turns" (1988, 9).

14. On military misogyny, see the first half (on U.S. Marine boot camp) of the film *Full Metal Jacket* (D. Stanley Kubrick, 1987).

15. Violence is also a problem for lesbian relationships in a homophobic society (Lobel 1986; Card 1988b, 1989), which creates situations for same-sex intimacy analogous to those misogyny creates for heterosexual intimacy.

16. On Hume as an exception, see Baier 1985a, 1987a.

17. I explore the concept of taking responsibility further in 1990 and further forward-looking senses of responsibility in unpublished c.

18. Laura Hobson's 1947 novel, *Gentlemen's Agreement*, portrays persistence of anti-Semitism in the U.S. despite formal equality of rights, by way of such things as "gentlemen's agreements" to exclude Jews from country clubs and other "friendly" organizations.

19. So-called "personal *obligations*" do not always involve personal *relationships*. Obligations may be called "personal" to contrast them with other obligations of the same person in an official capacity. My interest here is in the obligations of personal *relationships*.

20. For further discussion of paradigms of obligation, see Card 1988a.

21. On the ethics of friendships between parties very unequal in power, see Card 1988a.

References

Aristotle. 1925. *Nicomachean Ethics*. Translated by W. D. Ross. London: Oxford University Press.

Baier, A. 1985a. What do women want in a moral theory? *Noû* 19:53–63.

Baier, A. 1986. Trust and antitrust. *Ethics* 96:231–260.

Baier, A. 1987a. Hume, the women's moral theorist? In E. F. Kittay and D. T. Meyers (eds.), *Women and Moral Theory*. Totowa, N.J.: Littlefield, Adams.

Baier, A. 1987b. The need for more than justice. In M. Hanen and K. Nielsen (eds.), *Science, Morality, and Feminist Theory*. Calgary: University of Calgary.

Blum, L. 1980. *Friendship, Altruism, and Morality*. London: Routledge and Kegan Paul.

Brandt, R. B. 1964. The concepts of duty and obligation. *Mind*. 73:373–393.

Brandt, R. B. 1984. Utilitarianism and moral rights. *Canadian Journal of Philosophy* 14:1–19.

Card, C. 1972. On mercy. *Philosophical Review* 81:182–207.

Card, C. 1988a. Gratitude and obligation. *American Philosophical Quarterly* 25:115–127.

Card, C. 1988b. Lesbian battering. *American Philosophical Association Newsletter on Feminism and Philosophy* 88:3–7. (Review essay on Lobel 1986.)

Card, C. 1989. Defusing the bomb: Lesbian ethics and horizontal violence. *Lesbian Ethics* 3:91–100.

Card, C. 1990. Intimacy and responsibility: What lesbians do. In Martha Fineman and Nancy Thomadsen (eds.), *At the Boundaries of Law: Feminism and Legal Theory*. London: Routledge and Kegan Paul.

Card, C. Unpublished c. Responsibility and moral luck: Resisting oppression and abuse. Read at the 1989 Eastern Division Meetings of the American Philosophical Association.

Feinberg, J. 1970b. Justice and personal desert. In *Doing and Deserving: Essays in the Theory of Responsibility*. Princeton: Princeton University Press.

Flanagan, O., and Jackson, K. 1987. Justice, care, and gender: The Kohlberg-Gilligan debate revisited. *Ethics* 97:622–637.

Foot, P. 1978c. Virtues and vices. In Foot 1978a.

Freud, S. 1961. Some psychical consequences of the anatomical distinction between the sexes. In *The Standard Edition of the Complete Psychological Works of Sigmund Freud* (vol. 19), translated by J. Strachey. London: Hogarth. (First published in 1925.)

Friedman, M. 1987a. Beyond caring: The de-moralization of gender. In M. Hanen and K. Nielsen (eds.), *Science, Morality, and Feminist Theory*. Calgary: University of Calgary.

Gilligan, C. 1982. *In a Different Voice: Psychological Theory and Women's Development*. Cambridge: Harvard University Press.

Gilligan, C., Ward, J. V., and Taylor, J. M., with Bardige, B., eds. 1988. *Mapping the Moral Domain: A Contribution of Women's Thinking to Psychological Theory and Education*. Cambridge: Harvard University Press.

Held, V. 1984. *Rights and Goods: Justifying Social Action*. New York: Free Press/Macmillan.

Held, V. 1987a. Feminism and moral theory. In E. F. Kittay and D. T. Meyers (eds.), *Women and Moral Theory*. Totowa, N.J.: Littlefield, Adams.

Held, V. 1987b. Non-contractual society. In M. Hanen and K. Nielsen (eds.), *Science, Morality, and Feminist Theory*. Calgary: University of Calgary.

Hoagland, S. L. 1988. *Lesbian Ethics*. Palo Alto, Calif.: Institute for Lesbian Studies.

Hobson, L. 1947. *Gentleman's Agreement*. New York: Grosset & Dunlap.

Houston, B. 1987. Rescuing womanly virtues: Some dangers of reclamation. In M. Hanen and K. Nielsen (eds.), *Science, Morality, and Feminist Theory*. Calgary: University of Calgary.

Kant, I. 1948. *The Moral Law: Kant's Groundwork of "The Metaphysic of Morals."* Translated by H. J. Paton. London: Hutchinson. (First published 1785.)

Kant, I. 1960b. *Observations on the Feeling of the Beautiful and Sublime*. Translated by J. T. Goldthwait. Berkeley: University of California Press. (First published 1764.)

Kant, I. 1964b. *The Doctrine of Virtue: Part II of "The Metaphysic of Morals."* Translated by M. J. Gregor. New York: Harper & Row. (First published 1797.)

Kant, I. 1974. *Anthropology from a Pragmatic Point of View*. Translated by M. J. Gregor. The Hague: Nijhoff. (First published 1797.)

Kohlberg, L. 1981. *The Philosophy of Moral Development.* San Francisco: Harper & Row.

Lobel, K., ed. 1986. *Naming the Violence: Speaking Out about Lesbian Battering.* Seattle: Seal.

Mill, J. S. 1957. *Utilitarianism.* New York: Bobbs-Merrill. (First published 1861.)

Noddings, N. 1984. *Caring: A Feminine Approach to Ethics and Moral Education.* Berkeley: University of California Press.

Rawls, J. 1971. *A Theory of Justice.* Cambridge: Harvard University Press.

Raymond, J. 1986. *A Passion for Friends: Toward a Philosophy of Female Affection.* Boston: Beacon.

Rich, A. 1979b. Women and honor: Some notes on lying. In *On Lies, Secrets, and Silence: Selected Prose, 1966–1978.* New York: Norton.

Rich. A. 1980. Compulsory heterosexuality and lesbian existence. *Signs* 5:631–660.

Ringelheim, J. 1985. Women and the holocaust: A reconsideration of research. *Signs* 10:741–761.

Ross, W. D. 1930. *The Right and the Good.* Oxford: Oxford University Press.

Ruddick, S. 1989. *Maternal Thinking.* Boston: Beacon Press.

Schopenhauer, A. 1965. *On the Basis of Morality.* Translated by E. F. J. Payne. Indianapolis: Bobbs-Merrill. (First published 1841.)

Stocker, M. 1976a. The schizophrenia of modern ethical theories. *Journal of Philosophy* 73:453–466.

Stocker, M. 1986. Friendship and duty: Toward a synthesis of Gilligan's contrastive ethical concepts. In E. Kittay and D. Meyers (eds.), *Women and Moral Theory.* Totowa, N.J.: Rowman and Allanheld.

Telfer, 1970/1971. Friendship. *Proceedings of the Aristotelian Society* 71:223–241.

Williams, B. 1981b. Moral luck. In Williams 1981a.

Wollstonecraft, M. 1982. *A Vindication of the Rights of Women.* Harmondsworth: Penguin. (First published 1792.)

PART THREE

Extensions and Affirmations

6

Women and Caring: What Can Feminists Learn About Morality from Caring? [1989]

JOAN C. TRONTO

Embedded in our notions of caring we can see some of the deepest dimensions of traditional gender differentiation in our society. The script runs something like this: Men care about money, career, ideas, and advancement; men show they care by the work they do, the values they hold, and the provisions they make for their families (see Ehrenreich 1983). Women care for their families, neighbors, and friends; women care for their families by doing the direct work of caring. Furthermore, the script continues, men care about more important things, whereas women care about less important.

Some writers have begun to challenge this script. Caring has been defended in the first instance as a kind of labor, the "labor of love" (Finch and Groves 1983). Others have looked behind the work involved in women's caring to the attitudes and thinking involved in it. Sara Ruddick (1980) began the rehabilitation of one part of caring with her description of "maternal thinking" as a difficult and demanding practice. Further rehabilitation of caring has taken an explicitly moral direction (Elshtain 1982). The most widely read work on women's moral development, Carol Gilligan's *In a Different Voice* (1982), is often associated with the language of "an ethic of care." Other writers have suggested that caring grounds women in the world in such a way that they become and should remain immune from the appeals of abstract principles (McMillan 1982) or of religion (Noddings 1984:97).

In this essay I not only continue challenging the traditional script about men's and women's caring, but I also suggest that feminists must be careful about the direction their analysis of care takes. I shall argue that feminists cannot assume that any attribute of women is automatically a virtue worthy of feminists embracing it. Unless we adopt an uncritically profeminine position and say whatever women do is fine because women do it, we need to take a closer look at caring. In this essay I attempt to explore what a feminist approach to caring could be.

The task of disentangling feminine and feminist aspects of caring is not simple. First, we must clarify the nature of caring as understood today in the West. Then we will be in a position to evaluate how caring challenges contemporary notions in moral theory about what is desirable and virtuous. In both regards, feminine and feminist analyses of caring may overlap. In the final analysis, however, moral categories take on meaning in a broader context. Feminine analyses of caring can be distinguished in that they assume that the traditional script about caring is more or less correct. The truly transformative and feminist aspects of caring cannot be recognized unless we also revise our view of the political context in which we situate caring as a moral phenomenon.

Two Types of Caring: Caring About and Caring For

The language of caring appears in many settings in our daily language. Caring includes myriad actors and activities. Doing household tasks is taking care of the house. Doctors, nurses, and others provide medical care. We might ask whether a corporation cares for its workers. Someone might ask, who is taking care of this account? Historians care about the past. Judges care about justice. We usually assume that mothers care for their children, that nurses care for their patients, that teachers care for their students, that social workers care for their clients.

What all of these examples share can be distilled: Caring implies some kind of on-going responsibility and commitment. This notion accords with the original meaning of "care" in English, where care meant a burden; to care is to assume a burden. When a person or a group cares about something or someone, we presume that they are willing to work, to sacrifice, to spend money, to show emotional concern, and to expend energy toward the object of care. Thus, we can make sense of statements such as: he only cares about making money; she cries for her mother; this society does not care about the homeless. To the challenge, You do not care, one responds by showing some evidence of work, sacrifice, or commitment.

If caring involves a commitment, then caring must have an object. Thus, caring is necessarily relational. We say that we care for or about something or someone. We can distinguish "caring about" from "caring for" based on the objects of caring.[1] Caring about refers to less concrete objects; it is characterized by a more general form of commitment. Caring for implies a specific, particular object that is the focus of caring. The boundaries between caring about and caring for are not so neat as these statements imply. Nonetheless, this distinction is useful in revealing something about the way we think of caring in our society because this distinction fits with the engendered category of caring in our society.

Caring for involves responding to the particular, concrete, physical, spiritual, intellectual, psychic, and emotional needs of others. The self, another person, or a group of others can provide care. For example, I take care of myself, a mother cares for the child, a nurse for hospital patients, the Red Cross for victims of the earthquake. These types of care are unified by growing out of the fact that humans have physical and psychic needs (food, grooming, warmth, comfort, etc.) that require activity to satisfy them. These needs are in part socially determined; they are also met in different societies by different types of social practices.

In our society, the particular structures involving caring for grow especially out of the family; caring professions are often construed as a buttress to, or substitute for, care that can no longer be provided within a family. The family may no longer be intact, as a result of death, divorce, distance. Or the family may not be able to provide help; some caring requires expertise. The family may be or may be seen as the source of the problem—for example, families with patterns of substance abuse, incest, violence. Increasingly, then, care has been provided for by the state or in the market. Americans eat fewer meals at home, hire housekeepers, contract for others to wait in a line for them. In response to this increasingly market-oriented version of caring, some thinkers have pulled back in horror and suggested that caring cannot be provided if it disturbs the integrity of the self-other relationship (Elshtain 1981:330; Noddings 1984). The result is that in modern market society the illusion of caring is often preserved: providers of services are expected to feign caring (Hochschild 1983).

Caring is engendered in both market and private life. Women's occupations are the caring occupations, and women do the disproportionate amount of caretaking in the private household. To put the point simply, traditional gender roles in our society imply that men care about but women care for.

Because not all caring is moral, another distinction between caring about and caring for becomes obvious. When we wish to know if "caring about" is a moral activity, we inquire about the nature of the object of the care. To care about justice is a moral activity because justice is a moral concern; to care about one's accumulation of vacation days presumably is not a moral activity.

Caring for takes on moral significance in a different way. When we inquire about caring for, it is not enough to know the object of the care; presumably we must know something about the context of care, perhaps especially about the relationship between the caregiver and recipient of care. A dirty child is not a moral concern for most people, but we might morally disapprove of such a child's mother, who we might think has failed to meet her duty to care for her child. Note, of course, that such judgments are deeply rooted in social, classist, and cultural assumptions about mother's duties, about standards of cleanliness, and so on. The assignment of the responsibility of caring for someone, something, or some group, then might be a moral question. Thus, what typically makes "caring for" perceived as moral is not the activity per se but how that activity reflects upon the assigned social duties of the caretaker and who is doing the assigning.

The actual *activity* of caring for another person seems far removed from what we usually consider moral. Caring as an activity seems more tied to the realm of necessity than to the realm of freedom where moral judgments presumably have a place (see Arendt 1958; Aristotle 1981). One way in which recent theorists have tried to describe the value of caring is to deny that caring is simply banal activity devoid of judgment. Sara Ruddick (1980) describes maternal thinking as a kind of practice, that is, as a prudential activity where emotions and reason are brought to bear to raise a child. Like the theorists of care, Ruddick stresses that maternal thinking is a particular practice; the maternal thinker focuses on the single child before her or him. In order for children to grow, Ruddick explains, they must be preserved, they must grow physically and mentally, and they must be made aware of the norms and practices of the society of which they are a part. These goals will actually be in conflict in individual instances; for example, the toddler learning to climb threatens its preservation at the same time it develops its strength. Because raising children involves conflicting goals, the maternal thinker cannot simply rely upon instincts or receptivity to the child's wishes to achieve the ultimate goal of raising the child. Instead, a complex set of prudential calculations are involved, which Ruddick calls maternal thinking. Ruddick's point suggests that it might be worthwhile to explore at length the ways in which the practice of caring involves moral issues.

From the standpoint of much contemporary moral theory, caring poses a moral question only in deciding whether one ought to care, not in determining how one engages in the activity of caring. The "moral point of view," as described by moral philosophers such as William Frankena (1973), involves attributes of impartiality and universalizability. We might agree, universally, that special relationships such as being a parent entail certain duties toward our children, but this moral precept cannot then bring us any closer to how to engage in the practice of caring in a moral way. Furthermore, we often assume that morality concerns our interaction with other morally autonomous actors; in caring, the relationships between the caretakers and those cared for are often relations between unequals, where some amount of dependency exists.

Thus, in order to determine the moral dimensions of caring for others, the kind of caring most closely associated with women in our society, we must consider two aspects of caring for others. First, we must consider whether the activity of caring raises moral questions in and of itself. Second, and here a feminist analysis of caring will differ from a simply "feminine" analysis of caring, we must consider how the duties of caring for others are given moral significance in society as a whole. I shall explore these two concerns in the next two sections of this essay.

Moral Dimensions of the Activity of Caring for Others

In this section I shall suggest three ways in which caring for another raises questions about moral life. First, I shall discuss some aspects of moral life posed by the necessary attentiveness to [the] other's needs when caring for another. Second, I shall consider the way in which caring for another raises questions about authority and autonomy between carer and cared-for. And third, I shall examine how caring for another raises problems that grow out of the particularity of caring.

Attentiveness

Caring suggests an alternative moral attitude. From the perspective of caring, what is important is not arriving at the fair decision, understood as how the abstract individual in this situation would want to be treated, but at meeting the needs of particular others or preserving the relationships of care that exist (see Gilligan 1982). In this way, moral theory becomes much more closely connected to the concrete needs of others. How we come to know these needs raises several dimensions of concern for moral theory.

Knowledge. In order to engage in the practice of caring the nature of knowledge needed to act morally changes. At the most obvious level, the mode of philosophical discussion that starts from a philosopher's introspection is an inappropriate starting place to arrive at caring judgments. In the first instance one needs knowledge about others' needs, knowledge that comes from others.

It is not that contemporary moral theory ignores the needs of others, but in most moral discussion the needs of others are taken to reflect the understood needs of the thinking self if only he or she were in another's situation. In contrast, caring rests on knowledge completely peculiar to the particular person being cared for. Proper action for a nurse, faced with a patient who will not finish a meal, depends upon knowing the patient's medical condition, usual eating habits, and tastes. There is no simple way one can generalize from one's own experience to what another needs.

To provide such knowledge, the caring person must devote much attention to learning what the other person might need. Accounts of caring stress that an important part of the process of caring is attentiveness to the needs of others (see Weil 1951:72–73; Ruddick 1980:357–258). To achieve the proper frame of mind in which to care, Noddings stresses the need to be receptive to the needs of others (1984:24). At the moment when one wishes to care, it is impossible to be preoccupied with the self. This kind of selflessness is a key element of what Noddings calls the crucial moral question in caring, that is, how to meet the other morally.

How radically different the epistemological notion of attentiveness is from contemporary ways of thinking can be illustrated by reexamining the long-standing issue about the relationship of knowledge and interests from this perspective. Liberals commonly assume that no one knows your interests as well as you yourself do (see Mill 1975:187). Marxists and those inspired by Marx believe that a person's interests arise out of the objective circumstances in which one finds oneself or that one can posit some universal, or nearly universal, human interests, for example, "emancipatory interests" (Marx and Engels 1978; Habermas 1971; Cohen 1978). But from the standpoint of caring, these views are equally incomplete. There is some relationship between what the cared-for thinks he or she wants and his or her true interests and needs, although it may not be a perfect correspondence. A patient in the hospital who refuses to get up may be forced to do so. A child who wishes only to eat junk food may be disappointed by parents' reluctance to meet this wish. Genuine attentiveness would presumably allow the caretaker to see through these pseudo-needs and come to appreciate what the other really needs.

Such a commitment to perceiving the genuine needs of the other, though, is not so easy. Alice Miller suggests that many parents act not so much to meet the needs of their children as to work out unmet needs they continue to carry from when they were children (Miller 1981). If a caretaker has deficient self-knowledge about his or her own needs, then there is no way to guarantee that those needs have been removed in looking to see what the other's needs are. It may be very difficult to achieve the state of attentiveness, requiring first a tremendous self-knowledge so that the caretaker does not simply transform the needs of the other into a projection of the self's own needs.[2]

The Attentive Self.   To say that attentiveness requires a profound self-knowledge, though, does not yet capture how deeply attentiveness affects the self. The concern with attentiveness, with losing one's own concerns in order to see clearly the concerns of the cared-for, raises some difficult questions for the moral theory of caring: How much must one disregard one's own needs in order to be sufficiently attentive? How does one become adept at creating the condition of receptivity? If one is being solely receptive to the needs of others, how can one judge whether the needs are genuine, as serious as the one cared-for believes they are, and so on?

Furthermore, attentiveness involves a commitment of time and effort that may be made at a high price to the self. Noddings asserts that caring is not complete unless recognized by the cared-for person (1984:73–74), but this position is clearly wrong. As Noddings herself suggests, such recognition depends upon whether the cared-for person has the capacity to respond to caring. Although a mother's child may develop what Noddings would consider the proper responsiveness to caring over time, others, such as teachers and nurses, who provide care over a shorter duration, cannot expect that their commitment will be recognized and rewarded. Nodding's argument (1984:86) is seductive in its suggestion that we are always recognized for our sacrifices, but it is also dangerous in encouraging us to restrict caring only to those near to us on a continuing basis. For the rest of us, though, who are willing to attempt to care at some greater distance, attentiveness has a cost.

Another potential cost to the self is that caring is risky. As Sara Ruddick notes, the contingencies of the world will often cause disasters to befall those for whom we care (Ruddick 1980:350–351). If the self has become too committed to caring for the other, then the loss of the other may destroy the self. Thus caring cannot simply be a romanticized notion of selflessness, nor can it occur if the self remains aloof. A connection between the self and the other is necessary for the self to care, and the nature of this connection is a problem for any ethic of care.

Attentiveness and Market Relations. These questions about self-other relations and knowledge are not restricted to relations among individuals; there is a social and political dimension to attentiveness as well. I have noted that in order to be attentive to the needs of others one must relinquish the absolute primacy of the needs of the self. In this regard, attentive care is incompatible with the paradigmatic relationship of modern society, exchange (Hartsock 1983). The paradigm of market relations, of exchange, involves putting one's own interests first. It involves the assertion that one knows one's own interests best, another assumption inconsistent with the attitude of caring. It involves reducing complex relationships into terms that can be made equivalent. None of these premises is compatible with attentiveness.

The seriousness of this point depends upon whether market relationships and attentive care can coexist, and if so, how (see Lane 1986; Hardwig 1984; Walzer 1983; Schaar 1983). Theorists differ about how much the metaphors of exchange permeate all social relationships. Virtually all social relationships in modern life can be described in terms of exchange, but whether that means it is the only or the most illuminating way in which individuals conceive of those relationships is another matter.

If individuals are capable of using and discarding exchange and caring modes of thought at will, then to recognize a caring dimension provides important depth to our picture of moral life. If one cannot move easily from one mode to the other, however (see Hardwig 1984), then to suggest that caring is of value suggests several other disturbing possibilities. If people must either be predominantly caring or exchange-oriented, then the simplest way to arrange social institutions would be to create separate spheres for each mode of life. The ideological glorification of men in the cruel business world and women in the caring home is one obvious solution.

The advocate of caring might respond that if caring and market society cannot coexist, let us abolish market relations. The radicalness of this claim is immediately obvious, but the obviousness of its replacement to conduct life in a complex society is not.

Authority and Autonomy

The second area where caring raises fundamental questions opposed to contemporary moral theory is another issue that grows out of caring as providing help to meet the needs of others. Because caring occurs in a situation where one person is helping to meet the concrete needs of another, caring raises questions that cannot be easily accommodated by the starting assumption in most contemporary moral philosophy that we are rational, autonomous actors. Many conditions that we usually associate with care-giving belie this view because society does not consider all people we take care of to be rational and autonomous, either in an abstract moral sense (e.g., children) or in a concrete, physical sense (e.g., a bed-ridden parent, a disabled person) (see Fisher and Galler 1988). Furthermore, if the care-giver is considered rational and autonomous, then the relationship between the parties is unequal, and relationships of authority and dependency are likely to emerge. As I noted earlier, if the care-giver's needs are themselves met by providing care, then the care-giver might desire to keep the cared-for person dependent. How should care-givers understand their authoritative position in relation to those for whom they care?

However, the image of equal adults who rely upon other equal adults for care, not exchange, once again raises questions about what it means to be rational and autonomous. Two people in an equal relationship of care share an awareness of the concrete complications of caring. To maintain such a relationship will often entail making judgments that, from a more abstract point of view, might seem questionable. Is one wrong if one refuses to move for a better job because of an on-going situation for caring? Again one is forced to consider what autonomy actually means.

Previous writers about an ethic of care vary in whether they perceive authority and autonomy as an issue. The work of Carol Gilligan and Nona Lyons is useful in that it poses the nature of autonomy as an issue. Gilligan has identified an "ethic of care" characterized by a commitment to maintaining and fostering the relationships in which one is woven (Gilligan 1982:19). Her analysis leads her to suggest that without this dimension the account of morality found in enumeration of rights would be incomplete. Kohlberg's cognitive model of moral development, which Gilligan criticizes, stresses that a sense of the autonomous self, clearly differentiated from others, is crucial to developing a moral sense. In contrast, this ethic of care is based upon a different account of the self. Lyons's research suggests that only individuals who view themselves as connected to others, rather than as separate and objective, are able to use both an ethic of care and claims about justice to resolve real-life moral dilemmas. (Lyons 1983:140–141). Gilligan stresses that there may well be tension between the maintenance of self and of relationships; by her account moral maturity arrives when an individual can correctly balance concerns for the self and for others (Gilligan 1983:41–45).

Noddings's approach, on the other hand, seems to leave too little autonomy to the self and is unable to discern that relations of care might also be relations of authority. Noddings analyzes care as the relationship between the one caring and the one cared-for. The essential aspect of caring is that it involves a displacement from one's own interests to the interests of the one cared-for. "Our attention, our mental engrossment is on the cared-for, not on ourselves" (Noddings 1984:24). Caring affects both the one caring and the one cared-for. It affects the one caring because she must become engrossed in the other; it affects the cared-for because that individual's needs are met and because that individual must somehow respond and accept the care offered.

Caring challenges the view that morality starts where rational and autonomous individuals confront each other to work out the rules of moral life. Instead, caring allows us to see autonomy as a problem that people must deal with all the time, in their relations with both equals and those who either help them or depend upon them.

Particularity

Finally, let us consider how the particularity of caring challenges contemporary moral theory. Most contemporary moral theorists require universal moral judgments, that is, that if it is moral for a person to act in a given way in a given situation then it must be moral for any person so situated to act the same way[3] (Kohlberg 1981). Yet the decision we must make about how much care to provide and to whom cannot be so easily generalized or universalized. It is theoretically possible to spend all of one's time caring for others (see Blum 1976); the real decisions everyone will face then are decisions about both when to provide care and when to stop providing care. Because caring varies with the amount of time and kind of effort that a caring individual can expend as well as with the needs of the ones who need care, it is difficult to imagine that rules could ever be specified allowing us to claim that we had applied universal moral principles.

Consider, for example, a rule: always give aid to a person whose car is broken down on the highway. Suppose you are a nonmechanical woman alone and the stranger is a male? Always take care of your mother. Suppose she and your children rely on your income to keep the household together and caring for her will cost you your job? Thus, the moral judgments made in offering and providing care are much more complex than any set of rules can take into account. Any rule sufficiently flexible to cover all the complexities would probably have to take a form such as "do all that you can to help someone else." Such a form, though, does not serve as any guide to what morality requires. What may be "too much" care for a child to provide an elderly parent may seem too selfishly skimpy to another. This logical objection about the limits of rule-governed morality is familiar, yet it remains a practical difficulty.

The reason that rule-governed behavior is so often associated with moral life, though, is that if we are bound to follow the rules then we are bound to act impartially, not giving special favors to those nearest us. Another problem with caring from a moral point of view, then, is that we might, because of our caring relationship, provide special treatment to those closest to us and ignore others more deserving of care.

Nel Noddings pursues this problem in a disturbing way. Noddings is very restrictive about the conditions under which caring occurs. Although Noddings argues that it is natural for us to care for our children, when we extend care beyond our own children it becomes an ethical act (Noddings 1984:79–80). Noddings also suggests that caring must take place in a limited context or it is not properly understood as caring: Noddings's description of caring is very personal; her examples include caring for cats and birds, children and husbands, students and strangers who arrive at the door. Mother-child and teacher-pupil are paradigmatic caring relationships. But any expansion of caring beyond this sphere is dangerous because caring cannot be generalized. Thus, Noddings wishes to separate caring from many of its broader social connotations; she seems to exclude caretaking from caring for:

> The danger is that caring, which is essentially nonrational in that it requires a constitutive engrossment and displacement of motivation, may gradually or abruptly be transformed into abstract problem solving. There is, then, a shift of focus from the cared-for to the "problem." Opportunities arise for self-interest, and persons entrusted with caring may lack the necessary engrossment in those to be cared for. (Noddings 1984:25–26; compare Finch and Groves 1983)

Such caring can only be provided for a very limited number of others, and Noddings would probably exclude many relationships we might otherwise think of as caring. By Noddings's understanding of caring, nurses in hospitals do not necessarily care; indeed, by this view there are probably many mothers who would not qualify as carers. In this case, a moral question arises about the needs of the particular others we care for weighed against the needs of others more distant from us. To Noddings this problem is solved by saying that because everyone will be cared for by someone, it is not anyone else's concern to wonder about who is caring for whom in society

To say that we should only care for those things that come within our immediate purview ignores the ways in which we are responsible for the construction of our narrow sphere. When Noddings says that she will respond with caring to the stranger at her door but not to starving children in Africa, she ignores the ways in which the modern world is intertwined and the ways in which hundreds of prior public and private decisions affect where we find ourselves and which strangers show up at our doors. In an affluent community, where affluence is maintained by such decisions as zoning ordinances, the stranger at the door is less of a threat than in a dense city, where the stranger may wish to do you harm. Perhaps Noddings would have no problem with this point because in the city you do not have to care for strangers at the door. But the question then becomes, who does? Questions about the proximity of people to us are shaped by our collective social decisions. If we decide to isolate ourselves from others, we may reduce our moral burden of caring. Yet if moral life is only understood narrowly in the context of the exhibition of caring, then we can be absolved from these broader responsibilities.

One way to answer this objection is to say that the task of moral theory is to set out what the parameters of caring should be. Such an approach would soon blend into questions of social and political life. For caring to be an on-going activity, it is necessarily bounded by the activities of daily life because the entire complex of social institutions and structures determine with whom we come into contact on a regular enough basis to establish relationships of care.[4]

If caring is used as an excuse to narrow the scope of our moral activity to be concerned only with those immediately around us, then it does have little to recommend it as a moral theory. But the question of whom we should care for is not left entirely to individuals in our society.

A Feminist Approach to Caring: Caring About What We Care For

In the second section of this essay I explored some ways in which caring challenges contemporary moral theory. In each case, I realized that caring seems to provide a richer account of people's moral lives. Nevertheless, caring seems to suffer a fatal moral flaw if we allow it to be circumscribed by deciding that we shall only care for those closest to us. From this perspective, it is hard to see how caring can remain moral, rather than becoming a way to justify inconsideration of others at the expense of those for whom we care.

To solve this problem I must return to the way in which the activity of caring is situated in contemporary society. I noted at the beginning of this essay that the problem of who should care for whom is rooted in (often questionable) social values, expectations, and institutions. We do not hold everyone (anyone?) individually responsible for the homeless. Similarly, we do not hold just anyone responsible for the appearance of a child, but we do hold her mother (and father?) responsible. Nonetheless, I can make at least one generalization about caring in this society: men care about; women care for. Thus, by definition the traditional script on caring reenacts the division of male and female worlds into public and private. To raise the question about whether caring for is inevitably too particularistic is thus to return as well to the engendered nature of caring in our society and to a consideration of the difference between a feminist and feminine account of caring.

What does it mean to assert, as Nel Noddings does, that caring is a "feminine" approach to ethics? For Noddings, it means the celebration and legitimation of a part of women's lives. Yet we have seen that Noddings's formulation of caring cannot be satisfying as a model for moral theory. As Genevieve Lloyd (1984) argues about reason, the category of the feminine is quite problematic (see also Gilman 1979). Femininity is constructed as the antithesis of masculinity. Thus, what is constructed as the masculine, as the normal, is constructed in opposition to what is feminine. In this case, the construction of women as tied to the more particular activity of caring for others stands in opposition to the more public and social concerns about which men care.

I can make this argument still more pointed. Insofar as caring is a kind of attentiveness, it may be a reflection of a survival mechanism for women or others who are dealing with oppressive conditions, rather than a quality of intrinsic value on its own. Another way to understand caring is to see it as an ethic most appropriate for those in a subordinate social position. Just as women and others who are not in the central corridors of power in this society adopt a variety of deferential mannerisms (e.g., differences in speech, smiling, other forms of body language, etc.), so too it may have served their purposes of survival to have adopted an attitude that Noddings may approvingly call "attentiveness" but might otherwise be understood as the necessity to anticipate the wishes of one's superior.[5]

A feminine approach to caring, then, cannot serve as a starting point for a broader questioning of the proper role of caring in society. As with Temma Kaplan's (1982) description of "female consciousness," the feminine approach to caring bears the burden of accepting traditional gender divisions in a society that devalues what women do. From this perspective, caring will always remain as a corrective to morality, as an "extra" aspect of life, neither suggesting nor requiring a fundamental rethinking of moral categories.

A feminist approach to caring, in contrast, needs to begin by broadening our understanding of what caring for others means, both in terms of the moral questions it raises and in terms of the need to restructure broader social and political institutions if caring for others is to be made a more central part of the everyday lives of everyone in society. It is beyond the scope of this essay to spell out fully a feminist theory of care, but some points seem to suggest a starting place for further analysis.

In this essay I noted the way in which caring involves moral acts not usually comprehended in the framework of contemporary moral theory. The moral relevance of attentiveness belies the adequacy of the abstract, exchange-oriented individual as the moral subject. We noted earlier that to take attentiveness seriously questions our assumptions about our autonomy, the self, our knowledge of our interests, the effectiveness of the market. These issues are already topics that feminist political and moral philosophers consider. Caring may prove an especially useful way for feminist thinkers to try to ground their thoughts on these subjects.

Feminist theory will also need to describe what constitutes good caring. We have already noted that this task will be difficult because caring is so much tied to particular circumstances. Yet we need to rethink as well how those particular circumstances are socially constructed. Perhaps the impoverishment of our vocabulary for discussing caring is a result of the way caring is privatized, thus beneath our social vision in this society. The need to rethink appropriate forms for caring also raises the broadest questions about the shape of social and political institutions in our society.

To think of the social world in terms of caring for others radically differs from our present way of conceiving of it in terms of pursuing our self-interest. Because caring emphasizes concrete connections with others, because it evokes so much of the daily stuff of women's lives, and because it stands as a fundamental critique of abstract and often seemingly irrelevant moral theory, it is worthy of the serious attention of feminist theorists.

Notes

I gratefully acknowledge in writing this essay the help I received from Annmarie Levins, Mary Dietz, George Shulman, Berenice Fisher, and Alison Jaggar.

1. Note that my distinction between caring for and caring about differs from the distinction drawn by Meyeroff (1971) and Noddings (1984). Meyeroff wishes to conflate caring for ideas with caring for people. Not only does this parallel mask the traditional gender difference, but, as will become clear later, the kinds of activities involved in caring for other people cannot be easily used in this same sense. Noddings distinguishes caring for from caring about on a dimension that tries to get at the degree of commitment. We care more for what we care for than for what we care about (1984:86, 112), but Noddings also wishes to claim that we can care for ideas. I believe that the way I have formulated the distinction reveals more about caring and traditional assumptions of gender difference.

2. Nonetheless, in order for caring to occur, there must be more than good intentions and undistorted communication; the acts of caring must also occur. I believe this point may help to distinguish this approach from (at least early versions of) Habermas's approach. For the criticism that Habermas's work is too intellectualized, see Henning Ottmann (1982:86).

3. See, among other recent authors who question the dominant Kantian form of morality, Lawrence Blum (1980), Alasdair MacIntyre and Stanley Hauerwas (1983), John Kekes (1984), and Peter Winch (1972).

4. I am indebted here to Berenice Fisher's suggestion that one important element of a theory of care is the specification of the limits of caring.

5. Jack H. Nagel refined earlier analyses of power to include what C. J. Friedrich had called the "rule of anticipated reactions," the situation where "one actor, B, shapes his behavior to conform to what he believes are the desires of another actor, A, without having received explicit messages about A's wants or intentions from A or A's agents" (1975:16). See also Dahl (1984:24–25).

References

Aristotle. 1981. *The Politics.* Harmondsworth: Penguin Books.

Arendt, H. 1958. *The Human Condition.* Chicago: University of Chicago Press.

Blum, L. 1980. *Friendship, Altruism, and Morality.* Boston: Routledge and Kegan Paul.

Blum, L., M. Homiak, J. Housman, and N. Scheman. 1976. "Altruism and Women's Oppression." In *Women and Philosophy,* ed. C. Gould and M. W. Wartofsky. New York: G. P. Putnam.

Cohen, G. A. 1978. *Karl Marx's Theory of History: A Defence.* Princeton, N.J.: Princeton University Press.

Dahl, R. A. 1984. *Modern Political Analysis.* 4th ed. Englewood Cliffs, N.J.: Prentice-Hall.

Ehrenreich, B. 1983. *The Hearts of Men.* Garden City, N.Y.: Anchor Books.

Elshtain, J. B. 1981. *Public Man, Private Woman.* Princeton, N.J.: Princeton University Press.

———. 1982. "Antigone's Daughters." *democracy* 2:46–59.

Finch, J., and D. Groves, eds. 1983. *A Labour of Love: Women, Work and Caring.* London: Routledge and Kegan Paul.

Fisher, B., and R. Galler. 1988. "Friendship and Fairness: How Disability Affects Friendship Between Women." In *Women with Disabilities: Essays in Psychology, Politics and Policy,* ed. A. Asch and M. Fine. Philadelphia: Temple University Press.

Frankena, W. 1973. *Ethics.* Englewood Cliffs, N.J.: Prentice-Hall.

Gilligan, C. 1982. *In a Different Voice.* Cambridge: Harvard University Press.

———. 1983. "Do the Social Sciences Have an Adequate Theory of Moral Development?" In *Social Science as Moral Inquiry,* ed. N. Haan, et al. New York: Columbia University Press.

Gilman, C. P. 1979. *Herland.* New York: Pantheon.

Habermas, J. 1971. *Knowledge and Human Interests.* Boston: Beacon Press.

Hardwig, J. 1984. "Should Women Think in Terms of Rights?" *Ethics* 94:441–455.

Hartsock, N. C. M. 1983. *Money, Sex and Power: Toward a Feminist Historical Materialism.* New York: Longman.

Hochschild, A. 1983. *The Managed Heart: Commercialization of Human Feeling.* Berkeley: University of California Press.

Kaplan, T. 1982. "Female Consciousness and Collective Action: The Case of Barcelona, 1910–1918." In *Feminist Theory: A Critique of Ideology,* eds. N. Keohane, M. Rosaldo, B. Gelpi. Chicago: University of Chicago Press.

Kekes, J. 1984. "Moral Sensitivity." *Philosophy* 59:3–19.

Kohlberg, L. 1981. "From *Is* to *Ought:* How to Commit the Naturalistic Fallacy and Get Away with It in the Study of Moral Development." In his *The Philosophy of Moral Development: Moral Stages and the Idea of Justice.* Vol. 1 of *Essays in Moral Development.* New York: Harper & Row.

Lane, R. E. 1986. "Market Justice, Political Justice." *American Political Science Review* 80:383–402.

Lloyd, G. 1984. *The Man of Reason: "Male" and "Female" in Western Philosophy.* Minneapolis: University of Minnesota Press.

Lyons, N. P. 1983. "Two Perspectives: On Self, Relationships, and Morality." *Harvard Educational Review* 53:125–144.

MacIntyre, A., and S. Hauerwas, eds. 1983. *Revisions: Changing Perspectives in Moral Philosophy.* Notre Dame, Ind.: University of Notre Dame Press.

Marx, K., and F. Engels. 1978. "The German Ideology." In *The Marx-Engels Reader,* ed. R. C. Tucker. 2d ed. New York: Norton.

McMillan, C. 1982. *Women, Reason, and Nature: Some Philosophical Problems With Feminism.* Princeton, N.J.: Princeton University Press.

Meyeroff, M. 1971. *On Caring.* New York: Harper & Row.

Mill, J. S. 1975. "Considerations on Representative Government." In *Three Essays,* ed. R. Wollheim. Oxford: Oxford University Press.

Miller, A. 1981. *The Drama of the Gifted Child.* New York: Basic Books.

Nagel, J. H. 1975. *The Descriptive Analysis of Power.* New Haven, Conn.: Yale University Press.

Noddings, N. 1984. *Caring: A Feminine Approach to Ethics.* Berkeley: University of California Press.

Ottmann, H. 1982. "Cognitive Interests and Self-Reflection." In *Habermas: Critical Debates,* eds. J. B. Thompson and D. Held. Cambridge, Mass.: MIT Press.

Ruddick, S. 1980. "Maternal Thinking." *Feminist Studies* 6:342–367.

Schaar, J. 1983. "The Question of Justice." *Raritan Review* 3:107–129.

Walzer, M. 1983. *Spheres of Justice.* New York: Basic Books.

Weil, S. 1951. "Reflections on the Right Use of School Studies with a View to the Love of God." In *Waiting for God.* Trans. E. Craufurd. New York: Harper.

Winch, P. 1972. *Ethics and Action.* London: Routledge and Kegan Paul.

7

Black Women and Motherhood
[1991]

PATRICIA HILL COLLINS

Just yesterday I stood for a few minutes at the top of the stairs leading to a white doctor's office in a white neighborhood. I watched one Black woman after another trudge to the corner, where she then waited to catch the bus home. These were Black women still cleaning somebody else's house or Black women still caring for somebody else's sick or elderly, before they came back to the frequently thankless chores of their own loneliness, their own families. And I felt angry and I felt ashamed. And I felt, once again, the kindling heat of my hope that we, the daughters of these Black women, will honor their sacrifice by giving them thanks. We will undertake, with pride, every transcendent dream of freedom made possible by the humility of their love.

—June Jordan 1985, 105

June Jordan's words poignantly express the need for Black feminists to honor our mothers' sacrifice by developing an Afrocentric feminist analysis of Black motherhood. Until recently analyses of Black motherhood have largely been the province of men, both white and Black, and male assumptions about Black women as mothers have prevailed. Black mothers have been accused of failing to discipline their children, of emasculating their sons, of defeminizing their daughters, and of retarding their children's academic achievement (Wade-Gayles 1980). Citing high rates of divorce, female-headed households, and out-of-wedlock births, white male scholars and their representatives claim that

African-American mothers wield unnatural power in allegedly deteriorating family structures (Moynihan 1965; Zinn 1989). The African-American mothers observed by Jordan vanish from these accounts.

White feminist work on motherhood has failed to produce an effective critique of elite white male analyses of Black motherhood. Grounded in a white, middle-class women's standpoint, white feminist analyses have been profoundly affected by the limitations that this angle of vision has on race (Chodorow 1974, 1978; Flax 1978; Chodorow and Contratto 1982). While white feminists have effectively confronted white male analyses of their own experiences as mothers, they rarely challenge controlling images such as the mammy, the matriarch, and the welfare mother and therefore fail to include Black mothers "still cleaning somebody else's house or . . . caring for somebody else's sick or elderly." As a result, white feminist theories have had limited utility for African-American women (Joseph 1984).

In African-American communities the view has been quite different. As Barbara Christian contends, the "concept of motherhood is of central importance in the philosophy of both African and Afro-American peoples" (1985, 213). But in spite of its centrality, Black male scholars in particular typically glorify Black motherhood by refusing to acknowledge the issues faced by Black mothers who "came back to the frequently thankless chores of their own loneliness, their own families." By claiming that Black women are richly endowed with devotion, self-sacrifice, and unconditional love—the attributes associated with archetypal motherhood—Black men inadvertently foster a different controlling image for Black women, that of the "superstrong Black mother" (Staples 1973; Dance 1979). In many African-American communities so much sanctification surrounds Black motherhood that "the idea that mothers should live lives of sacrifice has come to be seen as the norm" (Christian 1985, 234).

Far too many Black men who praise their own mothers feel less accountable to the mothers of their own children. They allow their wives and girlfriends to support the growing numbers of African-American children living in poverty (Frazier 1948; Burnham 1985; U.S. Department of Commerce 1986, 1989). Despite the alarming deterioration of economic and social supports for Black mothers, large numbers of young men encourage their unmarried teenaged girlfriends to give birth to children whose futures are at risk (Ladner 1972; Ladner and Gourdine 1984; Simms 1988). Even when they are aware of the poverty and struggles these women face, many Black men cannot get beyond the powerful controlling image of the superstrong Black mother in order to see the very real costs of mothering to African-American women. Michele Wallace describes the tenacity of this controlling image:

> I remember once I was watching a news show with a Black male friend of mine who had a Ph.D. in psychology and was the director of an out-patient clinic. We were looking at some footage of a Black woman. . . . She was in bed wrapped in blankets, her numerous small, poorly clothed children huddled around her. Her apartment

looked rat-infested, cramped, and dirty. She had not, she said, had heat and hot water for days. My friend, a solid member of the middle class now but surely no stranger to poverty in his childhood, felt obliged to comment . . . "That's a *strong* sister," as he bowed his head in reverence. (1978, 108–9)

The absence of a fully articulated Afrocentric feminist standpoint on motherhood is striking but not particularly surprising. While Black women have produced insightful critiques of both white male and white feminist analyses of motherhood (King 1973; Davis 1981; Gilkes 1983a; Hooks 1981), we have paid far less attention to Black male views. This silence partly reflects the self-imposed restrictions that accompany African-Americans' efforts to present a united front to the dominant group. Part of Black women's reluctance to challenge Black men's ideas in particular stems from the vehement attacks sustained by those Black feminist scholars, such as Michele Wallace, Alice Walker, and Ntozake Shange, who have been perceived as critical of Black men (see, for example, Staples 1979). But much of our silence emanates from an unwillingness to criticize Black men's well-intentioned efforts to defend and protect Black womanhood. Glorifying the strong Black mother represents Black men's attempt to replace negative white male interpretations with positive Black male ones. But no matter how sincere, externally defined definitions of Black womanhood—even those offered by sympathetic African-American men—are bound to come with their own set of problems.

In the case of Black motherhood, the problems have been a stifling of dialogue among African-American women and the perpetuation of troublesome, controlling images, both negative and positive. As Renita Weems observes: "We have simply sat and nodded while others talked about the magnificent women who bore and raised them and who, along with God, made a way out of no way. . . . We paid to hear them lecture about the invincible strength and genius of the Black mother, knowing full well that the image can be as bogus as the one of the happy slave" (1984, 27).

African-American women need an Afrocentric feminist analysis of motherhood that debunks the image of "happy slave," whether the white-male-created "matriarch" or the Black-male-perpetuated "superstrong Black mother." Some of the classic sociological and ethnographic work on African-American families gives a comprehensive sense of how Black women mother (Herskovits 1941; Young 1970; Ladner 1972; Stack 1974; Aschenbrenner 1975; Dougherty 1978; Dill 1980). This emphasis on Black women's actions has recently been enriched by an outpouring of research on Black women's ideas by Black women scholars (McCray 1980; Joseph 1981, 1984; Rollins 1985; D. White 1985; *Sage* 1984, 1987). When coupled with the explorations of Black women's consciousness extant in Black women's autobiographies, fiction, and Black feminist literary criticism (Walker 1983; Washington 1984; Christian 1985), these sources offer the rich conceptual terrain of a Black women's standpoint from which an Afrocentric feminist analysis of African-American motherhood can emerge.

Exploring a Black Women's
Standpoint on Mothering

The institution of Black motherhood consists of a series of constantly renegoti-ated relationships that African-American women experience with one another, with Black children, with the larger African-American community, and with self. These relationships occur in specific locations such as the individual house-holds that make up African-American extended family networks, as well as in Black community institutions (Martin and Martin 1978; Sudarkasa 1981b). Moreover, just as Black women's work and family experiences varied during the transition from slavery to the post–World War II political economy, how Black women define, value, and shape Black motherhood as an institution shows comparable diversity.

Black motherhood as an institution is both dynamic and dialectical. An ongo-ing tension exists between efforts to mold the institution of Black motherhood to benefit systems of race, gender, and class oppression and efforts by African-American women to define and value our own experiences with motherhood. The controlling images of the mammy, the matriarch, and the welfare mother and the practices they justify are designed to oppress. In contrast, motherhood can serve as a site where Black women express and learn the power of self-defin-ition, the importance of valuing and respecting ourselves, the necessity of self-reliance and independence, and a belief in Black women's empowerment. This tension leads to a continuum of responses. Some women view motherhood as a truly burdensome condition that stifles their creativity, exploits their labor, and makes them partners in their own oppression. Others see motherhood as pro-viding a base for self-actualization, status in the Black community, and a catalyst for social activism. These alleged contradictions can exist side by side in African-American communities and families and even within individual women.

Embedded in these changing relationships are five enduring themes that characterize a Black women's standpoint on Black motherhood. For any given historical moment, the particular form that Black women's relationships with one another, children, community, and self actually take depends on how this dialectical relationship between the severity of oppression facing African-American women and our actions in resisting that oppression is expressed.

Bloodmothers, Othermothers, and
Women-Centered Networks

In African-American communities, fluid and changing boundaries often distin-guish biological mothers from other women who care for children. Biological mothers, or bloodmothers, are expected to care for their children. But African and African-American communities have also recognized that vesting one per-son with full responsibility for mothering a child may not be wise or possible. As a result, othermothers—women who assist bloodmothers by sharing mothering responsibilities—traditionally have been central to the institution of Black motherhood (Troester 1984).

The centrality of women in African-American extended families reflects both a continuation of West African cultural values and functional adaptations to race and gender oppression (Tanner 1974; Stack 1974; Aschenbrenner 1975; Martin and Martin 1978; Sudarkasa 1981b; Reagon 1987). This centrality is not characterized by the absence of husbands and fathers. Men may be physically present and/or have well-defined and culturally significant roles in the extended family and the kin unit may be woman-centered. Bebe Moore Campbell's (1989) parents separated when she was small. Even though she spent the school year in the North Philadelphia household maintained by her grandmother and mother, Campbell's father assumed an important role in her life. "My father took care of me," Campbell remembers. "Our separation didn't stunt me or condemn me to a lesser humanity. His absence never made me a fatherless child. I'm not fatherless now" (p. 271). In woman-centered kin units such as Campbell's—whether a mother-child household unit, a married couple household, or a larger unit extending over several households—the centrality of mothers is not predicated on male powerlessness (Tanner 1974, 133).

Organized, resilient, women-centered networks of bloodmothers and othermothers are key in understanding this centrality. Grandmothers, sisters, aunts, or cousins act as othermothers by taking on child-care responsibilities for one another's children. When needed, temporary child-care arrangements can turn into long-term care or informal adoption (Stack 1974; Gutman 1976). Despite strong cultural norms encouraging women to become biological mothers, women who choose not to do so often receive recognition and status from other mother relationships that they establish with Black children.

In African-American communities these women-centered networks of community-based child care often extend beyond the boundaries of biologically related individuals and include "fictive kin" (Stack 1974). Civil rights activist Ella Baker describes how informal adoption by othermothers functioned in the rural southern community of her childhood:

> My aunt who had thirteen children of her own raised three more. She had become a midwife, and a child was born who was covered with sores. Nobody was particularly wanting the child, so she took the child and raised him . . . and another mother decided she didn't want to be bothered with two children. So my aunt took one and raised him . . . they were part of the family. (Cantarow 1980, 59)

Even when relationships are not between kin or fictive kin, African-American community norms traditionally were such that neighbors cared for one anothers' children. Sara Brooks, a southern domestic worker, describes the importance that the community-based child care a neighbor offered her daughter had for her: "She kept Vivian and she didn't charge me nothin either. You see, people used to look after each other, but now its not that way. I reckon its because we all was poor, and I guess they put theirself in the place of the person that they was helpin" (Simonsen 1986, 181). Brooks's experiences demonstrate how the African-American cultural value placed on cooperative child care traditionally found institutional support in the adverse conditions under which so many Black women mothered.

Othermothers are key not only in supporting children but also in helping bloodmothers who, for whatever reason, lack the preparation or desire for motherhood. In confronting racial oppression, maintaining community-based child care and respecting othermothers who assume child-care responsibilities serve a critical function in African-American communities. Children orphaned by sale or death of their parents under slavery, children conceived through rape, children of young mothers, children born into extreme poverty or to alcoholic or drug-addicted mothers, or children who for other reasons cannot remain with their bloodmothers have all been supported by othermothers, who, like Ella Baker's aunt, take in additional children even when they have enough of their own.

Young women are often carefully groomed at an early age to become other-mothers. As a ten-year-old, civil rights activist Ella Baker learned to be an other-mother by caring for the children of a widowed neighbor: "Mama would say, 'You must take the clothes to Mr. Powells' house, and give so-and-so a bath.' The children were running wild. . . . The kids . . . would take off across the field. We'd chase them down, and bring them back, and put 'em in the tub, and wash 'em off, and change clothes, and carry the dirty ones home, and wash them. Those kind of things were routine" (Cantarow 1980, 59).

Many Black men also value community-based child care but exercise these values to a lesser extent. Young Black men are taught how to care for children (Young 1970; Lewis 1975). During slavery, for example, Black children under age ten experienced little division of labor. They were dressed alike and performed similar tasks. If the activities of work and play are any indication of the degree of gender role differentiation that existed among slave children, "then young girls probably grew up minimizing the difference between the sexes while learning far more about the differences between the races" (D. White 1985, 94). Differences among Black men and women in attitudes toward children may have more to do with male labor force patterns. As Ella Baker observes, "my father took care of people too, but . . . my father had to work" (Cantarow 1980, 60).

Historically, community-based child care and the relationships among blood-mothers and othermothers in women-centered networks have taken diverse in-stitutional forms. In some polygynous West African societies, the children of the same father but different mothers referred to one another as brothers and sis-ters. While a strong bond existed between the biological mother and her child—one so strong that, among the Ashanti for example, "to show disrespect towards one's mother is tantamount to sacrilege" (Fortes 1950, 263)—children could be disciplined by any of their other "mothers." Cross-culturally, the high status given to othermothers and the cooperative nature of child-care arrangements among bloodmothers and othermothers in Caribbean and other Black societies gives credence to the importance that people of African descent place on mothering (Clarke 1966; Shimkin et al. 178; Sudarkasa 1981a, 1981b).

Although the political economy of slavery brought profound changes to enslaved Africans, cultural values concerning the importance of motherhood and the value of cooperative approaches to child care continued. While older women served as nurses and midwives, their most common occupation was caring for the children of parents who worked (D. White 1985). Informal adoption of orphaned children reinforced the importance of social motherhood in African-American communities (Gutman 1976).

The relationship between bloodmothers and othermothers survived the transition from a slave economy to postemancipation southern rural agriculture. Children in southern rural communities were not solely the responsibility of their biological mothers. Aunts, grandmothers, and others who had time to supervise children served as othermothers (Young 1970; Dougherty 1978). The significant status women enjoyed in family networks and in African-American communities continued to be linked to their bloodmother and othermother activities.

The entire community structure of bloodmothers and othermothers is under assault in many inner-city neighborhoods, where the very fabric of African-American community life is being eroded by illegal drugs. But even in the most troubled communities, remnants of the othermother tradition endure. Bebe Moore Campbell's 1950s North Philadelphia neighborhood underwent some startling changes when crack cocaine flooded the streets in the 1980s. Increases in birth defects, child abuse, and parental neglect left many children without care. But some residents, such as Miss Nee, continue the othermother tradition. After raising her younger brothers and sisters and five children of her own, Miss Nee cares for three additional children whose families fell apart. Moreover, on any given night Miss Nee's house may be filled by up to a dozen children because she has a reputation for never turning away a needy child ("Children of the Underclass" 1989).

Traditionally, community-based child care certainly has been functional for African-American communities and for Black women. Black feminist theorist Bell Hooks suggests that the relationships among bloodmothers and othermothers may have greater theoretical importance than currently recognized.

> This form of parenting is revolutionary in this society because it takes place in opposition to the ideas that parents, especially mothers, should be the only childrearers. . . . This kind of shared responsibility for child care can happen in small community settings where people know and trust one another. It cannot happen in those settings if parents regard children as their "property," their possession. (1984, 144)

The resiliency of women-centered family networks illustrates how traditional cultural values—namely, the African origins of community-based child care—can help people cope with and resist oppression. By continuing community-based child care, African-American women challenge one fundamental assumption underlying the capitalist system itself: that children are "private property" and can be disposed of as such. Notions of property, child care, and gender differences in parenting styles are embedded in the institutional arrangements of any given political economy. Under the property model stemming from capitalist patriarchal families, parents may not literally assert that their children are pieces of property, but their parenting may reflect assumptions analogous to those they make in connection with property (J. Smith 1983). For example, the exclusive parental "right" to discipline children as parents see fit, even if discipline borders on abuse, parallels the widespread assumption that property owners may dispose of their property without consulting members of the larger community. By seeing the larger community as responsible for children and by giving othermothers and other nonparents "rights" in child rearing, African-Americans challenge prevailing property relations. It is in this sense that traditional bloodmother/othermother relationships in women-centered networks are "revolutionary."

Mothers, Daughters, and Socialization for Survival

Black mothers of daughters face a troubling dilemma. On one hand, to ensure their daughters' physical survival, mothers must teach them to fit into systems of oppression. For example, as a young girl Black activist Ann Moody questioned why she was paid so little for the domestic work she began at age nine, why Black women domestics were sexually harassed by their white male employers, why no one would explain the activities of the National Association for the Advancement of Colored People to her, and why whites had so much more than Blacks. But her mother refused to answer her questions and actually chastised her for questioning the system and stepping out of her "place" (Moody 1968). Like Ann Moody, Black daughters learn to expect to work, to strive for an education so they can support themselves, and to anticipate carrying heavy responsibilities in their families and communities because these skills are essential to their own survival and those for whom they will eventually be responsible (Ladner 1972; Joseph 1981). New Yorker Michele Wallace recounts: "I can't remember when I first learned that my family expected me to work, to be able to take care of myself when I grew up. . . . It had been drilled into me that the best and only sure support was self-support" (1978, 89–90). Mothers also know that if their daughters uncritically accept the limited opportunities offered Black women, they become willing participants in their own subordination. Mothers may have ensured their daughters' physical survival, but at the high cost of their emotional destruction.

On the other hand, Black daughters with strong self-definitions and self-valuations who offer serious challenges to oppressive situations may not physically survive. When Ann Moody became active in the early 1960s in sit-ins and voter registration activities, her mother first begged her not to participate and then told her not to come home because she feared the whites in Moody's hometown would kill her. Despite the dangers, mothers routinely encourage Black daughters to develop skills to confront oppressive conditions. Learning that they will work and that education is a vehicle for advancement can also be seen as ways of enhancing positive self-definitions and self-valuations in Black girls. Emotional strength is essential, but not at the cost of physical survival.

Historian Elsa Barkley Brown captures this delicate balance Black mothers negotiate by pointing out that her mother's behavior demonstrated the "need to teach me to live my life one way and, at the same time, to provide all the tools I would need to live it quite differently" (1989, 929). Black daughters must learn how to survive in interlocking structures of race, class, and gender oppression while rejecting and transcending those same structures. In order to develop these skills in their daughters, mothers demonstrate varying combinations of behaviors devoted to ensuring their daughters' survival—such as providing them with basic necessities and protecting them in dangerous environments— to helping their daughters go further than mothers themselves were allowed to go.

This special vision of Black mothers may grow from the nature of work women have done to ensure Black children's survival. These work experiences have provided Black women with a unique angle of vision, a particular perspective on the world to be passed on to Black daughters. African and African-American women have long integrated economic self-reliance with mothering. In contrast to the cult of true womanhood, in which work is defined as being in opposition to and incompatible with motherhood, work for Black women has been an important and valued dimension of Afrocentric definitions of Black motherhood. Sara Brooks describes the powerful connections that economic self-reliance and mothering had in her childhood: "When I was about nine I was nursin my sister Sally—I'm about seven or eight years older than Sally. And when I would put her to sleep, instead of me goin somewhere and sit down and play, I'd get my little old hoe and get out there and work right in the field around the house" (in Simonsen 1986, 86).

Mothers who are domestic workers or who work in proximity to whites may experience a unique relationship with the dominant group. For example, African-American women domestics are exposed to all the intimate details of the lives of their white employers. Working for whites offers domestic workers a view from the inside and exposes them to ideas and resources that might aid in their children's upward mobility. In some cases domestic workers form close, long-lasting relationships with their employers. But domestic workers also encounter some of the harshest exploitation confronting women of color. The work is low paid, has few benefits, and exposes women to the threat and reality of sexual harassment. Black domestics could see the dangers awaiting their daughters.

Willi Coleman's mother used a Saturday-night hair-combing ritual to impart a Black women's standpoint on domestic work to her daughters:

> Except for special occasions mama came home from work early on Saturdays. She spent six days a week mopping, waxing and dusting other women's houses and keeping out of reach of other women's husbands. Saturday nights were reserved for "taking care of them girls" hair and the telling of stories. Some of which included a recitation of what she had endured and how she had triumphed over "folks that were lower than dirt" and "no-good snakes in the grass." She combed, patted, twisted and talked, saying things which would have embarrassed or shamed her at other times. (Coleman 1987,34)

Bonnie Thornton Dill's (1980) study of the child-rearing goals of domestic workers illustrates how African-American women see their work as both contributing to their children's survival and instilling values that will encourage their children to reject their proscribed "place" as Blacks and strive for more. Providing a better chance for their children was a dominant theme among Black women. Domestic workers described themselves as "struggling to give their children the skills and training they did not have; and as praying that opportunities which had not been open to them would be open to their children" (p. 110). But the women also realized that while they wanted to communicate the value of their work as part of the ethics of caring and personal accountability, the work itself was undesirable. Bebe Moore Campbell's (1989) grandmother and college-educated mother stressed the importance of education. Campbell remembers, "[they] wanted me to Be Somebody, to be the second generation to live out my life as far away from a mop and scrub brush and Miss Ann's floors as possible" (p. 83).

Understanding this goal of balancing the need for the physical survival of their daughters with the vision of encouraging them to transcend the boundaries confronting them explains many apparent contradictions in Black mother-daughter relationships. Black mothers are often described as strong disciplinarians and overly protective; yet these same women manage to raise daughters who are self-reliant and assertive. To explain this apparent contradiction, Gloria Wade-Gayles suggests that Black mothers

> do not socialize their daughters to be "passive" or "irrational." Quite the contrary, they socialize their daughters to be independent, strong and self-confident. Black mothers are suffocatingly protective and domineering precisely because they are determined to mold their daughters into whole and self-actualizing persons in a society that devalues Black women. (1984, 12)

African-American mothers place a strong emphasis on protection, either by trying to shield their daughters as long as possible from the penalties attached to their race, class, and gender status or by teaching them skills of independence and self-reliance so that they will be able to protect themselves. Consider the following verse from a traditional blues song:

I ain't good lookin' and ain't got waist-long hair
I say I ain't good lookin' and I ain't got waist-long hair
But my mama gave me something that'll take me anywhere.
(Washington 1984, 144)

Unlike white women, symbolized by "good looks" and "waist-long hair," Black women have been denied male protection. Under such conditions it becomes essential that Black mothers teach their daughters skills that will "take them anywhere."

Black women's autobiographies and fiction can be read as texts revealing the multiple ways that African-American mothers aim to shield their daughters from the demands of being Black women in oppressive conditions. Michele Wallace describes her growing understanding of how her mother viewed raising Black daughters in Harlem: "My mother has since explained to me that since it was obvious her attempt to protect me was going to prove a failure, she was determined to make me realize that as a Black girl in white America I was going to find it an uphill climb to keep myself together" (1978, 98). In discussing the mother-daughter relationship in Paule Marshall's *Brown Girl, Brownstones.* Rosalie Troester catalogues the ways mothers have aimed to protect their daughters and the impact this may have on relationships themselves:

> Black mothers, particularly those with strong ties to their community, sometimes build high banks around their young daughters, isolating them from the dangers of the larger world until they are old and strong enough to function as autonomous women. Often these dikes are religious, but sometimes they are built with education, family, or the restrictions of a close-knit and homogeneous community. . . . This isolation causes the currents between Black mothers and daughters to run deep and the relationship to be fraught with an emotional intensity often missing from the lives of women with more freedom. (1984, 13)

Michele Wallace's mother built banks around her headstrong adolescent daughter by institutionalizing her in a Catholic home for troubled girls. Wallace went willingly, believing "I thought at the time that I would rather live in hell than be with my mother" (1978, 98). But years later Wallace's evaluation of her mother's decision changed: "Now that I know my mother better, I know that her sense of powerlessness made it all the more essential to her that she take radical action" (p. 98).

African-American mothers try to protect their daughters from the dangers that lie ahead by offering them a sense of their own unique self-worth. Many contemporary Black women writers report the experience of being singled out, of being given a sense of specialness at an early age which encouraged them to develop their talents. My own mother marched me to the public library at age five, helped me get my first library card, and told me that I could do anything if I learned how to read. In discussing the works of Paule Marshall, Dorothy West, and Alice Walker, Mary Helen Washington observes that all three writers make special claims about the roles their mothers played in the development of their creativity: "The bond with their mothers is such a fundamental and powerful source that the term 'mothering the mind' might have been coined specifically to define their experiences as writers" (1984, 144).

Black women's efforts to provide a physical and psychic base for their children can affect mothering styles and the emotional intensity of Black mother-daughter relationships. As Gloria Wade-Gayles points out, "mothers in Black women's fiction are strong and devoted . . . they are rarely affectionate" (1984, 10). For example, in Toni Morrison's *Sula* (1974), Eva Peace's husband ran off, leaving her with three small children and no money. Despite her feelings, "the demands of feeding her three children were so acute she had to postpone her anger for two years until she had both the time and energy for it" (p. 32). Later in the novel Eva's daughter Hannah asks, "Mamma, did you ever love us?" (p. 67). Eva angrily replies, "what you talkin' bout did I love you girl I stayed alive for you" (p. 69). For far too many Black mothers, the demands of providing for children in interlocking systems of oppression are sometimes so demanding that they have neither the time nor the patience for affection. And yet most Black daughters love and admire their mothers and are convinced that their mothers truly love them (Joseph 1981).

Black daughters raised by mothers grappling with hostile environments have to come to terms with their feelings about the difference between the idealized versions of maternal love extant in popular culture and the strict and often troubled mothers in their lives. For a daughter, growing up means developing a better understanding that even though she may desire more affection and greater freedom, her mother's physical care and protection are acts of maternal love. Ann Moody describes her growing awareness of the cost her mother paid as a domestic worker who was a single mother of three. Watching her mother sleep after the birth of another child, Moody remembers:

> For a long time I stood there looking at her. I didn't want to wake her up. I wanted to enjoy and preserve that calm, peaceful look on her face. I wanted to think she would always be that happy. . . . Adline and Junior were too young to feel the things I felt and know the things I knew about Mama. They couldn't remember when she and Daddy separated. They had never heard her cry at night as I had or worked and helped as I had done when we were starving. (1968, 57)

Moody initially sees her mother as a strict disciplinarian, a woman who tries to protect her daughter by withholding information. But as Moody matures and better understands the oppression in her community, her ideas change. On one occasion Moody left school early the day after a Black family had been brutally murdered by local whites. Moody's description of her mother's reaction reflects her deepening understanding: "When I walked in the house Mama didn't even ask me why I came home. She just looked at me. And for the first time I realized she understood what was going on within me or was trying to anyway" (1968, 136).

Another example of a daughter's efforts to understand her mother is offered in Renita Weems's account of coming to grips with maternal desertion. In the following passage Weems struggles with the difference between the stereotypical image of the superstrong Black mother and her own alcoholic mother's decision to leave her children: "My mother loved us. I must believe that. She worked all day in a department store bakery to buy shoes and school tablets, came home to curse out neighbors who wrongly accused her children of any impropriety (which in an apartment complex usually meant stealing), and kept her house cleaner than most sober women" (1984, 26). Weems concludes that her mother loved her because she provided for her to the best of her ability.

Othermothers often help to defuse the emotional intensity of relationships between bloodmothers and their daughters. In recounting how she dealt with the intensity of her relationship with her mother, Weems describes the women teachers, neighbors, friends, and othermothers she turned to—women who, she observes "did not have the onus of providing for me, and so had the luxury of talking to me" (1984, 27). Cheryl West's household included her brother, her lesbian mother, and Jan, her mother's lover. Jan became an othermother to West: "Yellow-colored, rotund and short in stature, Jan was like a second mother. . . . Jan braided my hair in the morning, mother worked two jobs and tucked me in at night. Loving, gentle, and fastidious in the domestic arena, Jan could be a rigid disciplinarian. . . . To the outside world . . . she was my 'aunt' who happened to live with us. But she was much more involved and nurturing than any of my 'real' aunts (1987, 43).

June Jordan offers an eloquent analysis of one daughter's realization of the high personal cost African-American women can pay in providing an economic and emotional foundation for their children. In the following passage Jordan offers a powerful testament of how she came to see that her mother's work was an act of love:

As a child I noticed the sadness of my mother as she sat alone in the kitchen at night. . . . Her woman's work never won permanent victories of any kind. It never enlarged the universe of her imagination or her power to influence what happened beyond the front door of our house. Her woman's work never tickled her to laugh or shout or dance. But she did raise me to respect her way of offering love and to believe that hard work is often the irreducible factor for survival, not something to avoid. Her woman's work produced a reliable home base where I could pursue the privileges of books and music. Her woman's work invented the potential for a completely different kind of work for us, the next generation of Black women: huge, rewarding hard work demanded by the huge, new ambitions that her perfect confidence in us engendered. (1985, 105)

Community Othermothers
and Political Activism

Black women's experiences as othermothers provide a foundation for Black women's political activism. Nurturing children in Black extended family networks stimulates a more generalized ethic of caring and personal accountability among African-American women who often feel accountable to all the Black community's children.

This notion of Black women as community othermothers for all Black children traditionally allowed African-American women to treat biologically unrelated children as if they were members of their own families. For example, sociologist Karen Fields describes how her grandmother, Mamie Garvin Fields, draws on her power as a community othermother when dealing with unfamiliar children: "She will say to a child on the street who looks up to no good, picking out a name at random, 'Aren't you Miz Pickney's boy?' in that same reproving tone. If the reply is, 'No, *ma'am,* my mother is Miz Gadsden,' whatever threat there was dissipates" (Fields and Fields 1983, xvii).

The use of family language in referring to members of the African-American community also illustrates this dimension of Black motherhood. In the following passage, Mamie Garvin Fields describes how she became active in surveying substandard housing conditions among African-Americans in Charleston. Note her explanation of why she uses family language:

> I was one of the volunteers they got to make a survey of the places where we were paying extortious rents for indescribable property. I said "we," although it wasn't Bob and me. We had our own home, and so did many of the Federated Women. Yet we still felt like it really was "we" living in those terrible places, and it was up to us to do something about them (Fields and Fields 1983, 195)

Black women frequently describe Black children using family language. In recounting her increasingly successful efforts to teach a boy who had given other teachers problems, my daughter's kindergarten teacher stated, "You know how it can be—the majority of children in the learning disabled classes are *our children.* I know he didn't belong there, so I volunteered to take him." In their statements both women use family language to describe the ties that bind them as Black women to their responsibilities as members of an African-American community/family.

In explaining why the South Carolina Federation of Colored Women's Clubs founded a home for girls, Mrs. Fields observes, "We all could see that we had a responsibility for those girls: they were the daughters of our community coming up" (Fields and Fields 1983, 197). Ms. Fields's activities as a community othermother on behalf of the "daughters" of her community represent an established tradition among educated Black women. Serving as othermothers to women in the Black community has a long history. A study of 108 of the first generation of Black club women found that three-quarters were married, three-quarters worked outside the home, but only one-fourth had children (Giddings 1984). These women emphasized self-support for Black women, whether married or not, and realized that self-sufficient community othermothers were important. "Not all women are intended for mothers," declares an 1894 edition of the *Woman's Era.* "Some of us have not the temperment for family life. . . . Clubs will make women think seriously of their future lives, and not make girls think their only alternative is to marry" (Giddings 1984, 108).

Black women writers also explore this theme of the African-American community othermother who nurtures the Black community. One of the earliest examples is found in Frances Ellen Watkins Harper's 1892 novel *Iola Leroy.* By rejecting an opportunity to marry a prestigious physician and dissociate herself from the Black community, nearly white Iola, the main character, chooses instead to serve the African-American community. Similarly, in Alice Walker's *Meridian* (1976), the main character rejects the controlling image of the "happy slave," the self-sacrificing Black mother, and chooses to become a community othermother. Giving up her biological child to the care of an othermother, Meridian gets an education, works in the civil rights movement, and eventually takes on responsibility for the children of a small southern town. She engages in a "quest that will take her beyond the society's narrow meaning of the word *mother* as a physical state and expand its meaning to those who create, nurture, and save life in social and psychological as well as physical terms" (Christian 1985, 242).

Sociologist Cheryl Gilkes (1980, 1982, 1983b) suggests that community othermother relationships can be key in stimulating Black women's decisions to become community activists. Gilkes asserts that many of the Black women community activists in her study became involved in community organizing in response to the needs of their own children and of those in their communities. The following comment is typical of how many of the Black women in Gilkes's study relate to Black children: "There were alot of summer programs springing up for kids, but they were exclusive . . . and I found that most of *our kids* were excluded" (1980, 219). For many women what began as the daily expression of their obligations as community othermothers, as was the case for the kindergarten teacher, developed into full-fledged actions as community leaders.

This community othermother tradition also explains the "mothering the mind" relationships that can develop between Black women teachers and their Black women students. Unlike the traditional mentoring so widely reported in educational literature, this relationship goes far beyond that of providing students with either technical skills or a network of academic and professional contacts. Bell Hooks shares the special vision that teachers who see our work in community othermother terms can pass on to our students: "I understood from the teachers in those segregated schools that the work of any teacher committed to the full self-realization of students was necessarily and fundamentally radical, that ideas were not neutral, that to teach in a way that liberates, that expands consciousness, that awakens, is to challenge domination at its very core" (1989, 50). Like the mother-daughter relationship, this "mothering the mind" among Black women seeks to move toward the mutuality of a shared sisterhood that binds African-American women as community othermothers.

Community othermothers have made important contributions in building a different type of community in often hostile political and economic surroundings (Reagon 1987). Community othermothers' actions demonstrate a clear rejection of separateness and individual interest as the basis of either community organization or individual self-actualization. Instead, the connectedness with others and common interest expressed by community othermothers models a very different value system, one whereby Afrocentric feminist ethics of caring and personal accountability move communities forward.

. . .

References

Aschenbrenner, Joyce. 1975. *Lifelines, Black Families in Chicago.* Prospect Heights, IL. Waveland Press.

Brown, Elsa Barkley. 1989. "African-American Women's Quilting: A Framework for Conceptualizing and Teaching African-American Women's History." *Signs* 14(4): 921–29.

Burnham, Linda. 1985. "Has Poverty Been Feminized in Black America?" *Black Scholar* 16(2): 14–24.

Campbell, Bebe Moore. 1989. *Sweet Summer: Growing Up with and without My Dad.* New York: Putnam.

Cantarow, Ellen. 1980. *Moving the Mountain: Women Working for Social Change.* Old Westbury, NY: Feminist Press.

"Children of the Underclass." 1989. *Newsweek* September 11, 16–27.

Chodorow, Nancy. 1974. "Family Structure and Feminine Personality." In *Woman, Culture, and Society,* edited by Michelle Zimbalist Rosaldo and Louise Lamphere, 43–66. Stanford: Stanford University Press.

———. 1978. *The Reproduction of Mothering.* Berkeley: University of California Press.

———, and Susan Contratto. 1982. "The Fantasy of the Perfect Mother." In *Rethinking the Family: Some Feminist Questions,* edited by Barrie Thorne and Marilyn Yalom, 54–75. New York: Longman.

Christian, Barbara. 1985. *Black Feminist Criticism, Perspectives on Black Women Writers.* New York: Pergamon.

Clarke, Edith. 1966. *My Mother Who Fathered Me.* 2d ed. London: Allen and Unwin.

Coleman, Willi. 1987. "Closets and Keepsakes." *Sage: A Scholarly Journal on Black Women* 4(2): 34–35.

Dance, Daryl. 1979. "Black Eve or Madonna? A Study of the Antithetical Views of the Mother in Black American Literature." In *Sturdy Black Bridges: Visions of Black Women in Literature,* edited by Roseann Bell, Bettye Parker, and Beverly Guy-Sheftall, 123–32. Garden City, NY: Anchor.

Davis, Angela Y. 1981. *Women, Race and Class.* New York: Random House.

Dill, Bonnie Thornton. 1980. "'The Means to Put My Children Through': Child-Rearing Goals and Strategies among Black Female Domestic Servants." In *The Black Woman,* edited by La Frances Rodgers-Rose, 107–23. Beverly Hills, CA: Sage.

Dougherty, Molly C. 1978. *Becoming a Woman in Rural Black Culture.* New York: Holt, Rinehart and Winston.

Fields, Mamie Garvin, and Karen Fields, 1983. *Lemon Swamp and Other Places: A Carolina Memoir.* New York: Free Press.

Flax, Jane. 1978. "The Conflict between Nurturance and Autonomy in Mother-Daughter Relationships and within Feminism." *Feminist Studies* 4(2): 171–89.

Fortes, Meyer. 1950. "Kinship and Marriage among the Ashanti." In *African Systems of Kinship and Marriage,* edited by A. R. Radcliffe-Brown and Daryll Forde, 252–84. New York: Oxford University Press.

Frazier, E. Franklin, 1948. *The Negro Family in the United States.* New York: Dryden Press.

Giddings, Paula. 1984. *When and Where I Enter . . . The Impact of Black Women on Race and Sex in America.* New York: William Morrow.

Gilkes, Cheryl Townsend. 1980. "'Holding Back the Ocean with a Broom': Black Women and Community Work." In *The Black Woman,* edited by La Frances Rodgers-Rose, 217–32. Beverly Hills, CA: Sage.

———. 1982. "Successful Rebellious Professionals: The Black Woman's Professional Identity and Community Commitment." *Psychology of Women Quarterly* 6(3): 289–311.

———. 1983a. "From Slavery to Social Welfare: Racism and the Control of Black Women." In *Class, Race, and Sex: The Dynamics of Control,* edited by Amy Swerdlow and Hanna Lessinger, 288–300. Boston: G. K. Hall.

———. 1983b. "Going Up for the Oppressed: The Career Mobility of Black Women Community Workers." *Journal of Social Issues* 39(3): 115–39.

Gutman, Herbert. 1976. *The Black Family in Slavery and Freedom, 1750–1925.* New York: Random House.

Herskovits, Melville J. [1941] 1958. *The Myth of the Negro Past.* Boston: Beacon.

Hooks, Bell. 1981. *Ain't I a Woman: Black Women and Feminism.* Boston: South End Press.

———. 1984. *From Margin to Center.* Boston: South End Press.

———. 1989. *Talking Back: Thinking Feminist, Thinking Black.* Boston: South End Press.

Jordan, June. 1985. *On Call.* Boston: South End Press.

Joseph, Gloria, 1981. "Black Mothers and Daughters: Their Roles and Functions in American Society." In *Common Differences,* edited by Gloria Joseph and Jill Lewis. 75–126. Garden City, NY: Anchor.

———. 1984. "Black Mothers and Daughters: Traditional and New Perspectives." *Sage: A Scholarly Journal on Black Women* 1(2): 17–21.

King, Mae. 1973. "The Politics of Sexual Stereotypes." *Black Scholar* 4(6–7): 12–23.

Ladner, Joyce. 1972. *Tomorrow's Tomorrow.* Garden City, NY: Doubleday.

———, and Ruby Morton Gourdine. 1984. "Intergenerational Teenage Motherhood: Some Preliminary Findings." *Sage: A Scholarly Journal on Black Women* 1(2): 22–24.

Lewis, Diane K. 1975. "The Black Family: Socialization and Sex Roles." *Phylon* 36(3): 221–37.

Martin, Elmer, and Joanne Mitchell Martin. 1978. *The Black Extended Family.* Chicago: University of Chicago Press.

McCray, Carrie Allen. 1980. "The Black Woman and Family Roles." In *The Black Woman,* edited by La Frances Rodgers-Rose, 67–78. Beverly Hills, CA: Sage.

Moody, Ann. 1968. *Coming of Age in Mississippi*. New York: Dell.

Morrison, Toni. 1974. *Sula*. New York: Random House.

Moynihan, Daniel Patrick. 1965. *The Negro Family: The Case for National Action*. Washington, DC: GPO.

Reagon, Bernice Johnson. 1987. "African Diaspora Women: The Making of Cultural Workers." In *Women in Africa and the African Diaspora*, edited by Rosalyn Terborg-Penn, Sharon Harley, and Andrea Benton Rushing, 167–80. Washington, DC: Howard University Press.

Rollins, Judith. 1985. *Between Women, Domestics and Their Employers*. Philadelphia: Temple University Press.

Sage: A Scholarly Journal on Black Women. 1984. "Mothers and Daughters I." Special Issue, 1(2).

———. 1987. "Mothers and Daughters II." Special Issue, 4(2).

Shimkin, Demitri B., Edith M. Shimkin, and Dennis A. Frate, eds. 1978. *The Extended Family in Black Societies*. Chicago: Aldine.

Simms, Margaret C. 1988. *The Choices that Young Black Women Make: Education, Employment, and Family Formation*. Working Paper No. 190, Wellesley, MA: Center for Research on Women, Wellesley College.

Simonsen, Thordis, ed. 1986. *You May Plow Here: The Narrative of Sara Brooks*. New York: Touchstone.

Smith, Janet Farrell. 1983. "Parenting as Property." In *Mothering: Essays in Feminist Theory*, edited by Joyce Trebilcot, 199–212. Totowa, NJ: Rowman & Allenheld.

Stack, Carol D. 1974. *All Our Kin: Strategies for Survival in a Black Community*. New York: Harper & Row.

Staples, Robert. 1973. *The Black Woman in America*. Chicago: Nelson-Hall.

———. 1979. "The Myth of Black Macho: A Response to Angry Black Feminists." *Black Scholar* 10(6): 24–33.

Sudarkasa, Niara. 1981a. "Female Employment and Family Organization in West Africa." In *The Black Woman Cross-Culturally*, edited by Filomina Chioma Steady, 49–64. Cambridge: MA: Schenkman.

———. 1981b. "Interpreting the African Heritage in Afro-American Family Organization." In *Black Families*, edited by Harriette Pipes McAdoo, 37–53. Beverly Hills, CA: Sage.

Tanner, Nancy. 1974. "Matrifocality in Indonesia and Africa and among Black Americans." In *Woman, Culture, and Society*, edited by Michelle Z. Rosaldo and Louise Lamphere, 129–56. Stanford: Stanford University Press.

Troester, Rosalie Riegle. 1984. "Turbulence and Tenderness: Mothers, Daughters, and 'Othermothers' in Paule Marshall's *Brown Girl, Brownstones*." *Sage: A Scholarly Journal on Black Women* 1(2): 13–16.

U.S. Department of Commerce, Bureau of the Census. 1986. *Money Income and Poverty Status of Families and Persons in the United States: 1985*. Series P-60, No. 154. Washington, DC: GPO.

———. 1989. *Money Income of Households, Families, and Persons in the United States: 1987*. Series P-60, No. 162. Washington, DC: GPO.

Wade-Gayles, Gloria. 1980. "She Who Is Black and Mother: In Sociology and Fiction, 1940–1970." In *The Black Woman*, edited by La Frances Rodgers-Rose, 89–106. Beverly Hills, CA: Sage.

———. 1984. "The Truths of Our Mothers' Lives: Mother-Daughter Relationships in Black Women's Fiction." *Sage: A Scholarly Journal on Black Women* 1(2): 8–12.

Walker, Alice. 1976. *Meridian*. New York: Pocket Books.

———. 1983. *In Search of Our Mothers' Gardens*. New York: Harcourt Brace Jovanovich.

Wallace, Michele. 1978. *Black Macho and the Myth of the Superwoman*. New York: Dial Press.

Washington, Mary Ellen. 1984. "I Sign My Mother's Name: Alice Walker, Dorothy West and Paule Marshall." In *Mothering the Mind: Twelve Studies of Writers and Their Silent Partners*, edited by Ruth Perry and Martine Watson Broronley, 143–63. New York: Holmes & Meier.

Weems, Renita. 1984. "'Hush. Mama's Gotta Go Bye Bye': A Personal Narrative." *Sage: A Scholarly Journal on Black Women* 1(2): 25–28.

West, Cheryl. 1987. "Lesbian Daughter." *Sage: A Scholarly Journal on Black Women* 4(2): 42–44.

White, Deborah Gray. 1985. *Ar'n't I a Woman? Female Slaves in the Plantation South*. New York: W. W. Norton.

Young, Virginia Heyer. 1970. "Family and Childhood in a Southern Negro Community." *American Anthropologist* 72(32): 269–88.

Zinn, Maxine Baca. 1989. "Family, Race, and Poverty in the Eighties." *Signs* 14(4): 856–74.

PART FOUR

Moral Epistemologies

8

Moral Understandings: Alternative "Epistemology" for a Feminist Ethics [1989]

MARGARET URBAN WALKER

When Annette Baier asked a few years ago what women wanted in a moral theory, the answer she arrived at was that moral *theory* was just what women *didn't* want, if a moral theory is a "fairly systematic account of a fairly large area of morality, with a keystone supporting all the rest" (Baier 1985, 55). Yet the latter is what a still dominant tradition of moral philosophy—stretching from Socrates through Sidgwick to Rawls—*does* want: a fairly compact system of very general but directly action-guiding principles or procedures. Current philosophical practice still largely views ethics as the search for moral knowledge, and moral knowledge as comprising universal moral formulae and the theoretical justification of these.

If one asks the somewhat different question of what a *feminist ethics* is, or should look like, one might have in mind some different things. One is that feminist ethics is one which clarifies the moral legitimacy and necessity of the kinds of social, political, and personal changes that feminism demands in order to end male domination, or perhaps to end domination generally.[1] Another conception of feminist ethics is that of one in which the moral perceptions, self-images, and senses of moral value and responsibility of women have been represented or restored. Philosophical ethics, as a cultural product, has been until recently almost entirely a product of some men's thinking. There are the usual reasons to suspect that those men will not have represented, or will not have represented truly, modes of life and forms of responsibility which aren't theirs, or which they could recognize fully only at the cost of acknowledging their interlocking gender, race and class privileges. While female voices alone may not be sufficient correctives to this, they promise to be important ones. Here the tasks of restoration, reconstruction, and new construction are not sharply divided; all involve suspension and re-examination of unquestioned assumptions and standard forms.

The reconstructive project has been pioneered in work by Baier (1985; 1986; 1987), Carol Gilligan (1982), Nel Noddings (1984), Adrienne Rich (1976; 1979), Sara Ruddick (1984), Caroline Whitbeck (1983), and others. While the result in each case is distinctive, a lattice of similar themes—personal relations, nurturance and caring, maternal experience, emotional responsiveness, attunement to particular persons and contexts, sensitivity to open-ended responsibilities— has become the object of sharp criticism from *other* feminist quarters. While the criticisms too are varied, they include a variety of cognate concerns about whether the values and paradigms valorized in the reconstructive work are not mistaken and politically retrograde. Jean Grimshaw (1986), Claudia Card (1985), Jeffner Allen (1986), Lorraine Code (1987), Barbara Houston (1987), and others have asked whether maternal paradigms, nurturant responsiveness, and a bent toward responsibility for others' needs aren't our oppressive history, not our liberating future, and whether "women's morality" isn't a familiar ghetto rather than a liberated space.[2] It is fair, if oversimple, to say that some feminists question whether the reconstructive project can meet and nourish the politically normative one.[3]

The many crossing strands of this conversation beg for close consideration, but I will pull one thread loose from the reconstructive project and commend it to our further deliberation as a part, but only part, of an adequate and flexible feminist ethic. The thread I refer to in the reconstructive work is a profound and original rebellion against the regnant paradigm of moral knowledge mentioned in my opening paragraph. Hence, it might be called an *alternative moral epistemology,* a very different way of identifying and appreciating the forms of intelligence which define responsible moral consideration. This view does not imagine our moral understandings congealed into a compact theoretical instrument of impersonal decision for each person, but as deployed in shared processes of discovery, expression, interpretation, and adjustment between persons. Facets of this alternative view which appear repeatedly in reconstructive discussions are: attention to the particular; a way of constructing morally relevant understandings which is "contextual and narrative" (Gilligan 1982, 19); a picture of deliberation as a site of expression and communication.

Here are my limited aims. First, I model this alternative epistemology of moral understandings by describing its three elements and their affinities. Second, I identify how its features challenge the still hardy mainstream universalist tradition on moral knowledge. Finally, too briefly, I indicate some ways this particular result of the reconstructive approach to feminist ethics answers to some concerns of the first, politically normative approach. Refusing the canonical "theory" option does not mean going without guidance in judgments and practices of countering domination. Neither does the alternative moral epistemology by itself require commitments to the specific moral values and paradigms lately in dispute among feminists.

I. Elements of an Alternative Moral Epistemology

A substantial number of contemporary women writers on morality have sounded the theme of attention to "particular others in actual contexts" (Held 1987, 118). Iris Murdoch (1970) sets an oft-cited precedent for this theme in her defense of *attention* ("loving regard" (40); "patient and just discernment" (38) as the "characteristic and proper mark of the active moral agent" (34). In pointed opposition to the emphasis in most moral philosophy on conscientious adherence to principle, Murdoch insists instead on the "endless task" (28) of "good vision: unsentimental, detached, unselfish, objective attention" (65–66), which she calls *love*.[4] More recent women writers who see acute and unimpeded perception of particular human beings as the condition of adequate moral response concur in Murdoch's epistemological point—her emphasis on a certain kind of understanding as central to morality.[5]

Ruddick (1984), for example, finds in the normative structure of maternal practices a rich display of that openness which allows for revelation of the particular individual. Maternal responsibility to foster growth, on Ruddick's account, requires certain recognitions: of the separate consciousness of another making its own sense of the world; of the common humanity of the other's familiar longings and impulses; of the need to give up expectations of repeatability in order to follow the distinct trajectory of a particular life (218–220). Such maternal virtues are ones Ruddick thinks it urgent to cultivate more widely. Whitbeck (1983) sees a similar sensibility enabling practices (such as teaching the young, nursing the sick, tending the body) for "the (mutual) realization of people" (65) which are typically considered "women's work." Related themes are sounded by others: Gilligan's reconstruction of the "care ethic" involves "the ability to perceive people in their own terms and to respond to their needs" (1984, 77); Benhabib (1987, 164) explores the "epistemic incoherence" of strategies of reversibility and universalization once the concreteness of other individuals has been covered over by the "generalized" conception of others in terms of an abstract *status*.[6]

Attention to particular persons as *a*, if not *the*, morally crucial epistemic mode requires distinctive sorts of understanding. Gilligan has usefully described the pattern of this thinking as "contextual and narrative" rather than "formal and ab-

stract," where the latter "abstracts the moral problem from the interpersonal situation" (1982, 32), while the former invokes a "narrative of relationships that extends over time" (1982, 28). Two elements are at work here: context and concreteness of individuals with specific "history, identity, and affective-emotional
constitution" (Benhabib 1987, 163), and the special context that is a relationship,
with *its* history, identity, and affective definition.

The two are linked by the notion of a narrative, of the location of human beings' feelings, psychological states, needs, and understandings as nodes of a
story (or of the intersection of stories) that has already begun, and will continue
beyond a given juncture of moral urgency. Conceptually, this means that we
don't and can't identify people's emotions, intentions and other mental states
with momentary (and especially not momentary inner, private) phenomena.
Instead, we identify these features of people by attending to how their beliefs,
feelings, modes of expression, circumstances and more, arranged in characteristic ways and often spread out in time, configure into a recognizable kind of story.
Practically, this means that individual embroideries and idiosyncracies, as well
as the learned codes of expression and response built up in particular relationships, and built up culturally around kinds of relationships, require of us very
acute attention to the minute and specific, to history and incident, in grasping
cases in a morally adequate way. If the others I need to understand really are actual others in a particular case at hand, and not repeatable instances or replaceable occupants of a general status, they will require of me an understanding of
their/our story and its concrete detail. Without this I really cannot know *how it is*
with others towards whom I will act, or what the meaning and consequence of
any acts will be.

Whitbeck argues for a relational view of persons, of their historical being as
"fundamentally a history of relationships to other people," and their actions as
responses to the "whole configuration of relations" (1983, 76). She connects this
view with the essentially responsive, discretionary character of moral responsibilities that relationships generate, responsibilities that cannot then be reduced
to obligations and specified in uniform terms. Sharon Bishop (1987) has also examined the different light cast on moral responsibilities, problems, deliberation,
resolution and guilt when one sees moral response as the attempt to mediate
multiple, sometimes conflicting, moral claims that arise out of our many actual
connections with other people and our needs to maintain them with integrity
and sensitivity. This intertwining of selves and stories in narrative constructions
which locate what is at stake, what is needed, and what is possible is at the heart
of moral thinking for many women and feminist writers. The understanding of
such stories requires many forms of intelligence; all are at work in the compe-
tent moral agent, according to these views.[7]

One form of intelligence that very often, if not typically, offers crucial resources for the resolution of moral problems is the *ability to communicate*
among persons involved or affected. While this avenue to understanding is not

always open, it often enough is, and its efficacy is so obvious that it is astonishing how little attention is paid it in most nonfeminist moral philosophy. Even in that strain of theory that postulates or simulates an original agreement or compact, the role of communication in, as it were, the moral event is routinely ignored, and the moral agent on the spot is depicted in lonely cogitations (or sometimes in admirable but solo display of fixed habits of virtue). Given the particularistic paradigm of understanding and the situated conception of responsibility already discussed, it is not surprising that the resource of communication is often stressed in women's writing on morality. Gilligan stresses the commitment in the "care" ethic she describes to "activating the network [of relationships] by communication" (1982, 30); and Bishop's reconstrual of moral response as "offering compensation and mediating settlements" (1987, 12) pictures us as engaging those affected by our moral choices in tight places in a common search for constructive ways of answering unsatisfiable or competing claims. Benhabib even more directly challenges the "monological model of moral reasoning" with a proposal for a "communicative ethic of need interpretation," in which actual dialogue replaces hypothetical methods and fixed, prior constraints on "admissible" concerns (1987, 167; 169). Murdoch speaks of a mutual "obscurity" which makes the work of love endless (1970, 33), and urges on us the study of literature as an education in how to "picture and understand human situations" (34). We need not make our obscurity to each other worse by unnecessarily unilateral decision. We might just try turning to each other: talking and listening and imagining possibilities together.

II. From Moral Knowledge to Moral Understandings

The three elements of attention, contextual and narrative appreciation, and communication in the event of moral deliberation might be seen, in their natural interdependence, as an alternative epistemology of moral understanding, or the basis of one. This view, gleaned from the works of a variety of female and feminist writers, provides an alternative to a now standard and canonical (which is to say: professionally institutionalized) view of the form and point of ethics (or its philosophical elaboration).[8] This view is both old and continuous enough to be called a tradition in the strongest sense, and we might call it the *universalist/impersonalist tradition.* In the words of one of its most explicit proponents, nineteenth-century utilitarian philosopher Henry Sidgwick,[9] its goal is systematization of moral understanding, and its ideal of system is that of "precise general knowledge of what ought to be" (1907, 1), encoded in "directive rules of conduct" (2) which are "clear and decisive" (199) and "in universal form" (228). The rationale for pursuing a "scientifically complete and systematically reflective form" (425) in morals is that it "corrects" and "supplements" our scat-

tered institutions, and resolves "uncertainties and discrepancies" in moral judgment. By useful abstraction it steers us away from, in Sidgwick's words, "obvious
sources of error" which "disturb the clearness" of moral discernment (214). For
Sidgwick, such distractions include complexity of circumstances, personal interests, and habitual sympathies. Thus, according to Sidgwick, only precise and
truly universal principles can provide for "perfection of practice no less than for
theoretical completeness" (262).

This capsule description of standard intent and methodology aims to bring
into relief its very general picture of morality as individuals standing before the
bar of impersonal truth. Moral responsibility is envisioned as responsiveness to
the impersonal truths in which morality resides; each individual stands justified
if he or she can invoke the authority of this impersonal truth, and the moral
community of individuals is secured by the conformity (and uniformity) guaranteed by obedience to this higher authority.[10] From an epistemological angle, one
might gloss this view as: adequacy of moral understanding increases as this understanding approaches systematic generality.

The alternative moral epistemology already outlined, holds, to the contrary,
that: adequacy of moral understanding decreases as its form approaches generality through abstraction. A view consistent with this will not be one of individuals standing singly before the impersonal dicta of Morality, but one of human
beings connected in various ways and at various depths responding *to each
other* by engaging together in a search for shareable interpretations of their responsibilities, and/or bearable resolutions to their moral binds. These interpretations and resolutions will be constrained not only by how well they protect
goods we can share, but also by how well they preserve the very human connections that make the shared process necessary and possible. The long oscillation
in Western moral thought between the impersonal and the personal viewpoints
is answered by proposing that we consider, fully and in earnest, the *interpersonal* view.

The result of this alternative epistemology is not, then, an "opposite number"
or shadow image of impersonalist approaches; it is instead a point of departure
for a *variety* of different problematics, investigations, focal concerns, and genres
of writing and teaching about ethics, many of which we have not, I suppose, yet
clearly imagined. Some philosophical endeavors are obviously relevant. We
might pay greater attention to the pragmatics of communication (of what people mean and do when they address each other, and not just what their words
mean). We could explore more fully how moral paradigms and exemplary particular cases are made points of reference for shareable judgments, how they are
explicated and how analogies are drawn with them. A lively interest in understanding how various factors (semantic, institutional, political) shape our ability
to arrive at shared interpretations is needed, as is a questioning of barriers between philosophical, literary, critical, and empirical investigations of moral life.

These endeavors can, however, be carried out in a cheerfully piecemeal fashion; we need not expect or require the results to eventuate in a comprehensive systematization.

The analogue of this on the practical level is the expectation of constant "moral remainders," to adopt a phrase in recent philosophical use. 'Moral remainders' refers to some genuine moral demands which, because their fulfillment conflicted with other genuine moral demands, are "left over" in episodes of moral choice, and yet are not just nullified.[11] Whether this sort of thing is even possible is an issue in contemporary moral philosophy.[12] But if moral life is seen as a tissue of moral understandings which configure, respond to, and reconfigure relations as they go, we should anticipate residues and carry-overs as the rule rather than the exceptions: one's choice will often be a selection of one among various imperfect responses, a response to some among various claims which can't all be fulfilled. So there will just as often be unfinished and ongoing business, compensations and reparations, postponements and returns. Moral problems on this view are nodal points in progressive histories of mutual adjustment and understanding, not "cases" to be closed by a final verdict of a highest court.

III. From Epistemology to Practice

Although I've cast the discussion here in terms of moral "epistemology," my point has been that there is a way of looking at the understanding critical to and distinctive of full moral capacity on which this understanding is *not* really an *episteme*, not a nomologically ordered theory. From the alternative view, moral understanding comprises a collection of perceptive, imaginative, appreciative, and expressive skills and capacities which put and keep us in unimpeded contact with the realities of ourselves and specific others.[13]

It's also true that a picture of moral understanding is not a whole moral view. Indeed, the alternative moral "epistemology" sketched here leaves open to consideration many questions about which sorts of values enable moral agents to express themselves and hear others, to interpret wisely, and to nourish each other's capacities for supple attentiveness. It also leaves open what other values not directly related to these expressive and receptive capacities are those a feminist ethics ought to endorse. It does not promote one kind of relationship as paradigmatic of moral encounter, and invites us to explore the resources and impediments to expression, reception, and communication in relationships of many kinds. Yet the priority it gives to voicing and hearing, to being answerable in and for specific encounters and relationships, promises, I believe, potent critical resources. The most obvious ones I see are its structural capacity to challenge "principled" moral stances in the concrete, where these are surrogates for, or defenses against, responsiveness in actual relationships; to export an insistence on the primacy of personal acknowledgement and communication to institutional and "stranger" contexts; and on a philosophical plane to pierce through the rhetoric of ethics to the *politics of ethics* as a routine matter.[14]

In the first instance, an ethic based on this alternative picture of moral understanding is set to challenge fundamentally and consistently the way the universalist tradition has institutionalized *indirect* ways of relating as moral *paradigms*. By "indirect" here I mean ways of appreciating persons and situations mediated through what are typically some few, entrenched parameters of status, right, principle, or duty. The alternative picture discussed here confronts this "policed sociability" (Skillen 1978, 170) of universalism with an alternative ideal of *moral objectivity:* that of unimpeded, undistorted, and flexible appreciation of unrepeatable individuals in what are often distinctive situations and relationships. Morally relevant categories on this view include the full, nuanced range of expressive resources for articulating and constructing interpersonal life. By contrast, the ways of describing and expressing to which universalist morality permits moral relevance are typically limited to those which are "repeatable," "universalizable," "impartial," or "impersonal," i.e., those that embody the forms of detachment that are taken by universalism as constitutive of "the moral point of view."

Universalism presses me to view you, for instance, as a holder of a certain right, or a promisee, or a satisfaction-function, or a focus of some specifiable set of obligatory responses. I am pressed to structure my response or appeal to you in terms which I can think of as applying repeatably to any number of other cases. If we step into the alternative framework, however, we see universalist morality as thus "curbing our imaginations" (Lovibond 1983, 199) by enforcing communicative and reflective strategies which are interpersonally *evasive*. Universalism, for example, tends to regiment moral thinking so that negligent or willful inattention to need and expectation in the course of daily life is readily seen as "mere insensitivity," a non-moral failing, when it is not in dereliction of explicit "duties." Worse, it legitimates *uniformly* assuming the quasi-administrative or juridical posture of "the" (i.e., universal) moral point of view. Yet in many cases assuming that viewpoint may foreclose the more revealing, if sometimes painful, path of expression, acknowledgement, and collaboration that could otherwise lead to genuinely responsive solutions.

A principled appeal to "fairness" or "what one promised" or what "right" one has to something or why "anyone" should expect a certain response may be a summarily effective arguing point. But if it is brought forth in an intricate situation of an ongoing relationship, it may also be the most effective way to stymie or silence your interlocutor—spouse, lover, friend, student, partner, patient— without addressing many questions. The avoided questions may include just the morally relevant ones about the particular needs and harms, the expectations and forms of trust, and the character and future of *that* relationship. Feminists have special and acute needs to fend off this systematic de-personalizing of the moral and de-moralizing of the personal. For on a practical level what feminists aspire to depends as much on restructuring our senses or moral responsibility in intimate partnerships, sexual relations, communities of personal loyalty, and day-to-day work relations as it clearly does on replacing institutional, legal, and political arrangements.

The alternative picture also invites us not to be too tempted by the "separate spheres" move of endorsing particularism for personal or intimate relations, universalism for the large-scale or genuinely administrative context, or for dealings with unknown or little-known persons. While principled, generalized treatments may really be the best we can resort to in many cases of the latter sort, it is well to preserve a lively sense of the *moral incompleteness* or inadequacy of these resorts. This is partly to defend ourselves against dispositions to keep strangers strange and outsiders outside, but it is also to prevent our becoming comfortable with essentially distancing, depersonalizing, or paternalistic attitudes which may not really *be* the only resorts if roles and institutions can be shaped to embody expressive and communicative possibilities. It is often claimed that more humanly responsive institutions are not practical (read: instrumentally efficient). But if moral-practical intelligence is understood consistently in the alternative way discussed (the way appropriate to relations among persons), it may instead be correct to say that certain incorrigibly impersonal or depersonalizing institutions are too morally impractical to be tolerated. It is crucial to examine how structural features of institutionalized relations—medical personnel, patients, and families; teachers, students, and parents; case workers and clients, for example—combine with typical situations to enable or deform the abilities of all concerned to hear and to be heard. Some characteristically modern forms of universalist thinking may project a sort of "moral colonialism" (the "subjects" of my moral decisions disappear behind uniform "policies" I must impartially "apply") precisely because they were forged historically with an eye to actual colonization—industrial or imperial.[15]

Finally, this kind of moral epistemology reminds us that styles of moral thinking are not primarily philosophical brain-teasers, data begging for the maximally elegant theoretical construction, but are ways of answering to *other people* in terms of some responsibilities that are commonly recognized or recognizable in some community. Philosophical representations of these styles will both reflect and reinforce the relations of authority, power, and responsibility they encode. Hence, for moral philosophy to be sincerely reflective, it must attend focally to questions heretofore considered "philosophically" inappropriate: questions about the rhetoric and politics of ethics. These are questions about the discursive and expressive formats which have been declared appropriate to the task of representing moral life, and about who has the standing (and the access to institutionalized forums) to make, and to challenge, the "rules" (including substantive assumptions) of the genre. When we construct and consider representations of our moral situations, we need to ask: what actual community of moral responsibility does this representation of moral thinking purport to represent? Who does it actually represent? What communicative strategies does it support? Who will be in a position (concretely, socially) to deploy these strategies? Who is in a position to transmit and enforce the rules which constrain them? In what forms of activity or endeavor will they have (or fail to have) an application, and who is served by these activities?

These questions are hard for philosophers to ask; it flies in the face of the professional self-image of supposedly disinterested searchers after timeless moral truth to recognize that a moral philosophy is a particular rhetoric too, situated in certain places, sustained and deployed by certain groups of people. Its apparent form may belie its real application and meaning. For example, philosophers have long insisted on "the universal" in ethics, and continue, I find, to insist on formal universality of norms, concepts, or procedures as the key moral bulwark against bias and injustice. Yet the rhetoric of universality has been entirely compatible, as feminist philosophers have repeatedly shown, with the most complete (and often intentional) exclusion of women as moral agents from such loftily universal constructs as the social contract, pure practical rationality, or the good life for man, and with bypassing altogether in application whole areas of life that are the province of women (voluntarily or not), such as the rearing of children.[16]

Further, not only the substance and presuppositions but also the standard discursive forms of moral philosophy—its canonical styles of presentation, methods of argument, characteristic problems—require pragmatic evaluation. These forms include stark absence of the second person and the plural in projections of philosophical deliberation; virtual exclusion of collaborative and communicative modes of formulating and negotiating moral problems; regimentation of moral "reasoning" into formats of deductive argument; reliance on schematic examples in which the few "morally relevant" factors have already been selected and in which social-political context is effaced; and omission of continuing narratives that explore the interpersonal sequels to moral "solutions." These are rhetorical conventions which curb the moral imaginations of academic philosophers drastically. Alarmingly, we visit them on our students as we "refine" their moral thinking, obscuring morally significant features of everyday life, personal relations, and the social conditions which structure them.

There are alternatives to the abstract, authoritarian, impersonal, universalist view of moral consciousness. The picture of direct mutual response and responsibility is not a whole ethics, but it is one way of rotating the axis of our investigation around the fixed point of our real need.[17]

Notes

1. This view of feminist ethics does not rule out in principle that some currently prominent view in philosophical ethics, properly applied, can be a feminist ethics. Although this

possibility seems less promising currently, early feminist discussions of issues like abortion, rape, and pornography often invoked standard notions of rights, respect, or the promotion of happiness. And it is still a fact that in our given political culture appeals to moral standards which cohere with liberal political ideas are potent and indispensable tools in pursuing feminist social and legal objectives.

2. Grimshaw is specially critical of claims that women's moral *thinking* is characteristically different; Code criticizes "maternalism"; Houston discusses objections by Card, Allen, and others. For critical reactions to Gilligan's work, see Nails et al. (1983), Kerber et al. (1986) and Michaels (1986).

3. I don't mean to make this dialogue sound too bipolar. Virginia Held (1987) is cautious on the issue of jettisoning principles to particularism. Marilyn Friedman (1987) combines a plea for the integration of justice and caring values with the view that the character of particularized moral commitments does not combine with rule-based respect. Both Held and Friedman tentatively suggest the application of different moral approaches to different "spheres" of life or different kinds of relationships. But see my section III, below, on the "separate spheres" idea.

4. Murdoch herself credits her conception of a "just and loving gaze directed upon an individual reality" (34) to Simone Weil, whose views are complicated enough, (and ambivalent enough, from the viewpoint I'm discussing here) to require quite separate consideration.

5. Many may not share the Platonism, Freudian psychology, theory of art, or other views to which Murdoch joins her views on love. One subtle critique of the deep social conservatism of Murdoch's views is provided by Sabina Lovibond (1983, 189–200).

6. See Held (1987); Noddings (1984, chapters 1 and 4). See also Nussbaum (1983) on reviving the Aristotelian notion of perception as "appropriate acknowledgment" of the particular person in the face of the blinding urge to preserve preconceived, harmonious orderings of abstracted value.

7. See also Diamond (1983) on the importance of grasping the moral "texture" of individuals (an idea she attributes to Iris Murdoch).

8. The difference between representing morality and "rationally reconstructing" it philosophically is not always clear, and this is itself a source of deep problems, substantively and methodologically. Addelson (1987), for example, deeply challenges the appropriateness and moral legitimacy of an academic practice of philosophical ethics (if I understand her correctly). I take this challenge quite seriously, even as I right now continue to do a version of academic philosophical ethics.

9. Sidgwick's work richly repays study if one wants to see in explicit and self-conscious form the "rules" of the genre of today's philosophical ethics. But one could find the same rules formulated (or implicitly honored) in any number of mainstream twentieth century authors.

10. Since writing this I have discovered a parallel characterization in Anthony Skillen's description of modern bourgeois moral consciousness as a blend of "abstract authoritarianism" and "generalized disciplinarianism" (Skillen 1978, 153).

11. A standard example would be that in which two promises, each sincerely and responsibly made, turn out to be contingently incapable of both being kept. In such cases, whichever commitment I fulfill, another will have been neglected. Bishop (1987, 13ff.) discusses the importance of taking the longer view of such cases.

12. A number of widely known essays which debate the issues about dilemmas and moral remainders are collected in Gowans (1987).

13. A moral epistemology of the sort described finds common or overlapping cause with a number of other contemporary deviations from dominant views. For critics of impartiality on behalf of the personal life, see Williams (1981), Blum (1980), and Stocker (1976). On interrogating moral views for their concrete social and historical conditions, see MacIntyre (1981). For insistence on the primacy of judgments in particular cases, see the new Aristotelians, Nussbaum (1986), and Wiggins (1978). For other versions of "responsibility ethics" which situate moral claims in relational structures of power and dependency, see Goodin (1985) and Jonas (1984). On morality as a tissue of acknowledgments and refusals, see Cavell (1979, Parts 3 and 4). And on morality as constituted by social practices and as expressive of relations of authority in, respectively, a Marxist and a Wittgensteinian-Hegelian vein see Skillen (1978) and Lovibond (1983). All these may be, used selectively, resources for a different kind of ethics. Yet feminists might remain wary of unwanted residues and omissions in some of these views.

14. On the political aspects of construction and deployment of modes of rationality and styles of thought with respect to gender, see essays by Ruddick, Addelson, and Harding in Kittay and Meyers (1987). See also Calhoun (1988) for a discussion of the way philosophers' neglect of certain topics reinforces moral ideologies.

15. In this connection see Skillen (1978, Chapter 4) on both Kantian and utilitarian disciplinarianism and Williams (1985, Chapter 6) on Sidgwickian "government house utilitarianism."

16. Baier (1986; 1987) is particularly humane and lucid on this topic.

17. Special thanks to Sandra Bartky for very good suggestions on an earlier and briefer draft of this paper, and to the editors and readers for helpful suggestion

References

Addelson, Kathryn. 1987. Moral passages. In *Women and moral theory.* Eva Feder Kittay and Diana T. Meyers, eds. Totowa, New Jersey: Rowman and Littlefield.

Allen, Jeffner. 1986. *Lesbian philosophy: Explorations.* Palo Alto, California: Institute of Lesbian Studies.

Baier, Annette. 1985. What do women want in a moral theory? *Nous* 19: 53–63.

Baier, Annette. 1986. Trust and anti-trust. *Ethics* 96: 231–260.

Baier, Annette. 1987. The need for more than justice. In *Science, morality & feminist theory.* Marsha Hanen and Kai Nielsen, eds. Calgary, Canada: University of Calgary Press.

Benhabib, Seyla. 1987. The generalized and the concrete other. In *Women and moral theory.* Eva Feder Kittay and Diana T. Meyers, eds. Totowa, New Jersey: Rowman and Littlefield.

Bishop, Sharon. 1987. Connections and guilt. *Hypatia* 2(1):7–23.

Blum, Lawrence. 1980. *Friendship, altruism and morality.* London: Routledge & Kegan Paul.

Calhoun, Cheshire. 1988. Justice, care, gender bias. *The Journal of Philosophy* 85: 451–463.

Card, Claudia. 1985. Virtues and moral luck. Working Series I, No. 4, Institute for Legal Studies, University of Wisconsin, Madison, Law School.

Cavell, Stanley. 1979. *The claim of reason.* Oxford: Oxford University Press.

Code, Lorraine. 1987. Second persons. In *Science, morality & feminist theory.* Marsha Hanen and Kai Nielsen, eds. Calgary, Canada: University of Calgary Press.

Diamond, Cora. 1983. Having a rough story about what moral philosophy is. *New Literary History* 15: 155–169.

Friedman, Marilyn. 1987. Beyond caring: The de-moralization of gender. In *Science, morality & feminist theory*. Marsha Hanen and Kai Nielsen, eds. Calgary, Canada: University of Calgary Press.

Gilligan, Carol. 1982. *In a different voice*. Cambridge: Harvard University Press.

Gilligan, Carol. 1984. The conquistador and the dark continent: Reflections on the psychology of love. *Daedalus* 113: 75–95.

Goodin, Robert. 1985. *Protecting the vulnerable*. Chicago: University of Chicago Press.

Gowans, Christopher. 1987. *Moral dilemmas*. New York: Oxford University Press.

Grimshaw, Jean. 1986. *Philosophy and feminist thinking*. Minneapolis: University of Minnesota Press.

Hanen, Marsha and Kai Nielsen, eds. 1987. *Science, morality & feminist theory*. Calgary, Canada: University of Calgary Press.

Held, Virginia. 1987. Feminism and moral theory. In *Women and moral theory*. Eva Feder Kittay and Diana T. Meyers, eds. Totowa, New Jersey: Rowman and Littlefield.

Houston, Barbara. 1987. Rescuing womanly virtues: Some dangers of moral reclamation. In *Science, morality & feminist theory*. Marsha Hanen and Kai Nielsen, eds. Calgary, Canada: University of Calgary Press.

Jonas, Hans. 1984. *The imperative of responsibility*. Chicago: University of Chicago Press.

Kerber, Linda, et al. 1986. On *In a different voice:* An interdisciplinary forum. *Signs* 11: 304–333.

Kittay, Eva Feder and Diana T. Meyers, eds. 1987. *Women and moral theory*. Totowa, New Jersey: Rowman and Littlefield.

Lovibond, Sabina. 1983. *Realism and imagination in ethics*. Minneapolis: University of Minnesota Press.

MacIntyre, Alasdair. 1981. *After virtue*. Notre Dame, Indiana: University of Notre Dame Press.

Michaels, Meredith. 1986. Morality without distinction. *The Philosophical Forum* 17: 175–187.

Murdoch, Iris. [1970] 1985. *The sovereignty of good*. London: Routledge & Kegan Paul.

Nails, Debra, Mary Ann O'Loughlin and James C. Walker, eds. 1983. *Social research* 50.

Noddings, Nel. 1984. *Caring: A feminine approach to ethics and moral education*. Berkeley and Los Angeles: University of California Press.

Nussbaum, Martha. 1983. Flawed crystals: James's *The golden bowl* and literature as moral philosophy. *New Literary History* 15: 25–50.

Nussbaum, Martha. 1986. *The fragility of goodness*. Cambridge: Cambridge University Press.

Rich, Adrienne. 1976. *Of woman born*. New York: W. W. Norton & Company.

Rich, Adrienne. 1979. *On lies, secrets, and silence*. New York: W. W. Norton & Company.

Ruddick, Sara. 1984. Maternal Thinking. In *Mothering*. Joyce Trebilcot, ed. Totowa, New Jersey: Rowman and Allanheld.

Sidgwick, Henry. [1907] 1981. *The methods of ethics*. Indianapolis: Hackett Publishing.

Skillen, Anthony. 1978. *Ruling illusions*. Atlantic Highlands, New Jersey: Humanities Press.

Stocker, Michael. 1976. The schizophrenia of modern ethical theories. *The Journal of Philosophy* 73: 453–466.

Whitbeck, Caroline. 1983. A different reality: Feminist ontology. In *Beyond domination*. Carol C. Gould, ed. Totowa, New Jersey: Rowman and Allanheld.

Wiggins, David. 1978. Deliberation and practical reason. In *Practical reasoning.* Joseph
    Raz, ed. Oxford: Oxford University Press.
Williams, Bernard. 1981. *Moral luck.* Cambridge: Cambridge University Press.
Williams, Bernard. 1985. *Ethics and the limits of philosophy.* Cambridge: Harvard
    University Press.

9

Feminist Moral Inquiry and the Feminist Future [1993]

VIRGINIA HELD

In historical terms, feminist inquiry is in its infancy. Of course we have not yet adequately worked out feminist moral theories with which to live our lives. And of course we are still groping for adequately developed views of the deep and fundamental ways in which culture and the organization of society and the pursuit of scientific knowledge will all have to be changed to be compatible with feminist morality. Feminist moral inquiry is an ongoing process that will need to continue far into the future. To get our methodological bearings in this process is a good first step.

Most feminists see morality as a matter of practice and art as well as of knowledge. Practice is involved both in understanding what we ought to do and in carrying out the norms of morality. I share this view, and I take moral inquiry to involve activity and feeling as well as thought and observation. Moral inquiry involves living our lives and actively shaping our relationships with others rather than accurately registering and theorizing about the impressions made upon us by what some take to be an external world. To engage in the development of feminist morality is to seek to improve practices in which knowledge is only one component, though an important one. It is to cultivate the art of living a life as admirable for women as for men.

Moral theories, I believe, should give us guidance in confronting the problems of actual life in the highly imperfect societies in which we live. We need moral theories about what to do and what to accept here and now. Ideal theories of perfect justice or purely rational theories for ideal societies leave the problems of what to do here and now unsolved, even unaddressed.

In my view, not only must moral theories be applicable to actual problems, they must in some way be "tested" in actual experience.[1] They must be made to confront lived reality; they must be found satisfactory in the actual situations people find themselves in. Otherwise they are intellectual exercises that may be intriguing and impressively coherent, but they are not adequate as *moral theories*.

The method of moral inquiry for which I argue makes room for what I call "moral experience." This is quite different from the "experience" of most philosophical writing, in ethics as well as in epistemology, where the term refers to empirical experience. Empirical observation is of course part of experience, but so is choosing what to do, so is the experience of feeling either disapproval or empathy, and so is the awareness that we share social relationships with other persons. In my view, moral theories need to be found to withstand the trials of actual moral experience, which is not at all the same as to advocate naturalistic moral theories that can meet the tests of empirical experience. To the extent that moral theories include judgments about empirical matters, the empirical component should of course be empirically accurate. But moral theories are not empirical theories; they address themselves to questions about what we *ought* to do, and they judge outcomes and feelings in distinctively *moral* terms.

Moral experience is the experience of consciously choosing to act, or to refrain from acting, on grounds by which we are trying conscientiously to be guided. *Moral* experience is the experience of accepting or rejecting moral positions for what we take to be good moral reasons or well-founded moral intuitions or on the basis of what we take to be justifiable moral feelings. *Moral* experience is the experience of approving or disapproving of actions or states of affairs of which we are aware and of evaluating the feelings we have and the relationships we are in. And it is experience as subjectively engaged in, not as studied by a scientific observer.

This view of moral experience and its relation to moral theory is entirely compatible with and strengthened by a feminist view of experience. The central category of feminist thought, at least in its contemporary phase, is experience. It is not the constricted experience of mere empirical observation. It is the lived experience of feeling as well as thinking, of acting as well as receiving impressions, and of connectedness to other persons as well as of self. Time and time again, feminist inquiry begins here and returns to the experience of women so inadequately reflected in the thought that has been taken as standard, which we can now so often recognize as constructed from points of view privileged in terms of gender as well as of race, class, and culture.

As Catharine Stimpson observes, "The trust in women's experience in North American feminist writing has been as common and as pervasive as city noise."[2] And Catharine MacKinnon writes of feminism that "its project is to uncover and claim as valid the experience of women."[3]

It is from experience that we adopt our critical stance toward what has been claimed as "knowledge" in male-dominated society. It is experience with which we confront and protest existing institutions and distributions of power. It is experience on which we trace suggested patterns for the future. And, I believe, it is moral experience to which we are now subjecting traditional moral theories and our own proposals for how we ought to live.

Moral experience, as I understand it, includes the sort of judgment we arrive at independently of moral theory. It includes the sort of choices we make about how to act, arrived at independently of general moral judgments to which we think we are committed. Sometimes we already have moral theories or general judgments recommending how we ought to act, and we act in accordance with them and judge that we acted rightly. Or, if we fail to act in accordance with them, we judge that we acted wrongly, out of weakness of will perhaps, but we maintain our belief in the theory or judgment. At other times, we choose to act because that particular act seems right to us regardless of any moral theory or abstract generality. And sometimes we continue to suppose that the particular act was morally justified. This may then require us to revise our moral beliefs because the act we judge right conflicts with what a theory we previously thought satisfactory would recommend. But rather than suppose that the act was wrong because the theory said so, we might *justifiably* retain the judgment arrived at in the moral experience of acting, and we might reject the theory. And if this is part of a sincerely pursued process of trying to develop a coherent network of moral beliefs by which to be guided, it need not be thought of as rationalization, but rather as part of an appropriate internal dialogue aiming to continually improve one's moral understanding.

Certainly not all our experience can serve as the kind of "test" of theory I am discussing. And the experience that can so serve need not be actively sought; sometimes we stumble upon an experience that clashes with our previous moral beliefs.[4] What is needed is that the moral inquirer interpret the experience, either before, during, or after its occurrence, as such a test and interpret the perspective in question, whichever it is, as the most valid.

This method resembles to some extent that of John Rawls's "reflective equilibrium" with a very significant difference.[5] The judgments between which equilibrium is to be sought will in my view deliberately include rather than deliberately exclude particular judgments based on feelings and arrived at in actual circumstances in which we are not necessarily impartial. This is a difference that also distinguishes the method I advocate from the "wide reflective equilibrium" frequently discussed among philosophers interested in moral theory.

"Reflective equilibrium" requires that coherence be sought between our particular judgments (about justice, for instance) and our general normative principles (of justice, for instance). "Wide reflective equilibrium" requires that these be coherent as well with our background philosophical ways of thinking—with contractualism, say, for those who find it persuasive—and with our reasons for subscribing to them.[6]

Rawls counsels us to seek equilibrium between our particular "considered" judgments and our general principles, such as our principles of justice and equality. He offers his principles of justice as a means for us to do so. But he counsels us to admit into our pool of "considered judgments" only those which have been laundered of their entanglements with self-interested or other emotional colorings. Rawls thinks we should discount any judgments we make "when we are upset or frightened, or when we stand to gain one way or the other."[7] I argue, in contrast, that judgments based on feelings can and should be included among those between which we seek coherence.

The Process of Moral Inquiry

Moral inquiry is an ongoing process. To see it as rational reflection providing theory, followed by the straightforward application of that theory to particular cases, is surely unsatisfactory. Rather, it should be seen as a process of continual adjustment of theory in the light of moral experience, as well as of particular judgments and actions in the light of theory.

I worked out these views some years ago chiefly in connection with examples of political decisions taken on moral grounds, such as whether to engage in civil disobedience to protest the war in Vietnam or whether government has an obligation to provide basic necessities for the poor and unemployed.

My first explorations into feminist moral theory were approached as if this were a new topic, and I remained unclear for some time about how to mesh moral theory developed from a feminist point of view with what I took to be moral theory as such, from any point of view. But gradually I came to recognize that what could be thought of as the methodology implicit in feminist moral theory coincided closely with what I had come to believe should be the method of moral inquiry appropriate from any point of view.

For instance, one of the claims made by many feminist moral theorists is that room must be made for what some call the moral emotions. The rationalism of many traditional moral theories, both the pure rationalism of Kantian ethics and the calculating rationalism of utilitarian approaches, is suspect in its denigration of emotion, in its advocacy of morality as involving a suppression of the emotions or a distancing of the self from feelings that may cloud what a rational man would hold or what an ideal observer would judge.

Feminists often insist on the importance of the emotions in moral understanding.[8] We value emotion not only in the way traditional moral theories do—as feelings to be cultivated to help us carry out the dictates of reason or as preferences setting goals toward which utilitarian calculations will recommend rational means. Although such theorists as Mill and Rawls applaud the cultivation of certain appropriate feelings, they value these feelings for their assistance in carrying out the requirements of morality, not in helping us to understand what these requirements are. And although utilitarianism and rational choice theory recognize the emotions as giving us the desires whose satisfaction we should seek to maximize, emotions are to be discounted in calculating how we morally ought to act so as to maximize the satisfaction of these desires among all those affected.

Many feminists argue, in contrast, that the emotions have an important function in developing moral understanding itself, in helping us decide what the recommendations of morality themselves ought to be. Feelings, they say, should be respected by morality rather than dismissed as lacking impartiality. Yes, there are morally harmful emotions, such as prejudice, hatred, desire for revenge, blind egotism, and so forth. But to rid moral theory of harmful emotions by banishing all emotion is misguided. Such emotions as empathy, concern for others, hopefulness, and indignation in the face of cruelty—all these may be crucial in developing appropriate moral positions. An adequate moral theory should be built on appropriate feelings as well as on appropriate reasoning. And that such a view requires us to suppose we already understand what feelings are appropriate is no more insurmountable an obstacle than that other views require us to suppose we already understand what train of reasoning is appropriate for morality. *Some* circularity may be inescapable on any plausible view of inquiry.

The emphasis of many feminists working in ethics and in moral development is on the concerns and implications of *caring:* caring for children, caring for the ill or infirm, caring about the feelings of others, and understanding how to care for human beings, including ourselves, enmeshed as we are in human relationships, and finally, also, caring about the globe. The caring so central here is partly emotional. It involves feelings and requires high degrees of empathy to enable us to discern what morality recommends in our caring activities.

Many philosophers emphasize the way reason and emotion are interconnected, pointing out that reasoning characteristically has an affective component and that our emotions characteristically have a cognitive content.[9] I am inclined to keep the concepts distinct for the sake of descriptive clarity but to acknowledge that the human moral experience against which we should test our moral theories characteristically involves both feeling and thought experienced together.

The practice of mothering brings out the way reason and emotion are entwined in the task of what Sara Ruddick names "preservative love":

> Rather than separating reason from feeling, mothering makes reflective feeling one of the most difficult attainments of reason. In protective work, feeling, thinking, and action are conceptually linked; feelings demand reflection, which is in turn tested by the feelings it provokes. Thoughtful feeling, passionate thought, and protective acts together test, even as they reveal, the effectiveness of preservative love.[10]

Returning to the method of moral inquiry sketched before, one can see how well it incorporates the feminist concern for emotion along with reason and the feminist appreciation of appropriate feelings. This method holds that when particular judgments are arrived at independently of moral theory, they may justifiably include judgments based on the feelings of care and concern that we experience. Instead of dismissing judgments based on such feelings as incompatible with the demands of impartial reason, the method of moral inquiry I advocate should develop theories that are capable of being as compatible with these particular judgments as with abstract principles divorced from emotional experience.

Experience and Impartiality

Let's consider the concern a parent may feel for her child. Plato, in *The Republic*, is perhaps the best known of those for whom parental feelings are seen as a threat to the moral well-being of the whole society, at which well-being the members of the society ought to aim. Hegel, appreciating women's devotion to our families but finding it threatening to the state, writes that the state "creates for itself in what it suppresses and what it depends upon an internal enemy—womankind in general."[11]

Many other moral theorists suggest that such feelings as parental concern are at best irrelevant to morality. They are simply part of the empirical given within which morality makes its recommendations. A Kantian approach will, for instance, from the perspective of pure reason, indicate what obligations to respect other persons any one person owes any other. Special feelings of affection between a parent and child are among the emotional attitudes to be discounted as a parent reasons about what the Categorical Imperative requires. *It* may require that all parents provide their children, to the best of their ability, with such necessities as food and shelter. But then the moral course of action would be to do so out of respect for the moral law, not because of parental feelings of affection. A utilitarian theory may also calculate that for parents to provide for their children will be conducive to maximizing the happiness of all, counting each person's happiness as of equal worth. But again, the judgment of what a parent ought to do will be based on the principle of utility, rationally applied, not on parental feelings except to the extent that the satisfaction of them enters into the calculation.

Feminist moral theorists might share the views of Charles Fried[12] and Bernard Williams[13] that the requirements of moral impartiality should not always be dominant and that one may give special consideration to one's spouse or child, but the feminist interpretation is apt to be different from that of nonfeminists. Instead of an individual man and his projects or attachments as the contrasting model opposing the dominance of impartiality, feminists tend to focus on relationships that contrast with impersonal impartiality and that are at least partially constitutive of the individuals in them.[14]

Feminist moral theories tend to acknowledge as central, rather than overlook or even condemn, relationships between actual persons. Hegel recognized relationships between parents and children and found the guarding of them appropriate for women, but he feared them as subversive of morality for male citizens, whose primary loyalty should be to the universal rationality realizable, in his view, only at the level of the state.[15] Other moral theories see family relationships as the natural bonds from which a rational individual will seek to free himself insofar as he is deciding what morality requires and is acting morally; the ideal of autonomy makes suspect relationships that are permanent and not chosen. Still other moral theories overlook family relationships altogether, employing such individualistic categories that relationships between persons become all but invisible.

In contrast, feminist moral theories almost never lose sight of such bonds as those of friendship and those that link parents and children. A feminist perspective would almost surely suggest that a parent who did not act to protect her own child might damage her relationship with that child in morally unacceptable ways. If we employ the method of moral inquiry recommended above, no moral theory would be acceptable that required a parent to disregard the relationship between her and her child or to fail to consider the health of that *relationship*, based as it needs to be on trust and concern. Moral theories would have to be tested for acceptability in the light of just those particular judgments of actual experience that might be based on a strong sense of the value of relationships between parents and children and on feelings about the importance of a child's trust.

Where the conflict is between actual relationship and abstract principle, a feminist approach to morality might give a felt relationship of trust priority over principle and seek a morality compatible with this priority.

Actual versus Hypothetical Experience

Another way in which a feminist approach to moral inquiry seems to differ from dominant approaches is in its greater reliance on actual rather than on hypothetical experience. Traditional moral theory is frequently built on what a person might be thought to hold from the point of view of a hypothetical ideal observer, or a hypothetical purely rational being. Morality is to reflect what Thomas Nagel calls "the view from nowhere."[16] A hypothetical moral being is thought able to distance himself from the particular selfish interests and distorting passions of actual, embodied human beings, located in particular social and historical contexts. Feminists have often been critical of these attempts to ignore the reality of embodiment. As Susan Bordo puts it, the view from nowhere embodies the ideal of being everywhere, and the individual who is everywhere is necessarily disembodied. And as Alison Jaggar argues, "We must never forget that consent given hypothetically is never the moral equivalent of actual consent. Constructions of hypothetical consent have no independent moral force, any more than hypothetical experiments have independent evidential force."[17]

The method of moral inquiry I advocate relies on actual rather than hypothetical moral experience. It is suspicious of the inapplicability or remoteness of the theory developed from a hypothetical point of view, and it is critical of the

inability of such theory to address actual moral problems as they arise for embodied, feeling human beings in specific historical and social contexts. In its development of relevant theory through a process of revising general principles in
the light of particular judgments, it values the particular judgments arrived at in
actual experience over those imagined to be acceptable in hypothetical circumstances.

Feminist moral inquiry often relies on actual, lived, moral experience. It pays
attention to the neglected experience of women and to such a woefully neglected though enormous area of human moral experience as that of mothering.
It attends to the actual experience of suffering domestic violence, of being conceptualized in terms of one's sexual availability or capacity to please men, of being exploited in the provision of care and affection. It suggests that moral theory
will be adequate only if it can address moral problems in this kind of actual experience as well as any other. And feminist moral inquiry suggests that women
must be listened to as we express our actual experience and our efforts to act
morally and to arrive at morally sound judgments in our actual, not hypothetical, lives.

Most feminist moral theory rejects a pure reliance on particular judgments.
General principles are recognized as necessary.[18] For instance, principles demanding equal respect for women and an end to gender oppression are basic to
almost all feminist theory. Feminist moral theory is thus seldom a kind of situation ethic; it does not embrace a pure case-by-case approach.[19] Neither is it
characteristically relativistic.[20] But it does suggest that the principles that might
be found adequate by feminist moral inquiry will have to be compatible with
particular judgments based, often enough, on feelings of empathy and on caring concern rather than on rational calculation or abstract reasoning. And it
does suggest that these judgments should be arrived at in actual rather than hypothetical experience, in the kind of experience which acknowledges the embodied and relational reality of human beings in actual historical contexts.

One way moral theory based on impartial rationality has managed to overlook
its unsuitability for much human moral experience has been through supposing
that emotional ties and interactions between family members are not matters of
moral import because they belong to the realm of "nature" rather than to the
realm of "morality." A mother caring for a child, for instance, has been supposed
to be acting on natural sentiment rather than moral principle. Behavior thus
"governed" by natural impulses and not subject to moral deliberation is then
treated as "outside morality." But how can the care of children possibly be imagined to lie outside morality? A parent trying to decide when to punish and when
to forgive, or how to divide her attention between several children, or what
ideals to hold up to her child, is of course engaged in acting morally. Certainly
she is involved in moral deliberation. That this whole vast region of human experience can have been dismissed as "natural" and thus as irrelevant to morality
is extraordinary. It may be outside moralities built entirely on abstract rational-

ity, modeled as these are on an abstraction of the supposed "public" realm. But that only shows how deficient these moralities are for the full range of human moral experience. This is not to say that rationality should be abandoned; it is to say that rationality must be tried out in and revised in the light of moral experience and must be supplemented by the moral understanding that can only be cultivated by embodied, empathetic actual persons.

The moral experience in which the principles of morality should be tried out, and revised in the light of, must include not only those regions traditionally thought of as providing arenas for moral choice and application—the regions of law and state and public policy—but also such neglected regions as those of friendship and of the family, of bringing up children and caring for the vulnerable. Then, it seems, to decide *what* morality counsels will require a much richer experience than that available to the abstract agent of so much traditional moral theory. We do not play with our children out of respect for the moral law. Though the moral law may provide moral minimums beneath which we should not sink, flourishing childhoods and joyful friendships rest on a wide range of moral considerations beyond what the moral law requires.

The experience needed for morality is the experience of persons who are at least partly constituted by relations with other persons, not autonomous individual agents as such. What we may look to morality to provide is guidance as we navigate within our actual, embodied, historically located relationships. The morality that will then give us unqualified reasons to act, when it can give us reasons at all, will be quite different from what would be prescribed for innumerable autonomous but essentially abstract and timeless and nonexistent individuals.

A Morality of Contexts

The moral theory that would result from reliance on a feminist method of moral inquiry would be highly unlikely to proclaim any single, simple principle such as the Categorical Imperative or the Principle of Utility as applicable to all moral problems. Much more likely would be a pluralistic ethics, containing some principles at an intermediate level of generality, relevant to given domains, and many particular judgments sensitively arrived at in these various domains. For instance, principles about how conflict ought to be settled nonviolently could be offered for small numbers of persons: children in a household, adolescents in school, rivals for a lover's affection. Different contexts might have different procedures. Principles advocating nonviolence would also be offered for conflicts among large numbers of persons, such as ethnic groups, and for methods of achieving social change. The principle would be more sound if approached from the point of view of those experienced with the former, rather than solely from the point of view of purely rational, nonexistent beings. As Sara Ruddick has shown in *Maternal Thinking,* the context of mothering can be a fruitful source of insight concerning how peace should be sought in other domains. And moral principles need to be appropriate for given domains, not so remote and abstract as to lose sight of the differences between different contexts and between the persons and groups in them.

Even principles that are only at an intermediate level of generality may be of no more than tentative use in interpreting actual complex moral problems. Sensitivity to a wide range of moral considerations may often be more important than rigid adherence to principle. While the dangers of arbitrary ad hoc decisions are real, so are the dangers of distorting actual situations in order to fit them into the abstract legalistic categories of general principles. Persons cannot increase the trust between them by misinterpreting each others' problems and pains.

It is quite true that subordinate groups have often used an abstract, clear principle of equality to argue against their subordination. They have not taken issue with the principle of equality but have argued that a widely accepted principle should apply to a previously excluded group—that their members are also entitled to the equality that has been denied them. In such cases, a call by the dominant group to recognize the complexity of particular situations is often used to distract the aggrieved and to excuse the exclusion, and should be rejected. In such cases, clear principles can be of the utmost importance. But as soon as we try to interpret what equality may require in given contexts, we must move beyond the abstract principle to a consideration of particular factors.[21] And we see that such principles can give us, at most, a view of certain moral minimums which have a high priority but which hardly constitute an adequate morality.

By now, many moral theorists have gone on to suggest, in behalf of previously subordinated groups, that there is more to an adequate morality than can be seen from the point of view of the autonomous individual agent as such, the rational man of liberal theory. What more is needed is not merely an optional extra which liberal theory can permit those so inclined to pursue. As Annette Baier explains, "The liberal morality, if unsupplemented, may *unfit* people to be anything other than what its justifying theories suppose them to be, ones who have no interest in each others' interests."[22] And such people will be unfit to care for and bring up with appropriate affection and concern the next generation in a suitably cared-for environment.

Feminist morality will develop its principles with awareness of the differences between the contexts for which such principles are deemed suitable and with attention to the moral experience of those actually in such contexts. It will be more open than theories which rely on a single, simple, universal moral principle that can be invoked for every moral problem.

Traditional approaches to moral theory often suggest that where individuals and groups have conflicting views on what ought to be done and how people ought to act, what they may be able to agree on are abstract principles, especially procedural ones, arrived at from the point of view of the abstract, rational individual. Thus John Rawls writes that "while men may put forth excessive demands on one another, they nevertheless acknowledge a common point of view from which their claims may be adjudicated."[23] From that point of view he offers his principles of justice as what would be agreed to. And Alan Gewirth, seeking even more clearly a moral rather than a merely political consensus, observes that "widely different ideals and conceptions of well-being and benefit have been upheld as morally relevant, right, or good by different persons or groups."[24] He argues that a supreme moral principle based entirely on the reasoning available to the rational individual is the only satisfactory solution to such conflict, and he offers his version of such a principle.

Many feminists, in contrast, suggest that agreement is much more likely, and much more likely to be satisfactory, if it rests on actual dialogue between actual persons. Iris Young defends a "dialogic conception of normative reason":

> Precisely because there is no impartial point of view in which a subject stands detached and dispassionate to assess all perspectives, to arrive at an objective and complete understanding of an issue or experience, all perspectives and participants must contribute to its discussion. Thus dialogic reason ought to imply reasons as contextualized, where answers are the outcome of a plurality of perspectives that cannot be reduced to unity. In discussion speakers need not abandon their particular perspective nor bracket their motives and feelings. As long as the dialogue allows all perspectives to speak freely, and be heard and taken into account, the expression of need, motive and feelings will not have merely private significance, and will not bias or distort the conclusions because they will interact with other needs, motives and feelings.[25]

And in an influential article on how to develop feminist theory that avoids cultural imperialism on the part of white Anglo women, Maria Lugones and Elizabeth Spelman present the voice of a woman of color:

> If white/Anglo women are to understand our voices, they must understand our communities and us in them . . . From within friendship you may be moved by friendship to undergo the very difficult task of understanding the text of our cultures by understanding our lives in our communities . . . [This learning] does not consist in a passive immersion in our cultures, but in a striving to understand what it is that our voices are saying. Only then can we engage in a mutual dialogue that does not reduce each one of us to instances of the abstraction called "woman."[26]

These calls do not ask that we all agree to take the point of view of the abstract rational man, or woman, but that we listen to each other in actual conversations in actual communities.

Many women of color have felt that in the women's movement in the United States, relatively privileged white women were presuming to speak for all women and that the claims made were often distorted versions of the experience of various minorities. The book entitled *All the Women Are White, All the Blacks Are Men, But Some of Us Are Brave: Black Women's Studies* is an example of black women expressing this resentment and seeking to give voice to actual experience.[27] By now many of us have learned to listen to each other across the divisions of race and class and ethnicity. The understanding we seek may be much more likely to arise out of actual conversation (some of it on paper) than out of a search for abstract principles to be chosen from the point of view of what some of us might think of as "woman as such."

It may well be that for *some* types of moral problems, the point of view of the autonomous agent as such *is* morally appropriate. But to make such a judgment we need a fuller and richer and more nuanced view of morality within which to decide that we have unqualified reasons to treat some but *not* all moral problems in that way. And the search for *that* morality and *its* justification must continue. A feminist approach offers better prospects for achieving such a morality than its predecessors.

The Decline of the Past

Lamentations about the decline of the social order, or Western Civilization, or the United States, abound. We are told repeatedly that stability is crumbling, that the center cannot hold, that the sources of authority have been undermined.

Although there are indeed extremely serious problems plaguing the United States, and Western civilization, and the world, it is often unclear how much such lamentations reflect genuine concern about the difficulties of confronting such problems, and how much they reflect nostalgia for unchallenged dominance by established male elites.[28]

Andreas Huyssen's description of turn-of-the-century associations between fear of the masses and fear of the feminine lends support to this conjecture. Over and over, the masses were identified with women, true culture with men:

> The notion . . . gained ground during the nineteenth century that mass culture is somehow associated with woman while real, authentic culture remains the prerogative of men . . . When the 19th and early 20th centuries conjured up the threat of the masses 'rattling at the gate,' to quote Hall . . . the masses knocking at the gate were also women . . . It is indeed striking to observe how the political, psychological, and aesthetic discourse around the turn of the century consistently and obsessively genders mass culture and the masses as feminine, while high culture, whether traditional or modern, clearly remains the privileged realm of male activities.[29]

Perhaps many of the changes we are seeing in contemporary society and culture reflect the decline of male dominance. It is probably true that the conceptual order of the barracks community is threatened, that the stability of masculine supremacy is being undermined, and that the traditional hierarchy of gender is in danger. Male dominance is surely being challenged. Few feminists will lament the decline of the old order of gender or pay heed to the attempts of some defenders of that order to blame feminism for the problems of the contemporary world. Feminists are indeed in the process of reshaping human relationships and rebuilding human lives; women are indeed changing our relationships with men, with children, with each other, and with the world. All the structures of thought that permeate human life and all the social arrangements that uphold male dominance are being reevaluated. But this is a promising renewal, an occasion for hope. If we are entering a postpatriarchal era, an era in which male domination will be overturned, that will be reason for rejoicing.

The changes which feminism and the women's movement have brought about in recent years and throughout the world have been revolutionary.[30] But they have involved on the part of women little vengeance and virtually no violence. They have built on the experience of women, on the practices and traditions of women reflectively analyzed, and on the thought and imagination of feminism experimentally put into practice. These changes have the potential to transform culture and thus society and to create a future that will be better for all children.

The threat of violence against women seeking change is real and alarming, but violence against women has been there all along. Means are being developed to combat it more effectively than in the past and to keep it from being concealed. Revolutions, it is true, cannot occur without pain, and women, as well as men, have suffered it. But by now very many women can attest to the changes having been well worth the pain. And many men are coming to appreciate rather than to resist the experience of mutuality with women and the joys of building such better relationships with their children as can only be achieved through involvement in their daily care. Many men want to share in developing the feminist future; those who do not may well be left behind.

The Future of Feminist Moral Inquiry

If we begin with the recommendations of feminist morality and include the rethinking of culture and society and politics implied by them, what might their implications be for the future?

I argued in my book *Rights and Goods* that we need different moral approaches for different domains of society, and those arguments seem still valid. The type of moral approach suitable for respecting rights in a legal context is not the best type for choosing various governmental policies. And the type of moral approach suitable for decisions in an economic marketplace is not the type best suited to decisions among family members and friends. I advocated a division of moral labor in which we would accept different moral considerations as salient for different domains of human activity, and I tried to delineate the approaches suitable for various domains.

However, such a view still leaves us with the difficulty of integrating the various approaches recommended and deciding which approach to follow for a specific problem when the approaches seem to conflict. It can be a serious diffi-culty, and we can hope that perhaps a feminist approach to morality can provide the framework or the more comprehensive moral theory within which the more specialized approaches can be fitted. But can feminist moral theory serve in this way to unify other approaches? Can it incorporate, for instance, a Kantian ap-proach for law, a utilitarian approach for public policy, an approach permitting a considerable degree of self-interested choice in the marketplace, and so forth? Can a feminist morality provide the sorts of recommendations suitable for those domains in which women have not been the primary moral agents, or will it be limited to such domains as the family, early education, and caring for the sick and elderly? Can feminist moral theory be the sort of theory that can, where nonfeminist theory cannot, appropriately provide recommendations for all do-mains and all contexts?

At the very least, feminist moral approaches will elevate to moral significance those contexts and problems neglected by nonfeminist moral theory, requiring that *any* moral theory claiming to be applicable to all moral problems be scruti-nized for its suitability for handling problems within the family, and in the con-text of giving care. Many traditional moral theories will fail this test. But feminist moral approaches will be more ambitious: they will ask for a reconsideration of all those other domains, such as of law and state and market, where moral prin-ciples recommended by nonfeminist moral theories have been thought applica-ble. They will ask how these domains might have to be reconstructed and trans-formed in the light of feminist approaches to morality. Since the latter are characteristically respectful of context, they may well allow what appear to be various traditional moral principles to be salient in various particular domains, if they can be embedded in a wider approach compatible with feminist con-cerns. But feminist approaches are not likely to lose sight of the way these prin-ciples should be limited to particular domains rather than generalized to all moral problems. To argue, for instance, that utilitarian recommendations to maximize the preference satisfaction of individuals can be suitable for certain governmental policy choices is not at all to subscribe to a utilitarian moral the-ory for all moral problems. But a feminist approach to morality might agree that after its requirements and most urgent goals had been met—for the flourishing of children, say—then perhaps utilitarian principles would be the appropriate ones to employ in a limited region of human activity. This would, however, be because utilitarian principles in this domain could be justified in terms of femi-nist moral inquiry, not because, as utilitarianism has characteristically claimed, the right course of action is always just what will maximize the satisfaction of in-dividuals.

Since feminist approaches to morality are suspicious of rather than eager to offer highly abstract theories and simple principles, they are more likely to em-phasize methods of moral inquiry and processes of moral improvement than to propound finished, comprehensive theories. But feminist approaches to moral-ity will seek, I believe, to develop patterns of moral concern and expression suitable for any and all contexts. Then, within these patterns, more limited recommendations may be acceptable for particular domains.

For instance, a feminist approach might hold that within a pattern of morality recognizing a more satisfactory, relational concept of persons, it is acceptable to treat persons, in some contexts and some of the time, as if the artificially abstract individualistic terms of the Kantian and utilitarian traditions were satisfactory for that domain. As long as we do not lose sight of the way we are abstracting from reality, and as long as we keep our understanding of the limited aspects of this way of thinking, we may find the use of individualistic liberal conceptions to be a helpful device.

Similar arguments could be made about various nonfeminist moral principles. Such abstract principles as those of freedom and equality may well be acceptable for various domains if embedded in patterns of morality arrived at through the course of feminist moral inquiry. But what the latter can be expected to provide is an understanding of which principles are suitable for which contexts, and why traditional nonfeminist moral principles that have been claimed to be universally valid are often not suitable for many contexts when the experience of women is accorded its proper due.

Let us now try to develop further what some feminist recommendations for the future might include.

Conceptualizing Feminist Society

First, how should we conceptualize feminist society? The major prefeminist conceptions include three alternative views.

(1) Law is supreme. Whatever the law does not forbid, it permits; thus law covers everything. The state has a monopoly on the legitimate use of violence to uphold law. The state enforces law and thus has ultimate authority in the society. Economic activity and cultural production and education are permitted to develop under law as participants in them choose; they are not directly controlled by the state but may be regulated by it. Government is legitimate only if it rests on the consent of the governed (who are formally or effectively male heads of household); when it does, it is supreme. This is a picture of society offered by, among others, the liberal tradition of political thought.

(2) The economic base determines everything else in society. A capitalist economic system will have a capitalist state, law that upholds capitalist economic relations, and a government that reflects the economic interests of the dominant class. Cultural production and educational institutions will be structured to reinforce the economic system. Society is built on an economic foundation and the means and relations of production in this foundation bring about the characteristics of other segments of society. This is the model of society provided, roughly, by Marxist analyses.

(3) The segments of society are overlapping but relatively independent; none determines or is supreme over all others. The political system can be distinguished from the economic system, but neither determines the other; other segments of society such as the cultural or the educational are also distinguishable and relatively independent. Society is seen as pluralistic with multiple sources of influence. Interests conflict; none overpower with regularity. A number of recent empirical theories in sociology and political science present this depiction of society.

None of these familiar descriptions of society includes recognition of the centrality of the gender structure of society. A feminist description of past and current social reality will assure that gender will be attended to as a central factor organizing society in fundamental and pervasive ways, and feminist evaluations of society will include assessments of the aspects of gender in them. Feminist recommendations for the future may show why the influence of gender should be greatly reduced as we strive for a society that is genuinely democratic. Or we may recommend that the values incorporated in the gender structure be transformed so that feminist concerns have priority.

To say that feminist concerns should have priority is not to advocate female dominance or a replacement of men by women in the gender structure of existing societies. Among feminist values is a rejection of domination itself. As we have seen repeatedly, most feminists do not aim to integrate women on equal terms into the structures of male-dominated society; we seek to change these structures into ones hospitable to and reflective of feminist values. Among the implications of a feminist aim to overcome domination are a commitment to the liberation of culture and to the development of social arrangements that will shape the future of society through cultural imagination and free discussion rather than through organized violence and economic power.

Of the three conceptions referred to, the first—a pyramidal one—is incompatible with a feminist view of how society ought to be organized. It unduly elevates, for law, a supremacy brought about by force, and it unduly privileges the power of the state to determine the shape of society. It ignores the coercion produced by economic power, and it overlooks the unsuitability of law and legalistic approaches for dealing with a wide range of human problems. As description, it seems to miss many other important sources of influence in society, such as social movements and cultural innovation, as well as family relationships and racial or ethnic or other group ties.

The view that an economic foundation determines all the layers of society built upon it also seems inadequate from a feminist point of view. It is descriptively insufficient and normatively pallid. Surely there are political forces other than economic effects. And the women's movement itself has shown the influence of changed consciousness on social change. Although the surge of women into the labor force has undoubtedly been a strong influence on that consciousness and on the women's movement, at least some of the shift of women from the household to the workplace has been brought about by consciously chosen values rather than by economic causes. And Marxism cannot explain such aspects of the women's movement as the resistance to the sexual objectification of women and the determination to oppose rape, sexual harassment, and domestic violence. Moreover, the society for which feminists strive will be one going far beyond the ending of economic class privilege.

The third view—that of society as composed of partially overlapping but relatively independent domains or segments—is more compatible with feminist views of society than the others. It is unsatisfactory all the same: not only has it ignored the structure of gender domination that affects all these segments, as have the other models, but it may obscure even more than the others do the way domination has operated throughout society.

Let us imagine a feminist alternative to these views. To understand society as it exists at present, a feminist view would first of all recognize the centrality and pervasiveness of the gender structure of society. It would see the way male dominance operates throughout society. Now let us suppose male dominance were to be overcome. What would all the different segments of society be like, and what would the relations between them be like? How they fit together would in all likelihood be transformed as would each domain. Is there any point in trying to imagine all this?

Much philosophical and theoretical effort has been devoted to prescribing ideal liberal alternatives to existing society. But the elaborate delineation of ideal societies of perfect justice, an enterprise which has dominated mainstream political philosophy for some time, has seemed to many critics to be of limited usefulness. Many feminists have shared these reservations about ideal theory along with our objections to the various ideals promoted.[31] It may thus be appropriate to question the point of imagining what an ideal feminist society might be like. From the perspective of many of the draining political struggles which need to be fought in society as it is, such a utopian sketch might appear distracting. Countless women struggle to survive, and to allow children to survive, in economic conditions that became even more grim in the Reagan-Bush era than they were before the women's movement. When women need desperately to have actual conditions improve, ideal conditions may seem irrelevantly remote.[32] Still, to the extent that a tentative depiction of goals to be sought is useful to guide cultural and political effort and to lend it encouragement, its absence may be missed. Images of possible feminist society should be part of the cultural stage, and can grow out of feminist practices.

Looking Ahead

Suppose we change the gender domination the previously outlined conceptualizations of society obscure. We might then be left with some segments of society relatively intact and distinguishable from other segments—a democratic political system, say, with true equality for women at all levels. But if all such segments are infused with feminist values, and if all are embedded in a society hospitable to feminism, then the relative positions of the segments might change in fundamental ways, as well as many of their internal characteristics.

A feminist society would be fundamentally different from a society composed of individuals each pursuing his own interest, especially his own economic interest, and evaluating public institutions by how well they facilitate or contribute to his own advancement—the traditional model of liberal and pluralistic society. It would be different as well from Marxist conceptions of society with their neglect of the issues of women and the family, and different as well from conservative communitarian views with their upholding of patriarchy.

Feminist society might be seen as having various relatively independent and distinct segments, with some not traditionally thought of as especially central and influential now being so, and with all such segments embedded in a wider network of social relations characterized by social caring and trust. Certainly the levels of caring and trust appropriate for the relations of all members of society with all others will be different from the levels appropriate for the members of a family with one another. But social relations in what can be thought of as society as a whole will not be characterized by indifference to the well-being of others, or an absence of trust, as they are in many nonfeminist conceptions. What kinds and amounts of caring and trust might characterize the relations of the most general kind in society should be decided on the basis of experience and practice with institutions that have overcome male dominance.

From the point of view of the self-interested head of household, the individual's interest in his own family may be at odds with the wider political and public interest. And aspects of mothering in patriarchal society have contributed to parochialism and racism. But from a satisfactorily worked-out feminist and moral point of view, the picture of the particularistic family in conflict with the good of society is distorted. The postpatriarchal family can express universal emotions and can be guided by universally shared concerns. A content and healthy child eager to learn and to love elicits general approval. A child whose distress can be prevented or alleviated should elicit universal efforts to deal with the distress and prevent its recurrence. Any feminist society can be expected to cherish new persons, seeing in each child both the specialness of a unique person and the universal features of a child's curiosity and hope. It should seek to build institutions and practices and a world worthy of that hope, and needed for each child to flourish.

Although feminist society would be likely to have democratic political processes, an independent judicial system to handle the recalcitrant, and markets to organize some economic activity, these and other institutions would be evaluated in terms of how well they worked to realize feminist values. And other segments of society might be recognized as far more central in doing so. Cultural expression would continually evaluate imaginative alternatives for consideration. It would provide entertainment not primarily to serve commercial interests or to relieve for a few hours the distress of persons caught in demeaning and exploitative jobs or with no jobs at all, but to enrich the lives of respected members of cultural and social communities.

The major implications of a feminist ethic on such areas of human activity traditionally noticed as having specifically moral significance—the state, the law, and the market—might be to limit drastically their influence rather than to change completely the principles by which they are guided. Consider the principles of democracy on which there is such widespread agreement around the globe. A feminist ethic would almost surely agree that government should be founded on the consent of the governed, though it might require the consent to be interpreted in actual rather than hypothetical terms.[33] But as soon as we moved to questions of what government should do, we would hear questions about the reach of law and of bureaucratic authority, as well as questions about adequate social support for the kinds of social activity a feminist ethic would recognize ought to be undertaken. And a feminist approach would differ significantly from a nonfeminist one. If nongovernmental efforts do not succeed in meeting needs, government should be called on to do so itself. Everyone should have, by right, access to the means to live and to develop. On the other hand, government might often do better to empower families—in various and expanded senses—to provide for their members rather than to multiply its own bureaucratic layers.

With respect to many social programs, the United States is especially backward compared with those industrialized countries which have a background of strong social democratic influence. A comparison of provisions for maternal health care, child care, paternal leave, and early education makes this clear.[34] Certainly a feminist view of how society ought to be restructured may have a harder time realizing its goals in a society as ideologically overcommitted to capitalism as is the United States. But in other ways, such as awareness of sexual victimization, feminist transformations may have gone further in the United States than elsewhere. In any case, all societies will need fundamental change along feminist lines. And the changes to improve the future of children should be motivated not by the desire to win the competition, which may now be the economic competition with Japan and Germany rather than the military competition with the Soviet Union, but by the understanding that all children deserve the care that will enable them to flourish.

A society organized along feminist lines might put the proper care and suitable development of all children at the very center of its concerns. Instead of allowing, as so often at present, family policies and arrangements for child care and for the education and health of children to be marginal concerns, vastly less important than military strength and corporate profits, a feminist society might understand the future of children to be its highest priority. As the children grew up with the levels of concern and attention needed for all to flourish and with feminist values guiding their development, the needs for the traditional functions of state power might greatly diminish; fewer children would grow up to be lawbreakers or irresponsible agents in need of ever more detailed legal restraints.

Among the most important transformations needed in the ways human beings organize their lives are changes in prevailing relationships between "man" and "nature." Feminists have shown the connections between the attitudes that nature is to be conquered and dominated and the association of nature with the feminine. Prior to the sixteenth century, there had been a reluctance to violate an earth seen as a generative and nurturing mother. But by the seventeenth century, sexual metaphors burgeoned: the earth was seen as a female to be dominated, a woman who should be mastered.[35] Many feminists believe that there remain connections between men's domination of women and their exploitation and destruction of the environment, and that achieving respect for nature will require achieving respect for women.[36] Feminist concerns for the well-being of future children include awareness of the urgent need for harmonious relationships between human beings and the global environment.

Of course feminist moralities and the arrangements they will recommend will not of themselves provide solutions to all problems, but they may make remarkable contributions compared to previous moralities and arrangements.

From Family to Society

Long before we reach anything resembling feminist society we can indicate the directions, from where we are, that a feminist ethic would suggest we move in. We need to consider how we should connect a feminist morality most appropriate for moral problems that arise within a family, or among persons with close ties to one another, with what we think of as the moral foundations of the state, law, politics, and interactions among strangers. A feminist ethic will not be blind to the need for procedural principles to settle disputes among strangers or to the appeal of principles of justice and equality as prima facie starting points for reaching agreements among conflicting positions. And a feminist ethic will of course be concerned with increasing the general happiness. But a feminist ethic will never forget that such principles and starting points and concerns should not be more than a part, perhaps a rather small part, of morality. A feminist ethic will not try to generalize these principles and approaches to all other domains.

Generalizing from the "public" domain of law and politics to the whole of morality has been the dominant tendency of philosophical ethics in the modern era. The rationalistic moralities exemplified by Kantian moral theories have taken a conception of law needed for public rationality in the modern world and have supposed it to be applicable to the whole of personal morality as well. Utilitarian and rational choice theories reflect a generalization to the moral level of assumptions and motivations thought suitable for the marketplace. The moral agent must consider the interests of others as well as of himself, but the starting assumptions of discrete individuals with their conflicting interests are carried over from the economic realm to the realm of moral theory.

Any feminist ethic will be likely to resist such expansions as these of moral concepts and approaches developed for law and politics and the marketplace. And it will call for significant rethinking of them for the legal and political and economic domains themselves.

It is certainly true, as Marilyn Friedman and Susan Okin argue, that justice is relevant to arrangements within the family. The fact that so often "men do not serve women as women serve men" is a violation of distributive justice; wife battering and child abuse are occasions for corrective justice.[37] But we can at the same time recognize that justice in the family sets little more than the moral minimums to be observed. Bringing this about is no easy matter, still, most of what families should provide is in a range over and above these moral minimums. Building relations of trust and consideration far exceeds what justice can assure. When we consider the activity of mothering we see how many of its values are "beyond justice." The activity is not a one-way giving that can be divided up equally between women and men, though many of the minimal tasks involved can and should be. As Nel Noddings writes, "Infants contribute to the mother-child relationships by responding in characteristic (and idiosyncratic) ways to their mothers." Their smiles and attention contribute to the relation and show how mutuality or reciprocity can characterize relations even when one member is weaker than another. In Noddings's view, "much of the energy required to maintain caring relations comes from the cared for."[38]

Certainly the activity of mothering can be exploitative if women are confined to it or expected to perform it at the expense of pursuing other activities. But the activity itself is potentially among the most humanly promising, as it allows future persons to flourish and satisfying human relationships to grow. Friedman emphasizes that relationships can be exploitative and harmful as well as enriching, and she suggests that our aim should be "to advance 'beyond caring,' that is, beyond *mere* caring dissociated from a concern for justice."[39] We can agree that caring relationships need a floor of justice if they lack it. But what those who seek to develop an ethic of care often suggest is that we should progress beyond mere justice, which has been so dominant a focus of so much traditional moral theory.[40] And we need to do this not only within the family, where care has prevailed and justice has not, but in the society as well. We need to work towards a future where feminist moral inquiry and feminist culture reshape the organization of society. This will require fundamental reorderings and rethinkings of dominant practices and theories.

Notes

1. See Virginia Held, "The Political 'Testing'of Moral Theories," *Midwest Studies in Philosophy* 7 (Spring 1982): 343–63; and Virginia Held, *Rights and Goods: Justifying Social Action* (New York: Free Press, 1984; Chicago: University of Chicago Press, 1989), Chaps. 4 and 15.

2. Catharine R. Stimpson, *Where the Meanings Are: Feminism and Cultural Spaces* (New York: Routledge, 1990) 181.

3. Catharine A. MacKinnon, *Toward a Feminist Theory of the State* (Cambridge: Harvard University Press, 1989) 116.

4. Mary Stevenson (Personal correspondence, 8 December 1991) describes several incidents where agents are "taken by surprise" by such experience.

5. John Rawls, *A Theory of Justice* (Cambridge: Harvard University Press, 1971).

6. See Norman Daniels, "Wide Reflective Equilibrium and Theory Acceptance in Ethics," *Journal of Philosophy* 76 (May 1979): 256–82; and Richard Brandt, "The Science of Man and Wide Reflective Equilibrium," *Ethics* 100 (January 1990): 259–78.

7. J. Rawls, *Theory of Justice*, 47.

8. See Nel Noddings, *Caring: A Femine Approach to Ethics and Moral Education* (Berkeley: University of California Press, 1984); Carol Gilligan, *In a Different Voice: Psychological Theory and Women's Development* (Cambridge: Harvard University Press, 1982); Eva Feder Kittay and Diana T. Meyers, eds., *Women and Moral Theory* (Totowa N.J.: Rowman and Littlefield, 1987); Claudia Card, ed., *Feminist Ethics* (Lawrence: University Press of Kansas, 1991); and Margaret Urban Walker, "Moral Understandings: Alternative 'Epistemology' for a Feminist Ethics," *Hypatia* 4 (Summer 1989): 15–28.

9. See Amélie Oksenberg Rorty, ed., *Explaining Emotions* (Berkeley: University of California Press, 1980). See also Anthony Kenny, *Action, Emotion and the Will* (London: Routledge, 1963); and Irving Thalberg, *Perception, Emotion and Action* (Oxford: Blackwell, 1977).

10. Sara Ruddick, *Maternal Thinking: Toward a Politics of Peace* (Boston: Beacon Press, 1989), 70.

11. G. W. F. Hegel, *The Phenomenology of Mind*, pt. 6, A, b, trans. J. Baillie (New York: Harper, 1967), 496.

12. Charles Fried, *An Anatomy of Values* (Cambridge: Harvard University Press, 1970).

13. Bernard Williams, *Moral Luck: Philosophical Papers 1973–1980* (Cambridge, Eng.: Cambridge University Press, 1981), 18.

14. See Marilyn Friedman, "The Social Self and the Partiality Debates," in *Feminist Ethics*, ed. C. Card. See also Lawrence A. Blum, "Gilligan and Kohlberg: Implications for Moral Theory," *Ethics* 98 (April 1988): 474–91.

15. See G. W. H. Hegel, *Philosophy of Right*, trans. T. Knox (Oxford: Clarendon Press, 1952).

16. Thomas Nagel, *The View from Nowhere* (New York: Oxford University Press, 1986).

17. Alison M. Jaggar, "Taking Consent Seriously: Feminist Ethics and Actual Moral Dialogue," in *The Applied Ethics Reader*, ed. Earl Winkler and Jerrold Coombs (Oxford: Blackwell, 1993).

18. An exception may be N. Noddings, *Caring*.

19. See Susan Sherwin, "Feminist and Medical Ethics: Two Different Approaches to Contextual Ethics," *Hypatia* 4 (Summer 1989): 57–72.

20. See Kathryn Pauly Morgan, "Strangers in a Strange Land: Feminists Visit Relativists," in *Perspectives on Relativism*, ed. D. Odegaard and C. Stewart (Toronto: Agathon Press, 1990).

21. For discussion of both the limitations of abstract legal categories and the utility for African Americans of the concept of rights, see Patricia J. Williams, *The Alchemy of Race and Rights* (Cambridge: Harvard University Press, 1991), esp. chap. 8.

22. Annette C. Baier, "The Need for More than Justice," in *Science, Morality and Feminist Theory*, ed. Marsha Hanen and Kai Nielsen (Calgary: University of Calgary Press, 1987) 53.

23. J. Rawls, *Theory of Justice*, 5.

24. Alan Gewirth, *Reason and Morality* (Chicago: University of Chicago Press, 1978), 10.

25. Iris Marion Young, "Impartiality and the Civic Public," in *Feminism as Critique: On the Politics of Gender*, ed. Seyla Benhabib and Drucilla Cornell (Minneapolis: University of Minnesota Press, 1987), 69. See also Mari J. Matsuda, "Affirmative Action and Legal Knowledge: Planting Seeds in Plowed-Up Ground," *Harvard Women's Law Journal* 11 (Spring 1988): 1–17.

26. Maria C. Lugones and Elizabeth V. Spelman, "Have We Got a Theory for You! Feminist Theory, Cultural Imperialism and the Demand for 'The Woman's Voice,'" *Women's Studies International Forum (Hypatia)* 6, no. 6 (1983): 581. See also Uma Narayan, "Working across Difference: Some Considerations on Emotions and Political Practice," *Hypatia* 3 (Summer 1988): 31–47.

27. Gloria T. Hull, Patricia Bell Scott, and Barbara Smith, eds. *All the Women Are White, All the Blacks Are Men, But Some of Us Are Brave* (New York: Feminist Press, 1982).

28. For a related view, see Rosi Braidotti, "The Subject in Feminism," *Hypatia* 6 (Summer 1991): 155–72.

29. Andreas Huyssen, *After the Great Divide: Modernism, Mass Culture, Postmodernism* (Bloomington: Indiana University Press, 1986) 47.

30. See Vivian Gornick, "Who Says We Haven't Made a Revolution?" *New York Times Magazine*, 15 April 1990, 24.

31. Starting with *The Public Interest and Individual Interests* (New York: Basic Books, 1970), most of my work has considered what we ought to do from where we are here and now, rather than what ideal principles of perfect justice or equality would hold.

32. For a portrayal of how far women still have to go to attain even minimal levels of respect and equality, see Marilyn French, *The War against Women* (New York: Simon and Schuster, 1992).

33. A. Jaggar, "Taking Consent Seriously."

34. See *Beyond Rhetoric: A New American Agenda for Children and Families*. Final Report of the National Commission on Children (Washington, D.C.: U.S. Government Printing Office, 1991); *Who Cares for America's Children?* Report of the National Academy of Sciences (National Academy Press, 1990); Fred M. Hechinger, "Why France Outstrips the United States in Nurturing Its Children," *New York Times*, 1 August 1990; and report by Robert Pear on the Report of the White House Task Force on Infant Mortality, *New York Times*, 6 August 1990, A1, B9.

35. Carolyn Merchant, *The Death of Nature: Woman, Ecology, and the Scientific Revolution* (New York: Harper and Row, 1982) 170–89.

36. See Karen Warren, "Feminism and Ecology: Making Connections," *Environmental Ethics* 9 (1987): 3–20.

37. Marilyn Friedman, "Beyond Caring: The De-Moralization of Gender," in *Science, Morality and Feminist Theory*, ed. M. Hanen and K. Nielsen, 101, quoting Marilyn Frye; see also Susan Moller Okin, *Justice, Gender, and the Family* (New York: Basic Books, 1989).

38. Nel Noddings, "A Response," *Hypatia* 5 (Spring 1990): 123.

39. M. Friedman, "Beyond Caring," 105.

40. A good example of such an argument is A. Baier's "The Need for More Than Justice."

PART FIVE

New Integrations

10

Caring as a Feminist Practice of Moral Reason [1995]

ALISON M. JAGGAR

In less than two decades, the ethics of care has achieved a spectacular rise to fame and fortune, at least in North America.[1] Almost unheard of in 1980, today caring is widely regarded as a moral perspective that is both distinctively feminine and peculiarly appropriate for feminists; it has even been institutionalized in establishments such as the Center for Human Caring, run by the School of Nursing at my own University of Colorado.[2] Although the ethics of care has been variously described, it is typically portrayed as a moral orientation that not only produces assessments of action different from those provided by traditional Western moralities, especially the ethics associated with the European Enlightenment, but that also arrives at those assessments through an alternative process of moral thinking.[3] My present interest is not in care as a moral ideal or value or virtue but rather in the potential of care thinking as a feminist mode or "style" of practical moral reasoning (Hacking 1985).

Practical moral reasoning is intended to identify morally desirable, or at least morally permissible, actions and practices, although it cannot, of course, be expected to do so infallibly. Since feminism, by definition, revolves around moral opposition to women's subordination, a mode of moral reasoning adequate for feminism should be capable of critiquing conventionally accepted practices of male dominance and identifying actions and practices that promote feminist ideals and values. Since male dominance is manifested in both institutional arrangements and personal relationships and in both the so-called public and private domains, feminist moral reasoning must be able to address all these aspects of social life. In addition, since feminist thought and action occur by definition in a world that is morally imperfect, a feminist mode of moral reasoning must be applicable to circumstances that are less than morally ideal.

This chapter discusses what I find to be two limitations of care thinking as a practice of moral reasoning suitable for feminism. My arguments suggest that although care thinking may have considerable utility for feminists, feminist practical ethics cannot rely exclusively on care but must supplement it with other modes of moral reasoning.

Distinctive Features of Care Reasoning

As a practice of moral thinking, care involves a distinctive moral orientation toward another person or persons. This orientation has both affective and cognitive dimensions: the caring individual is simultaneously concerned about the other's welfare and perceives acutely and insightfully how it is with the other. The carer recognizes and takes pleasure in the other's happiness and identifies and is concerned about her needs (Blum 1992). Descriptions of care thinking often take as paradigmatic situations in which the other is in need, but Sara Ruddick notes that participants in caring relations also strive to delight and empower each other (Ruddick, personal correspondence).

Care thinking is generally explained by contrasting it with so-called justice thinking. One contrast lies in the structure of moral reasoning attributed to each mode of thinking. Justice thinking is portrayed as appealing to rational and universalizable moral principles, applied impartially, whereas accounts of care thinking emphasize its responsiveness to particular situations whose morally salient features are perceived with an acuteness thought to be made possible by the carer's emotional posture of empathy, openness, and receptiveness (Blum 1992). Care theorists' emphasis on moral perception is sometimes taken to imply that care is immediate rather than deliberate, but several authors assert that it may be thoughtful and reflective (Blum 1991:706). However, rather than validating its responses by reference to general principles, care reasoning is likely to take the form of a narrative in which the concrete details of specific situations become intelligible in the context of people's ongoing lives and relationships (Walker 1992:167).

Perhaps the most distinctive and controversial feature attributed to care thinking is its particularity, which means not only that it addresses the needs of others in their concrete specificity but that it is unmediated by general principles. Addressing the needs of others in their concrete specificity is understood as responding to them as unique, irreplaceable individuals rather than as "generalized" others regarded simply as representatives of a common humanity (Benhabib 1986). Such responsiveness requires paying as much moral attention to the ways in which people differ from each other as to the ways in which they are the same (Dillon 1992). Care's intense focus on particular others is taken to entail the denial that it is impartial in the sense of universalizable; thus, asserting the moral propriety of a particular caring response is claimed to carry no implication that someone else in a similar situation should do something similar (Walker 1987).

Care and justice thinking have sometimes been portrayed by contrasting allegedly dispassionate justice with supposedly nonrational care, but in fact such portrayals caricature both justice and care. Although traditional accounts of moral reason often neglected or disparaged the moral significance of emotion, recent accounts increasingly acknowledge that even justice involves characteristic emotions such as respect and indignation. Similarly, theorists of care resist reducing it to a simple feeling, insisting that its cognitive elements be recognized. They consider care not simply as a motivation to right action, itself conceived as established through a process of rational calculation, but also as a distinct moral capacity with cognitive dimensions, necessary to determining what actions are morally appropriate (Blum 1992:125). The significant contrast seems to be not that care is emotional whereas justice is rational but rather that, as Virginia Held points out, the emotions play a different epistemic role in each perspective: the justice perspective limits the role of emotion to that of motivating actions whose moral permissibility must be determined by reason; the care perspective regards emotions as having "an important function in developing moral understanding itself, in helping us decide what the recommendations of morality themselves ought to be." Specifically, caring "involves feelings and requires high degrees of empathy to enable us to discern what morality recommends in our caring activities" (Held 1993:30).

Care is not rational in the senses of being purely intellectual, deductive, or even egoistic, but Nel Noddings asserts that "rationality and reasoning involve more than the identification of principles and their deductive application" (Noddings 1990a:27). Proponents of care thinking regard it as rational in a broader, honorific sense of being a distinctively human way of engaging with others that produces morally appropriate action.

Women and the Ethics of Care

There is nothing new in the assertion that women are uninterested in—often, indeed, neglectful of—justice. This claim has been made not only by antifeminists, such as Sigmund Freud, who thought that lack of concern for justice was inherent in women's nature (Freud 1933), but also by feminists, such as John Stuart Mill, who thought that women would develop a greater concern for justice if they were allowed to extend their sphere of activity beyond the home (Mill 1980). Until the 1970s, antifeminists and feminists alike assumed that to establish women's lack of concern about justice would be tantamount to demonstrating that women were morally inferior to men. The contemporary feminist counterclaim, that an exclusive preoccupation with *justice* reflects a moral sensibility that is also defective, is quite uncharacteristic of modern Western moral philosophy—although we shall see that it is not entirely unprecedented in it.

Even though the ethics of care is widely associated with women, some critics contend that the alleged connection between women and caring cannot be validated empirically. Some studies have found no sex differences emerging on tests of moral development when subjects are matched for education and occupation: with the exception of women who work in the home, males and females are said to achieve almost identical scores on Kohlbergian tests (Walker 1984:677–691). Moreover, many men as well as women have been asserted to employ care thinking, including members of traditional African societies (Harding 1987), African Americans migrating back from the northern to the southern United States (Stack 1986:321–324), and the members of some Native American cultures—not to mention so-called new age men.

Even within male-dominated Western philosophy, the themes that define the ethics of care are not entirely novel. Apart from Christ's injunction to love our neighbors, we may think of Aristotle's remark in Book VIII of his *Nicomachean Ethics* that "when we have justice, we also need friendship but when we have friends, we no longer need justice" echoed by Aquinas's assertion in his ethics commentaries that "a moralist should be more profoundly concerned with friendship than justice." Annette Baier regards David Hume's moral thought as congenial with Gilligan's account of the ethics of care (Baier 1987b), and Joan Tronto finds caring themes in the work of two other Scottish Enlightenment thinkers, Francis Hutcheson and Adam Smith (Tronto 1993).[4] Such examples are more than sufficient to discredit any simple claims that the ethics of justice and care reflect invariable differences between the moral thinking of men and women.

None of the major theorists of care makes any such simple claim, though many have been misread as doing so. Even in her early work, Carol Gilligan[5] asserted that as men and women age, their moral thinking converges, and in a later study of "educationally advantaged Americans" she found that a third of the women focused on justice, a third on care, and a third raised considerations of both justice and care (Gilligan 1987:25–26). Even though men thought about situations almost exclusively in terms of justice and failed to raise concerns of care spontaneously, both sexes were able to recognize both moral orientations when these were suggested to them. Virginia Held and Sara Ruddick both associate care thinking with mothering, but Ruddick asserts that men as well as women are able to mother and Held speaks of "mothering persons" with pointed gender neutrality. Noddings attributes care thinking to those who saved Jews during the Holocaust, people who certainly included men as well as women (Noddings 1990a:27–28).

Although feminist proponents of the ethics of care recognize that some women think in terms of justice and some men think in terms of care, they still associate caring with women because they believe that the care perspective emerges from forms of socialization and experience that, in contemporary

Western society, are predominantly feminine. Gilligan suggests that women's affinity for the ethics of care and men's preference for the ethics of justice may be explained at least partly in terms of Nancy Chodorow's version of neo-Freudian object relations theory, which claims that because children are reared primarily by women, girls' gender identity is defined through connection with others whereas boys' gender identity must be established through separation from others (Gilligan 1987:28). Although Held and Ruddick both assert that mothering may be performed by men, they are clear that male mothering is the exception rather than the rule. Noddings connects care with the feminine work of raising children, tending to the elderly, maintaining a supportive home environment, nursing, and teaching (Noddings 1990a:26).

Joan Tronto argues that in contemporary Western society, care is linked not only with gender but also with race and class. Defining care as those practices aimed at "maintaining, continuing and repairing the world," she associates the moral perspective of care with the work of cleaning up after bodily functions, tasks that in Western history have been relegated primarily to women, but not to women exclusively and not to all women (Tronto 1993:104). Tronto asserts that in "modern industrial societies, these tasks of caring continue to be disproportionately carried out by the lowest ranks of society: by women, the working class, and in most of the West, by people of color" (Tronto 1993:113). She argues, therefore, that it is misleading to associate care with femininity *simpliciter:* the ethics of care reflects primarily the experience of women of certain races and classes— as well as of some racial/ethnic men of those classes (Tronto 1993:112). Tronto's analysis of the social genesis of care thinking fits well with Lawrence Blum's characterization of two prominent versions of the ethics of justice, the moral rationalisms of Kant and Hegel, as expressing a juridical-administrative perspective that, in modern Western societies, is typically masculine (Blum 1982). Blum's view suggests that the justice orientation does not reflect the moral perspective of men universally, but only the perspective of men from the professional, administrative, and managerial classes—leaving open the possibility that the ethics of justice may well be adopted by the increasing numbers of women currently entering professional and administrative occupations. Tronto's and Blum's work suggests several reasons that caring themes are recessive rather than dominant in modern Western moral philosophy; such themes appear to characterize the thinking not only of women but also of people in premodern societies and of lower-class people, including people of color—none of whom are well represented among modern Western philosophers.

In addition to reflecting a social experience that is usually but not invariably or inevitably feminine, care may also be feminine in a symbolic or normative sense. Marilyn Friedman asserts that the genders are "moralized" in that

> specific moral ideals, values, virtues, and practices are culturally conceived as the special projects or domains of specific genders. These conceptions determine which commitments and behaviors are to be considered normal, appropriate, and expected of each gender, which commitments and behaviors are to be considered re-

markable or heroic, and which commitments and behaviors are to be considered deviant, improper, outrageous, and intolerable. (Friedman 1993:123)

Friedman reports that the moralization of gender is commonplace at the level of popular perception in contemporary Western societies. Both men and women expect women to be more empathic and altruistic, to display concern for the welfare of others, to be caring and nurturant and, to a lesser extent, to be interpersonally sensitive, emotionally expressive, and gentle in personal style. By contrast, men are expected to be assertive, dominant, independent, self-confident, personally efficacious, and direct and adventurous in personal style (Friedman 1993:124). Friedman concludes that the ethics of care is feminine not simply in springing from types of labor assigned generally to women but also in reflecting moral ideals that are culturally feminine.

That the ethics of care is in some plausible senses feminine does not of course establish it as a mode of moral reasoning that is especially appropriate for feminism. Although Western feminists in both the nineteenth and twentieth centuries have occasionally attempted to reclaim the culturally feminine, including the domestic and the emotional,[6] most feminists, and certainly most Western philosophers who have promoted women's equality, such as Plato, Marx, and Mill, have been concerned to challenge and even reject the feminine (Coole 1988). Developing the ethics of care is clearly one means of reappropriating the feminine in the area of moral philosophy, but to evaluate the possibilities for the success of this project requires a critical examination of the strengths and weaknesses of care reasoning for feminist purposes.

Are Care and Justice Thinking Compatible?

In her early accounts of the ethics of care, Gilligan spoke of the need to marry care with justice, but she did not explain how this might be possible (Gilligan 1982:174). Several philosophers have explored how such a marriage might be consummated, suggesting ways in which care and justice might not only coexist but even presuppose each other. Susan Okin, for instance, argues both that justice is needed to frame caring relationships and that care for others is the value implicit in impartiality (Okin 1989). Friedman argues both that being just is one form of caring and that caring should be done justly so that, for instance, one partner does not bear most of the burden of sustaining the personal relationship or accomplishing the family or parenting labor (Friedman 1993:127–130).

If care and justice are construed as values or ideals, there seems no reason to doubt that both may be part of the same value system and compatibility in this sense is not threatened by occasional uncertainty over which ideal should take precedence, just as liberty and equality may both be part of a single value system even though there may be occasional tension between them. But when care and justice are construed as alternative modes of moral thinking or reasoning, it is harder to see how they may be compatible. As Friedman expresses the opposition between them, care thinking emphasizes moral commitments to particular individuals and justice thinking, to general principles (Friedman 1993:136). Although Friedman asserts that the two modes of thinking may be integrated, her own argument, which recognizes the difficulty of choosing between them, suggests that they are compatible only in the sense that a moral agent may elect at one time to use one mode of thinking, at another time, the other (Friedman 1993:138–139). Friedman does not show that care and justice thinking are compatible in that both may be used on the same occasion, let alone that each implies the other.

Some philosophers have attempted to make precisely such an argument, suggesting that care and justice reasoning be interpreted not as independent practices of moral thinking but rather as aspects of a single practice. With such an interpretation, the ethics of care would not identify a different voice, new at least to philosophy, but would rather present a somewhat different way of listening to a familiar voice, emphasizing elements previously ignored by moral philosophers.

Various suggestions have been offered for construing care as one aspect of a complex practice of moral reasoning. Some Kantian feminists have suggested that care might be interpreted as a moral motive operating within a framework of morally permissible action determined by the Categorical Imperative (Herman 1983; Baron 1984; O'Neill 1984). Other philosophers have suggested that care be equated with the faculty that Kant calls judgment, which is a direct and non-rule-governed but nonetheless moral assessment of the nature of the situation (Kant 1965:177). Still other moral theorists redescribe care reasoning as universalizable, whether or not agents appeal consciously to the Categorical Imperative, arguing that it involves a suppressed major premise (Kohlberg 1982:513–528; Sher 1987:187–188). If accounts of care thinking do not designate a hitherto unrecognized mode or practice of moral reasoning but instead highlight unremarked aspects of a familiar practice, it is plausible to suppose that both aspects must be included in a complete account of moral reasoning and thus that justice and care are not only logically compatible with but even logically indispensable to each other.

Suggesting that justice and care ethics each represent different aspects of moral reasoning is not the only way of arguing for their compatibility. Another approach is to recognize them as distinct practices of moral thinking but, assuming that they originate in the experience of public and private life respectively, to suggest that they complement each other in the sense of being appropriate for different domains. Not only Kohlberg and his colleagues (Kohlberg, Levine, and Hewer 1983) but also Blum (1992:126) have suggested that care is especially appropriate for intimate relations or one-to-one encounters.

A third strategy for viewing care and justice as compatible and even complementary is to construe each as addressing a different set of issues. Jürgen Habermas suggests that care thinking is concerned with "evaluative questions of the good life" and "the evaluation of personality types and modes of action." He regards these as "personal" issues of self-realization, not truly moral, unlike the questions of universal obligation, which he takes to be the subject of justice thinking. For Habermas, care is distinguished from justice in reflecting *Sittlichkeit* rather than *Moralitaet* and addressing questions of the good rather than the right, the content of morality rather than its form (Habermas 1990:178–180).

Although compatibility claims are accepted by some advocates of the ethics of care, they are made more frequently by those committed to the primacy of justice. Often compatibility claims are presented in a way that is deflationary, minimizing the moral and theoretical significance of care by reducing it to one aspect of a morality whose essential constituents are the impartiality and universalizability thought to be defining characteristics of the ethics of justice. George Sher, for instance, denies firmly that the articulation of the ethics of care provides any reason to suppose that moral theory needs radical revision; he states that "far from being novel, this approach [making moral decisions on the basis of care and sympathy] . . . is central to the existing tradition" (Sher 1987:184).

Advocates of care thinking are especially resistant to compatibility proposals that trivialize the concerns raised by the ethics of care, proposals that Barbara Houston has diagnosed as expressing a "politics of dismissal" (Houston 1988). Blum, for instance, has objected to several attempts to assimilate caring to one aspect of justice thinking. He insists that care cannot be reconstructed in terms of rules that are in principle universalizable (Blum 1987:326–327), and he distinguishes moral perception from the Kantian notion of moral judgment on the grounds that its task is not to apply moral principles but rather to individuate the situations in which moral judgment operates (Blum 1991:708–714). Margaret Walker argues that some moral reasoning is irreducibly particular and nonuniversalizable because those practicing it assign a discretionary weight, rank, or value to moral particulars, in the process defining their own moral personae, the kind of persons they are (Walker 1987).

Many care advocates reject also the suggestion that care and justice are each appropriate for a different domain. Apart from Noddings's attempt to extend care thinking to handle all moral concerns in all domains (Noddings 1991:97), some argue that justice as well as care is needed in the household (Ruddick, this volume) and many assert that care as well as justice is needed in the public domain (Walker 1991; Tronto 1993; Held 1993, this volume; Ruddick, this volume). Dividing the moral labor so that justice and care regulate the public and private domains, respectively, makes justice primary over care because justice regulates the domain that not only has the higher status but also controls how the domains are demarcated. Care ethics, symbolically gendered feminine, then becomes analogous to housework: despite its indispensability, its contribution to the larger economy is disregarded or marginalized.

Although Seyla Benhabib retains a strong commitment to a universal ethics of justice, she seeks to rescue care thinking from what she calls Habermas's relegation of it "to the margins of ethical theory." Benhabib complains that, on Habermas's construal, the issues with which he takes care to be concerned become "'anomalies' or residual problems of an otherwise adequate scientific paradigm" (Benhabib 1992:183). She challenges Habermas's sharp distinction between the right and the good, noting, "The line between matters of justice and those of the good life is not given by some moral dictionary, but evolves as a result of historical and cultural struggles" (Benhabib 1992:75). In her view, questions of the good life are also susceptible to intersubjective debate and reflection, although she concedes that consensus here may not be possible, and she insists, in opposition to Habermas, that "questions of care are moral issues" (Benhabib 1992:186).

Most proponents of the ethics of care now dispute the possibility of any easy synthesis of care with justice. They note that in her later work, Gilligan presents care and justice as "two moral perspectives that organize thinking in different ways" (Gilligan 1987:20), dropping her early metaphor of a marriage in favor of explaining care and justice by reference to ambiguous figures that may be given alternative and incompatible interpretations. Rather than seeking to include care and justice in a unified account of moral reasoning, most contemporary advocates of an ethics of care are committed to exploring care's strengths as an independent style or practice of moral thinking. They present the ethics of care as a complete moral orientation or perspective or outlook, "a unified perspective on morality" (Walker 1989:123). In this view, care and justice both involve distinctive ontological, epistemological, and practical commitments, though this is not to deny that the concepts, themes, and priorities associated with both orientations are often loosely defined, permitting considerable disagreement between them. Sara Ruddick speaks for many in asserting that "justice" and "care" are "two non-assimilable moral orientations . . . which foster distinctive cognitive capacities, appeal to distinctive ideals of rationality, elicit distinctive moral emotions, presume distinctive conceptions of identity and relationships, recognize distinctive virtues and make distinctive requirements on institutions." On Ruddick's view, "justice" and "care" each offer

> "a point of view from which alone a certain sort of understanding of human life is possible." That is to say, each orientation is genuinely moral; neither can be replaced by or subsumed under the other; each covers the whole of the moral domain and therefore can check and inform the other; there is no third, "mature," single integrative moral perspective within which each orientation has its place. (Ruddick, this volume)

Care Thinking's Significance
for Moral Philosophy

Even if the new interest in caring did no more than focus philosophical attention on previously disregarded aspects of moral thinking, it would have considerable significance for moral philosophy. Cheshire Calhoun has argued that the historical neglect of these aspects has produced a distorted and misleading representation of moral life (Calhoun 1988). For instance, focusing exclusively on people's shared humanity and equal membership in the moral community diverts attention from the ways in which people's basic interests and empirical desires may differ depending on their social location. Focusing exclusively on the adult capacity for consistent and universalizable moral reflection diverts attention from the indispensability of moral motivation and education and from the social availability of morally relevant information. Focusing exclusively on the dangers of egoism and partiality to one's own diverts attention from the dangers of self-sacrifice and devalues the moral significance of special relations. Calhoun argues that the traditional focus of Western moral philosophy has created a lopsided ideology of moral life and thought that reflects the moral preoccupations of propertied males and obscures the moral concerns of (among others) many women. The ethics of care, construed as a focus on hitherto neglected aspects of moral life and thought, can help to redress this gendered bias in moral theory.

If care thinking is construed in a stronger sense, as an independent style or practice of moral reasoning, then its advocates contend that it may generate actions morally superior to those that result from a concern for justice. Many examples purport to illustrate how people motivated primarily by justice frequently ignore the pressing needs of real people, often those closest to them, or subordinate individuals to abstract principle, with a "blind willingness to sacrifice people to truth" (Gilligan 1982:104; compare Baier 1987a and Noddings 1984). Care's ability to generate actions morally preferable to those produced by justice reasoning is credited in part to its reliance on the direct perception of particular situations. This direct perception is said to facilitate action that is more context-sensitive than actions guided by moral rules that, because of their generality, are necessarily indeterminate.

Care is also asserted to be more reliable than justice thinking in motivating right action because justice often presents right action as requiring the sacrifice of one's own self-interest, whereas care thinking regards the interests of the self as inseparable from those of others. Unlike acting from a concern for justice, therefore, acting caringly does not require a prior act of moral will strong enough to overcome one's inclinations, and so caring action, unlike justice-motivated action, can hardly be inhibited by "weakness of the will." For instance, Noddings reports that of the non-Jews who risked their own safety to save Jews during the Holocaust, only 11 percent acted on principle; the rest "responded either directly out of compassion or from a sense of themselves as decent, caring people" (Noddings 1990a:27).

Finally, the process of responding in a caring manner itself is said to have moral value, unlike the intellectual appeal to principle characteristic of the ethics of justice. As Blum observes, "Accurate moral perception is a good in its own right," expressing a praiseworthy moral sensitivity (Blum 1991:714).

Many of these claims seem to me persuasive, but rather than developing them here, I intend to discuss two features of care reasoning that I find especially problematic. Gilligan chose the analogy of the ambiguous figure to suggest that the ethics of care draws attention to some things only at the expense of obscuring others. I am concerned about two of care thinking's apparent blind spots, which hamper and may even disable care from addressing certain questions crucial for feminist ethics.

Justifying "True Care"

In this section, I criticize the care tradition for failing to explain how care thinking may be properly critical of the moral validity of felt, perceived, or expressed needs, so that it can avoid permitting or even legitimating morally inadequate responses to them. I attribute this failure to the relative lack of attention to moral justification given so far by theorists of care ethics.

It would not be true to say that the tradition of care ethics fails to acknowledge any distinction between real necessities and objects of empirical desire, between felt or expressed needs, on the one hand, and genuine needs, on the other. On the contrary, such a distinction runs through the work of Gilligan, it is implicit in Ruddick's definition of caring in terms of what may usefully be given and received (Ruddick, this volume), and it is explicit in Tronto's observation that "a patient in the hospital who refuses to get up may be forced to do so. A child who wishes only to eat junk food may be disappointed by parents' reluctance to meet this wish" (Tronto 1989:177). But although most accounts of care reasoning assume such a distinction, they have provided only scanty explanations of how it should be drawn.

Accounts of care thinking that emphasize the directness of caring perception sometimes discourage even raising this epistemological question by treating care as a "success" concept. On this construal, caring perception of another's need is by definition veridical; if someone fails to assess another's situation accurately, she is not practicing care thinking. Tronto's assertion that hospital patients may be forced to get up and children prevented from eating junk food is followed immediately by the remark, "Genuine attentiveness would presumably allow the caretaker to see through these pseudo-needs and come to appreciate what the other really needs" (Tronto 1989:177). Such comments tend to obscure the question of how we distinguish "pseudo-needs" from "real needs" by suggesting that "genuine attentiveness," which Tronto takes as central to caring, is self-authenticating. From here, it is easy to slide into paternalism, authoritarianism, and dogmatism.

Many care theorists, including Tronto, are aware of these dangers and discuss such concerns as vicarious identification, projection, and carers' desires to control those for whom they care or to maintain them in a state of dependence. Frequently, care theorists maintain that these dangers may be avoided through improved practices of attentiveness, portraying attentiveness as a kind of discipline whose prerequisites include attitudes and capacities such as openness, receptivity, empathy, sensitivity, and imagination. Margaret Walker writes, "Acuity of moral perception, especially as regards the interests and perspectives of people, must result from the exercise of many complex, learned, and indefinitely improvable skills of attention, communication, and interpretation" (Walker 1991:771).

Among contemporary care theorists, Walker is probably the most insistent on the need that caring intentions be validated through communication with those cared-for. But Ruddick also mentions mothers attempting to figure out how to care for their children by talking with each other (Ruddick 1989), and Held emphasizes the need "to listen to each other in actual conversations in actual communities" (Held 1993:41). Noddings's argument that there must be fairly tight limits on the circle of those for whom we care depends partly on her insistence that the caring relation be completed by the recognition of those who are cared-for, and this insistence is in turn at least partially motivated by an epistemological concern. She says that if we do not "check on the effects of our efforts" and attend to a "living other speaking to us directly—informing us, persuading us, getting us to change our minds," we can be led into "a dangerous inauthenticity" (Noddings 1991:98). In a similar vein, Walker writes, "A great deal of our best evidence about how it is with others requires talking with and listening to them. . . . Asking, telling, repeating, mutually clarifying, mulling over, and checking back are the most dependable, accessible, and efficient devices for finding out how it is with others" (Walker 1991:769).

Theorists influenced by Simone Weil and Iris Murdoch sometimes speak as though care thinking requires forgetting the self; Noddings, for instance, asserts that "our attention, our mental engrossment is on the cared-for, not on ourselves" (Noddings 1984:24). But other theorists emphasize that care thinking also requires self-awareness and self-knowledge; Tronto says that attentiveness requires "a tremendous self-knowledge so that the caretaker does not simply transform the needs of the other into a projection of the self's own needs" (Tronto 1989:178).

The care perspective's attention to the subjects of moral consciousness contrasts with the justice perspective's efforts to disregard or bracket individual subjectivity through ingenious theoretical devices designed to approximate an impersonal "view from nowhere." Not only that strand of the justice tradition concerned primarily with rights but also the strand that concerns itself with welfare or utility typically focuses on relations "out there" in the world external to the self. This is not to say that the justice tradition dismisses all questions about the interests and obligations of the moral subject or about personal relationships but that, in both teleological and neo-Kantian deontological ethics, relationships between particular selves and particular others are regarded as likely to be epistemologically subversive or morally corrupting. Theoretical postulates such as the ideal observer, the disinterested judge, the archangel, the original position, and the view from nowhere are designed to correct for the assumed bias of particular points of view.

Care reasoning is unlike justice reasoning in that it does not attempt to bracket or disregard the self, whose appropriate motivations, attitudes, sensibilities, and qualities of character are thought indispensable to morally acute perception. Furthermore, these qualities are regarded not simply as instrumental to producing a morally desirable outcome but as intrinsic to the quality of the caring relationship. Care thinking thus not only pays more attention than justice thinking to the subject or moral consciousness but also conceptualizes differently the relation between that subject and the objects of her moral concern. Justice thinking is impersonal and general because it regards both moral subjects and the objects of their moral concern in terms of their moral status as representatives of humanity or as beings capable of pleasure and pain rather than in terms of their concrete specificity; care thinking is personal and particularized in that both carers and those cared-for regard each other as unique, irreplaceable individuals.

The justice perspective's concern to depersonalize moral thinking reflects its interest in epistemological issues and its eagerness to identify a method for discovering which moral principles are most objectively just. Justice thinking often prides itself on being objective precisely insofar as it distances itself from the self and particular relationships and dismisses care thinking as subjective and therefore unreliable precisely because successful caring by definition involves particular relations between carers and those cared-for. However, it is mistaken to assume that bracketing subjectivity is the best way of achieving moral objectivity, in the sense of trustworthy moral responses.

Care's focus on the relation between the carer and the cared-for is valuable in raising questions often ignored by justice reasoning, questions that are important both morally and epistemologically. Turning our attention inward as well as outward encourages reflexive consideration of what the agent brings to the situation, her interests, her location, the context, her warrant for intervention. Conceiving moral reasoning as interactive encourages reflection not only on the moral implications for others of action or inaction but also on the implications for the self, how it expresses or develops her moral character. As Walker puts it, it encourages us to ask, What kind of person do I want to become? (Walker 1987). Acknowledging the moral dimension of perception and the epistemic dimension of emotion also encourages consideration of how people may develop the moral abilities for morally sensitive perception and loving attention. Finally, insisting on the importance of checking with the one cared-for, rather than as-

suming that we know her needs in advance, avoids the arrogance and presump-
tiveness of postulating hypothetical consent in what Walker calls "round robins
of role-taking" in what she regards as the "alarming" "philosophical predilection
for the game of imagination" (Walker 1991:769).

Although it is not true that moral objectivity is best achieved by bracketing
subjectivity, it is equally mistaken to suppose that morally appropriate responses can be determined by focusing exclusively either on the attitude of the
moral subject or even on the caring relationship. Yet care theorists often seem to
assume that even if adequate caring cannot be guaranteed by the carer's intentions alone, the carer/cared-for dyad between them can be counted on to identify truly caring behavior.

On reflection, it is immediately evident that such an assumption is unwar-
ranted. Overindulgence or "spoiling" are only the least of the moral mistakes
that may be carried out in the name of care. Other, more clearly gendered,
abuses include incest and even footbinding. Incestuous fathers often portray
themselves as caring for their daughters, even as nurturing or initiating them,
and the Chinese women who bound the feet of their daughters and grand-
daughters also equated the pain they caused with care (Blake 1994:682).[7] These
examples show not only that appropriate caring is not guaranteed by the intentions of the one who claims to care but that such a guarantee is not supplied
even by agreement on the part of the one who is cared-for. Children characteristically retain a tenacious trust in the goodness of their "caretakers'" intentions,
finding it less psychologically devastating to interpret neglect or abuse as care
than to believe that they are not cared for. Abused women also often regard violence as an expression of caring or love, and they may even identify empathically
with their abusers. "Co-dependents" appeal to care to justify their facilitation of
destructive or self-destructive behavior on the part of others. These examples
demonstrate clearly that so long as care thinking focuses exclusively on the
carer/cared-for dyad, it cannot reliably assess the adequacy and appropriateness of responses that claim to be caring.

The care perspective is not necessarily without resources for addressing this
issue, but so far few care theorists have given it more than perfunctory attention,
perhaps because they have not yet clearly acknowledged it as a problem. The
care literature contains relatively few direct discussions of how to identify care
that is morally appropriate and has shown limited interest in moral justification.
Noddings, here as often elsewhere the most radical of the care theorists, even explicitly rejects traditional concerns about justification. She writes,

> An ethic of caring does not emphasise justification. As one-caring, I am not seeking
> justification for my action; I am not standing alone before some tribunal. What I seek
> is completion in the other—the sense of being cared-for and, I hope, the renewed
> commitment of the cared-for to turn about and act as one-caring in the circles and
> chains within which he is defined. Thus, I am not justified but somehow fulfilled and
> completed in my own life and in the lives of those I have thus influenced. (Noddings
> 1984:95)

This passage may be read as expressing lack of concern for any perspectives external to the caring relation.

The recent work of Joan Tronto is one exception to care theorists' lack of interest in justification. Because she recognizes that identifying and ranking needs is inherently contestable, Tronto asserts that care is a desirable political ideal only in the context of a just, pluralistic, democratic society in which open and equal discussion about needs and justice occurs (Tronto 1993:154–172). But in asserting the necessity of societywide dialogue about needs, which presumably involves assessing and ranking the needs of classes of people rather than specific individuals, Tronto seems to be concerned primarily with care as a political ideal and to depart from classic accounts of care thinking that describe it as distinguished by its focus on particular others.

These considerations suggest that care thinking, at least as it has been described so far in the literature, is incomplete as a feminist account of moral rationality. The suggestion that dyadic relations of care are somehow self-justifying, a suggestion more often implied than explicit, is not only mystifying but evidently false. I suggest that claims to care, like other perceptual and moral claims, can be justified only by widening the circle of intersubjective validation.

Care's Focus on the Particular

Care reasoning is often described as responding directly to particular persons and situations, whereas justice reasoning is supposedly concerned with universal principles. Like several other alleged contrasts between care and justice, this contrast is often overstated, since justice and care reasoning each necessarily recognize both particular and universal aspects of situations. Justice reasoning, as we have seen already, requires perceiving and assessing the morally salient features of particular situations in order to know which general principles should be brought to bear. Similarly, care's recognition of particular situations necessarily utilizes general concepts; for instance, recognizing a particular individual's need for companionship presupposes an ability to deploy the concepts of person and loneliness in a range of relevantly similar situations. Since both care and justice reasoning logically involve reference to both particular and universal aspects of situations, this distinction between them may be regarded as one of degree rather than kind, a difference of emphasis or attention or focus.

Justice reasoning regards particular situations as tokens of more general types and so attends to what they have in common with other situations. Care reasoning, by contrast, focuses on the specificities of each situation, emphasizing the ways in which it is unique and responding to those involved as particular in the sense of nonsubstitutable or irreplaceable (Friedman 1993:136–137). Accounts of care reasoning emphasize its attentiveness to detail, its deep and rather narrow focus, whereas justice reasoning, which requires explicit comparisons, tends to have a wider but shallower focus. Although the state of the nation, the world, and the universe are all, in a logical sense, particular states of affairs, care reasoning, with its emphasis on detail, depth, and specificity, is typically practiced in small-scale or micro situations involving a very few people whom the carer knows or comes to know personally. Justice reasoning, by contrast, has often been thought inappropriate for small-scale situations involving personal relations (Sandel 1982) and is paradigmatically used to address large-scale or macro situations involving people not known by the agent in their concrete specificity. On those somewhat exceptional occasions when agents apply justice reasoning to situations in which they are personally acquainted with those involved, they are expected to bracket or discount their personal knowledge and feelings. Care thinking celebrates minute perception of detail, but justice is supposed to be blind to all aspects of situations other than the limited number of generalizable features taken to be morally salient.

Some critics of the ethics of care complain that care thinking is unable to address large-scale social or global problems, but that is not precisely my concern here. Instead, I want to discuss one limitation of care reasoning not in terms of its applicability or otherwise to large-scale situations or the so-called public realm but rather in terms of what care makes visible in any situation regardless of scale or publicity. Accepting that one strength of care reasoning lies in its ability to draw moral attention to aspects of situations often disregarded by justice reasoning, I shall argue that its weakness lies in its inability to bring into focus other morally salient features of situations. When some things are foregrounded, others recede into the background; in making some things visible, care obscures others.

The distinctive feature of care reasoning that I address here is its focus on the specificities of particular situations, especially the needs of particular individuals. This focus is valuable in encouraging awareness of the moral complexities of situations, which are always open to a variety of interpretations, and of individuals' responsibilities within situations. Its weakness is that its attention to situations' specificity and particularity diverts attention away from their general features such as the social institutions and groupings that give them their structure and much of their meaning (Card 1990:205; Hoagland 1991:253, 260). For instance, care's emphasis on responding to immediate needs simultaneously takes those needs as givens, failing to question their source or why they are presently unfulfilled.

My point is not that the care perspective excludes awareness of social identities and structures; on the contrary, care presupposes such awareness, since the identity of particular individuals is constituted partly by their group membership and since particular actions or situations are made possible by and gain their meaning from social structures. Thus, recognizing a situation of racial privilege or sexual abuse inevitably presupposes an awareness of the race or sex of the individuals involved and of the way that these aspects of their identity influence particular situations. In an example of Lawrence Blum's, for instance, when a taxi driver chooses a white male customer over an African American woman, it would be impossible to perceive the affront to the dignity of the African American woman unless one were aware of the social meanings assigned to the skin colors of those involved; without this awareness, one's perception would be aesthetic rather than moral. Conversely, social structures, such as race and sex, exist only in their specific manifestations, and understanding them requires recognizing their operation in particular situations and experiences. The universal and particular aspects of situations, what might be called their form and content, thus presuppose each other in a way that the images of the duck and the rabbit in the ambiguous duck-rabbit figure do not presuppose each other. It is no more than a contingent fact that the outline of the duck can also be seen as the shape of a rabbit and vice versa, whereas it is not contingent that particular situations gain their meaning from social structures and that social structures exist only through their instantiation in particular situations. Despite this disanalogy, reference to the ambiguous duck-rabbit figure helps illustrate one important feature of the relationship between justice and care. This is that even when one is aware of the presence of both images, one cannot focus on both at once; when one is visible, the other becomes invisible. Similarly, when an agent is focusing on the concrete specificities of a situation, she is not attending directly to the social institutions that structure it and vice versa. When one is at the center of her consciousness, the other is at the margins. In care thinking, social structure occupies a place comparable to the frame of a picture one is viewing; one must be aware of it in some sense but one pays it little direct attention.

From a feminist perspective, care's exclusive focus on particularity is sometimes a significant liability, since an important concern of feminist ethics must be the ways in which male-dominant social structures limit the life chances of women and men. Close attention to the specificities of small-scale situations may well obscure perception of the larger social context in which they are embedded. For instance, focusing on particular examples of oppression may facilitate perception of insensitive and bullying behavior on the part of individuals, but it can also divert moral attention away from the social structures of privilege that legitimate such behavior. Moral thinking that focuses on the specificities of particular situations is likely to see the source of problems as lying in the personal attitudes of individual men, whites or heterosexuals who benefit, sometimes unwittingly or unwillingly, from sexism, racism, and heterosexism, rather than in those larger institutions that give some individuals power and privilege over others. Similarly, attending to an individual's immediate needs for food, shelter, comfort, or companionship is likely to distract from moral scrutiny of the social structures that create those needs or leave them unfulfilled.

I do not wish to argue that individual attitudes and immediate needs are morally insignificant. On the contrary, social structures and institutions are human inventions that survive only because people conform their behavior to them; racism and sexism outlive legal prohibition because of individuals' insensitivity or callousness. Care reasoning encourages personal accountability and individual resistance to oppressive structures. But care's emphasis on individual responses to immediate needs also encourages what are sometimes called band-aid or social work approaches to moral problems rather than efforts to solve them institutionally or prevent their occurrence through social changes.

The characteristic strengths and limitations of the care perspective are revealed in Noddings's response to the criticism most commonly made of caring, namely, that it is partial or parochial because attention to intimates and proximate strangers can lead to neglecting those who are further away. Noddings readily acknowledges the legitimacy of moral concern for distant strangers or humanity at large but insists it is not properly addressed in ways such as giving money to famine-relief organizations, which she calls "caring about." "Caring about" is "a poor second-cousin to caring," in Noddings's view, (1984:112) because caring, as she defines it, is an interactive relation in which people recognize each other as particular individuals. When others are too distant or too numerous for personal caring relations to be established with them, Noddings suggests that we either press their neighbors to care for them or seek to empower them to help themselves (Noddings 1991:97–98). "Instead of presenting ourselves to the world as heroes, gangbusters, or saviors, we would act as friends and partners, carefully building and maintaining stable relations on which we as well as others could depend in times of need" (Noddings 1991:97).

> From the perspective of caring, when we empower a group, we do not just give them things. Rather we help them to gain control over their own lives and, especially, to develop the resources and commitment to help others. The process of empowering is thus a part of caring. It necessarily requires a sort of "staying with" or "holding" as Sara Ruddick describes it, and this is a longterm program that involves the continuous construction and maintenance of caring relations. *It is still limited in the individualist sense.* I have to trust others to do the direct work of caring when I cannot be present." (1991:98, emphasis added)

Care's insistence on personal engagement and individual responsibility is a useful corrective to the impersonality, insensitivity, and frequent ineffectiveness of social engineering. It reminds us not only that a new society needs new people to make it work but that social change requires individual action and challenges each of us to act now rather than wait for the authorities or the revolution. Noddings's rejection of the masculine models of hero, gangbuster, and savior is a characteristically feminist response to the "grandiose universality" of the justice orientation (Friedman 1993:109) and the posturing of leaders, paradigmatically male (Fisher 1980:12–13), who infantilize and disempower their followers, positioning them as victims awaiting rescue or salvation.

Despite the virtues of care thinking, its emphasis on the quality of individual relations seems to preclude its addressing the structural oppositions between the interests of social groups that make caring difficult or unlikely between members of those groups. Similarly, care's reliance on individual efforts to meet individual needs disregards the social structures that make this virtually impossible in many cases. Care thinking seems unable to focus on the social causes of many individual problems, such as widespread homelessness and hunger, both of which have disproportionately severe effects on women.

I am not aware that care theorists have addressed the question of homelessness in North America, but it seems compatible with the spirit of care ethics to encourage moral responses such as personally helping homeless individuals or families rehabilitate or build houses or even taking them into one's own home, as opposed to challenging zoning and credit restrictions, pressing for governmental provision of housing, or even questioning why so many people, especially women, lack the money for housing. With respect to the question of Third World hunger, we have seen that care thinking encourages local people to give food to individuals with whom they are acquainted and even to help them grow their own food. But care thinking does not question why some "neighbors" have food while others do not, let alone identify the larger social forces causing peasant dislocation and dispossession, the assignment of land to cash crops for export rather than food for local people, Third World deforestation and desertification, and the draining of Third World resources to service its debt to international financial institutions. Even if caring is capable eventually of producing a social transformation that is evolutionary rather than revolutionary, the slowness and uncertainty of this approach make it morally inadequate for tackling existing problems of homelessless or hunger, given the level and extent of dislocation, malnutrition, and starvation as well as the interlinked and accelerating social and environmental crises.

Some care theorists have talked about making care applicable to large-scale social or global issues by enlarging our moral imagination, learning to care for distant others, including large populations with whom we have no personal contact. But this is to treat care merely as a moral motive, not as a distinctive mode of moral response, and it is incompatible with the characteristically interactive and personal relation that defines care thinking. At best, it is what Noddings calls "caring about." At worst, it appropriates the language of caring to refer to "caring that is *directed toward* inert and unknown recipients" and is thus a form of colonization, "oblivious to the possibility that [its] 'targets' might experience the proffered caring as insulting and invasive" (Code 1992:1–2).

Significantly improving the lives of the world's women certainly requires the empathy, imagination, and responsiveness that distinguish care thinking; but it also requires a kind of moral thinking that focuses not only on meeting immediate needs but on problematizing the structures that create those needs or keep them unfulfilled. This is as true on the familial and local levels as it is on the national and international levels, and it presents a major challenge for care theorists.

To note care thinking's difficulty in addressing some crucial questions of feminist practical ethics is not necessarily to assume that justice thinking is capable of dealing adequately with those questions. For instance, care reasoning addresses instances of rape and domestic violence by "strongly disapproving" of them (Noddings 1990b:125) and tries to protect victims and survivors by establishing moral authority over their assailants; justice reasoning, as commonly construed, is likely to condemn these assaults as violations by individuals of other individuals' rights. In order to fully comprehend sexual violence, however, its meanings and functions as a systematic social practice must be addressed, together with the ways in which many social institutions implicitly condone and legitimate it. Neither care nor justice reasoning, as ordinarily construed, constitutes the kind of hermeneutical moral thinking capable of questioning conventional definitions of assault as well as of exploring the complex assumptions about sexuality, aggression, and gender that make rape not only thinkable but predictable and even normal. The feminists of the late 1960s called this kind of thinking consciousness-raising.

Conclusion

At least as so far described by its theorists, care thinking has severe limitations. Its inability to focus on social structures restricts the scope of its moral critiques, and its lack of theoretical interest in justification renders its critical perspective unreliable even on those issues that it does address. Despite these shortcomings, the recent recognition of care thinking has made valuable contributions to philosophical understandings of moral rationality. Through studying empirical examples of moral thinking, care theorists have raised questions hitherto largely neglected by moral philosophers and revealed that the conception of practical reason associated with the European Enlightenment has its own limitations. Among these are an inadequate portrayal of moral thinking that exaggerates the significance of principles and fails to recognize that affectively laden aspects of moral thinking have epistemic as well as motivational functions. In addition, and because care is generally associated with the personal realm, the ethics of care has contributed to rehabilitating personal life as an arena for moral scrutiny; it has thus expanded the domain of practical morality, exposing further limitations in traditional theory. Finally, the ethics of care has revealed damaging biases, including gender biases, in Enlightenment moral theory, which has not only devalued the caring work assigned primarily to women, especially women of the lower classes, but also functioned as an ideology to rationalize selfishness as natural and normal.

Notes

1. Virginia Held and Sara Ruddick both read several earlier drafts of this essay and discussed them with me at length. I am deeply grateful for their help, although I must make the usual disclaimer that the views expressed here are still, in the end, not theirs but mine.

2. The Center for Human Caring was established in 1986 and its history and mission statement describes it as "the nation's first interdisciplinary center with an overall commitment to develop and use knowledge of human caring and healing as the foundation for transforming the health care system."

3. The contemporary ethics of care was pioneered by Milton Mayeroff's 1971 book, *On Caring,* (New York: Harper & Row) but this did not explore care's gendered dimensions and so was largely ignored by feminists. The name most widely associated with the contemporary feminist ethics of care is that of Nel Noddings (1984, 1989) but other philosophers who have endorsed some version of this approach to ethics include, but are not limited to Annette Baier (1987a, 1987b, 1994), Lawrence Blum (1988, 1991), Marilyn Friedman (1993), Virginia Held (1993), Rita Manning (1992), Sara Ruddick (1987, 1989, 1995), Joan Tronto (1993), and Margaret Urban Walker (1987, 1989, 1991, 1992).

4. There also appear to be convergences between the ethics of care and some non-Western moral thought. For instance, a recent article likens the ethics of care to the Confucian ethics of *Jen* (Chenyang Li 1994).

5. Contemporary feminist claims that women's morality is different from men's were foreshadowed in theories developing the neo-Marxist notion of a feminist standpoint (Smith 1974; Hartsock 1983), but the claims became best known in their psychological versions, through the work of Jean Baker Miller (1976), Nancy Chodorow (1978) and especially Carol Gilligan. In two influential articles published in the late 1970s in the *Harvard Educational Review,* followed by her landmark book, *In a Different Voice,* Gilligan argued that most accepted accounts of moral development were male biased not simply in focusing primarily on males but, more seriously, in measuring the development of both males and females by a standard derived exclusively from the study of men and boys (Gilligan 1982). Reflecting on the responses of girls and women interviewed initially about their abortion decisions, Gilligan claimed to hear "a different voice" expressing an understanding of morality that she called the ethics of care. She argued that this understanding contrasted in significant ways with what she called the ethics of justice assumed by her teacher and mentor Lawrence Kohlberg, whose own studies of moral development had drawn on the Kantian conception of morality embodied in the work of Jean Piaget and John Rawls.

6. Some suffragists argued for the vote on grounds that women's moral superiority would encourage cleaning up politics, and the "moral mothers" in Britain and the United States drew on cultural myths of women's innate peacefulness to oppose World War I. Contemporary feminist peace and environmental activists have sometimes portrayed their political work as a kind of global housekeeping.

7. The Chinese word *teng* may mean "pain," "care," or a conflation of both, as in the proverb that translates as "Beating is caring, scolding is loving" (Blake 1994).

References

Baier, Annette C. 1987a. "The Need for More than Justice." *Science, Morality and Feminist Theory*, edited by Marsha Hanen and Kai Nielsen. Calgary, Canada: University of Calgary Press (*Canadian Journal of Philosophy*, Supplementary Volume 13).

———. 1987b. "Hume, the Women's Moral Theorist?" In *Women and Moral Theory*, edited by Eva Feder Kittay and Diana T. Meyers. Totowa, NJ: Rowman and Littlefield.

———. 1994. *Moral Prejudices: Essays on Ethics*. Cambridge, MA: Harvard University Press.

Baron, Marcia. 1984. "The Alleged Moral Repugnance of Acting from Duty." *Journal of Philosophy* 81:4 (April), 197–220.

Benhabib, Seyla. 1986. "The Generalized and the Concrete Other: The Kohlberg-Gilligan Controversy and Feminist Theory." *Praxis International* 5:4 (January), 402–424.

———. 1992. *Situating the Self: Gender, Community and Postmodernism in Contemporary Ethics*. New York: Routledge.

Blake, C. Fred. 1994. "Footbinding in Neo-Confucian China and the Appropriation of Female Labor." *Signs: Journal of Women in Culture and Society* 19:3 (Spring).

Blum, Lawrence. 1982. "Kant's and Hegel's Moral Rationalism: A Feminist Perspective." *Canadian Journal of Philosophy* 12:2 (June), 287–302.

———. 1987. "Particularity and Responsiveness." *The Emergence of Morality in Young Children*, edited by Jerome Kagan and Sharon Lamb. Chicago: University of Chicago Press.

———. 1988. "Gilligan and Kohlberg: Implications for Moral Theory." *Ethics* 98 (April), 472–491.

———. 1991. "Moral Perception and Particularity." *Ethics* 101:4 (July), 701–725.

———. 1992. "Care." In *Encyclopedia of Ethics*, edited by Lawrence C. Becker. New York: Garland.

Calhoun, Cheshire. 1988. "Justice, Care, Gender Bias." *Journal of Philosophy* 85:9 (September).

Card, Claudia. 1990. "Gender and Moral Luck." In *Identity, Character and Morality*, edited by Owen Flanagan and Amelie Oksenberg Rorty. Cambridge, MA: MIT Press.

Chodorow, Nancy. 1978. *The Reproduction of Mothering: Psychoanalysis and the Sociology of Gender*. Berkeley: University of California Press.

Code, Lorraine. 1992. "Who Cares? The Poverty of Objectivism for a Moral Epistemology." *The Annals of Scholarship* 9: 1–2, 1–17.

Coole, Diana. 1988. *Women in Political Theory: From Ancient Misogyny to Contemporary Feminism*. Brighton, UK, and Boulder, CO: Wheatsheaf and Lynne Rienner.

Dillon, Robin S. 1992. "Care and Respect." In *Explorations in Feminist Ethics: Theory and Practice*, edited by Eve Browning Cole and Susan Coultrap McQuin. Bloomington and Indianapolis: Indiana University Press.

Fisher, Berenice. 1980. "Who Needs Woman Heroes?" *Heresies* 3:1 (issue 9).

Flanagan, Owen, and Kathryn Jackson. 1987. "Justice, Care and Gender: The Kohlberg-Gilligan Debate Revisited." *Ethics* 97, 622–637.

Freud, Sigmund. 1933. "Femininity." In *New Introductory Lectures on Psychoanalysis*, translated from the German and edited by James Strachey. New York: W. W. Norton.

Friedman, Marilyn. 1993. *What Are Friends For? Feminist Perspectives on Personal Relationships and Moral Theory*. Ithaca: Cornell University Press.

Gilligan, Carol. 1982. *In a Different Voice: Psychological Theory and Women's Development*. Cambridge, MA: Harvard University Press.

———. 1987. "Moral Orientation and Moral Development." In *Women and Moral Theory,* edited by Eva Feder Kittay and Diana T. Meyers. Totowa, NJ: Rowman and Littlefield.

Habermas, Jürgen. 1990. "Moral Consciousness and Communicative Action." In *Moral Consciousness and Communicative Action,* translated by Christian Lenhardt and Shierry Weber Nicholsen. Boston: MIT Press, pp. 178–180.

Hacking, Ian. 1985. "Styles of Scientific Reasoning." In *Post-Analytic Philosophy,* edited by John Rajchman and Cornel West. New York: Columbia University Press.

Harding, Sandra. 1987. "The Curious Coincidence of Feminine and African Moralities: Challenges in Feminist Theory." In *Women and Moral Theory,* edited by Eva Feder Kittay and Diana T. Meyers. Totowa, NJ: Rowman and Littlefield.

Hartsock, Nancy. 1983. *Money, Sex and Power: Toward a Feminist Historical Materialism.* New York: Longman.

Held, Virginia. 1993. *Feminist Morality: Transforming Culture, Society and Politics.* Chicago: University of Chicago Press.

Herman, Barbara. 1983. "Integrity and Impartiality." *Monist* 66, 233–250.

Hoagland, Sarah Lucia. 1991. "Some Thoughts About 'Caring.'" In *Feminist Ethics,* edited by Claudia Card. Lawrence: University of Kansas Press.

Houston, Barbara. 1988. "Gilligan and the Politics of a Distinctive Women's Morality." In *Feminist Perspectives: Philosophical Essays on Method and Morals,* edited by Lorraine Code, Sheila Mullett, and Christine Overall. Toronto: University of Toronto Press.

Kant, Immanuel. 1965. *Critique of Pure Reason,* translated by L. W. Beck. New York: St. Martin's Press, p. 177:A133–A134.

Kohlberg, Lawrence. 1982. "A Reply to Owen Flanagan." *Ethics* 92, 513–528.

Kohlberg, Lawrence, Charles Levine, and Alexandra Hewer. 1983. *Moral Stages: A Current Reformulation and Response to Critics.* Basel: S. Karger.

Li, Chenyang. 1994. "The Confucian Concept of *Jen* and the Feminist Ethics of Care: A Comparative Study." *Hypatia* 9:1 (Winter), 70–89.

Mill, John Stuart. 1980. *The Subjection of Women.* Arlington Heights, IL: Harlan Davidson. Originally published in 1869.

Miller, Jean Baker. 1976. *Toward a New Psychology of Women.* Boston: Beacon Press.

Noddings, Nel. 1984. *Caring: A Feminine Approach to Ethics and Moral Education.* Berkeley: University of California Press.

———. 1989. *Women and Evil.* Berkeley: University of California Press.

———. 1990a. "Feminist Fears in Ethics." *Journal of Social Philosophy* 21:2–3 (Fall-Winter), 25–33.

———. 1990b. "A Response." *Hypatia* 5:1 (Spring).

———. 1991. "The Alleged Parochialism of Caring." *American Philosophical Association Newsletter on Feminism and Philosophy* 90:2 (Winter).

Okin, Susan. 1989. "Reason and Feeling in Thinking About Justice." *Ethics* 99:2 (January), 229–249.

O'Neill, Onora. 1984. "Kant After Virtue." *Inquiry* 26, 387–405.

Ruddick, Sara. 1987. "Remarks on the Sexual Politics of Reason." In *Women and Moral Theory,* edited by Eva Feder Kittay and Diana T. Meyers. Totowa, NJ: Rowman and Littlefield.

———. 1989. *Maternal Thinking: Towards a Politics of Peace.* Boston: Beacon Press.

Sandel, Michael. 1982. *Liberalism and the Limits of Justice.* Cambridge: Cambridge University Press.

Sher, George. 1987. "Other Voices, Other Rooms? Women's Psychology and Moral Theory." In *Women and Moral Theory*, edited by Eva Feder Kittay and Diana T. Meyers. Totowa, NJ: Rowman and Littlefield.

Smith, Dorothy. 1974. "Women's Perspective as a Radical Critique of Sociology." *Sociological Inquiry* 44.

Stack, Carol. 1986. "The Culture of Gender: Women and Men of Color." *Signs: Journal of Women in Culture and Society* 11:2 (Winter), 321–324.

Tronto, Joan. 1989. "Women and Caring: What Can Feminists Learn About Morality from Caring?" In *Gender/Body/Knowledge: Feminist Reconstructions of Being and Knowing*, edited by Alison M. Jaggar and Susan R. Bordo. New Brunswick, NJ: Rutgers University Press.

———. 1993. *Moral Boundaries: A Political Argument for the Ethics of Care*. New York: Routledge.

Walker, Lawrence J. 1984. "Sex Differences in the Development of Moral Reasoning." *Child Development* 55:3, 677–691.

Walker, Margaret Urban. 1987. "Moral Particularity." *Metaphilosophy* 18:3–4 (July–October).

———. 1989. "What Does the Different Voice Say? Gilligan's Women and Moral Philosophy." *Journal of Value Inquiry* 23, 123–134.

———. 1991. "Partial Consideration." *Ethics* 101:4 (July), 758–774.

———. 1992. "Moral Understandings: Alternative 'Epistemology' for a Feminist Ethics." In *Explorations in Feminist Ethics: Theory and Practice*, edited by Eve Browning Cole and Susan Coultrap McQuin. Bloomington and Indianapolis: Indiana University Press.

11

Injustice in Families:
Assault and Domination
[1995]

SARA RUDDICK

I begin, as one does, in *medias res*, in this case in the midst of a conversation among feminists about justice and families. Hitherto, theorists of justice have tended to ignore families or else have explicitly contrasted the "private domain" of the family with the "public" world of justice.[1] Feminists have claimed in response that sheltering families from the demands of justice legitimates the exploitation of children by adults and women by men. But, at the same time, some feminists also argue that there are serious incongruities between moral experience in families and dominant (so-called liberal) theories of distributive justice.[2] This disparity has provided one motive for developing an alternative "ethics of care"[3] that seems suited for, indeed is often inspired by, central relations and moral dilemmas that arise within families.

Whatever the intentions of its proponents, the presence of an ethics of care has tended to reinforce the separation between families and justice for several reasons. At least in the United States, an "ethics of care" has been explicitly contrasted with an "ethics of justice." A long history of separate public and private spheres as well as recent attempts to develop domain or practice sensitive ethics makes it easy to construe care as "feminine" and domestic and justice as remaining in its traditional public domain. And finally, although certain ethicists have been creatively translating principles of care into public domains and languages,[4] few have revised dominant "liberal" conceptions of justice in order to make them suitable to the moral experience of families.[5]

There are at least three ways to bring justice more securely into the family. One might assimilate or subordinate the concerns of care to justice and then ar-

gue that families should be subject to distributive justice as it is best conceptualized in current theories.[6] Alternatively one could develop an ethics of care that
subordinates but adequately addresses the concerns of justice.[7] Or one could
maintain the distinction between the ethics of justice and of care, without subordinating either to the other, and reconceptualize justice in ways more suitable
to the moral experience and relationships of families. It is the third way that I
pursue here.[8]

Accordingly I assume a conceptual framework that distinguishes moral orientations of "justice" and "care". This framework is neither exhaustive nor exclusive
but offers one among several ways of thinking about moral phenomena.[9] My
reading of the justice-care distinction follows a suggestion of Carol Gilligan's[10]
that the whole of the moral domain can be likened to an ambiguous figure.
"Justice" and "care" refer to unassimilable ways of identifying, interpreting, and
responding to moral phenomena that can be seen from two perspectives, as a
single figure can be seen alternatively as a duck or rabbit, a vase or two faces. In
this view, each moral orientation offers a "point of view from which alone a certain sort of understanding of human life is possible";[11] each is genuinely moral;
neither can be replaced by or subsumed under the other; each covers the whole
of the moral domain and therefore can check and inform the other; there is no
third, "mature," single integrative moral perspective within which each orientation has its place.[12]

Characteristics of "justice" and "care," when contrasted with each other, are
complex. The two moral orientations foster distinctive cognitive capacities, appeal to distinctive ideals of rationality, elicit distinctive moral emotions, presume distinctive conceptions of identity and relationships, recognize distinctive
virtues, and make distinctive demands on institutions. For the purposes of this
discussion, I waive these complexities and, presuming familiarity, draw a simple
contrast between the requirements of just relationships and those of caring relationships as a family member might see them.

From the perspective of justice, relationships require *restraint* of one's own
aggression, intrusion, and appropriation and *respect* for the autonomy and bodily integrity of others. Participants attempt to devise and agree upon procedures
for resolving fairly inevitable conflicts. A primary temptation, according to the
perspective of justice, is to flout the rules of fair play, taking whatever you can
get, what you are strong or lucky enough to be able to exact. Correlatively, a person may be tempted (as well as forced) to submit to injustice without protest.
She may also be tempted to watch, without protest, when injustice is inflicted on
others.

From the perspective of care, relationships require *attentiveness* to others and
response to their needs. Each participant should endeavor to give what can usefully be received and to receive what can usefully be given. A primary temptation, according to the perspective of care, is to neglect others or to project one's

own needs onto them. Correlatively, a caring person may be destructively self-sacrificial, unwilling or unable to be the recipient of care. Or he may be tempted to watch with indifference when others are neglected or abandoned.

I believe that "justice" and "care," when more appropriately elaborated, usefully mark alternative moral visions, conflicts, virtues, and ways of reasoning. I also believe that the capacity to welcome irreducible differences of perspective, as much as the insight each affords, illuminates moral conflict in both personal and public contexts. If there are two irreducible orientations, individuals can learn to shift between them while discussants can acknowledge that they "see" the same situation yet see so differently that they cannot at once understand each other's moral reasoning. Because there are two contrasting perspectives rather than a multiperspectival array, a disruptive and illuminating shift of moral perspective in regard to the same phenomena becomes possible.

In developmental and social psychology the contrast between "justice" and "care" has, notoriously, been associated with gender.[13] In developmental theory, it was women listening primarily to women who identified a "care" perspective. According to these developmental theorists, although most women and men shift appropriately between the two orientations as particular moral circumstances suggest, most also tend to "focus" on or consistently adopt one rather than the other perspective. Some men adopt a care orientation, but most men and many women reflect a justice focus that, at least until recently, was the dominant orientation of public moral discourse in the United States. But few women adopt only a justice perspective and many (perhaps more than a third) reason primarily in the subordinated, marginal "different" voice of care. These findings are controversial and continuously modified. Moreover, whatever their current associations with gender, these orientations are, according to Carol Gilligan, the principal researcher, rooted in human childhood experiences: powerlessness and inequality in the case of justice, attachment and fruitful interdependence in the case of care.[14] Accordingly, each orientation would normally be employed in any individual's or group's moral thinking, although particular sociopolitical experiences of inequality as well as disparate family forms would almost certainly produce systematic differences among racial, ethnic, national, and class as well as gender groups. Whatever the social or psychological origins of justice or care perspectives, the values of each orientation are (in my view) meant to be binding on women and men. Although "care" is not better than "justice"—any more than a duck is better than a rabbit, a face better than a vase—it is disturbing that a humanly rooted, feminine-identified orientation of care has been submerged both in public discussion and in the moral reasoning of many individuals.

Partly because care is associated with femininity, and partly because dominant theories of justice seem to bypass much of family moral life, feminists have sometimes used the justice-care framework to separate the familial from the political. My reading of "care" and "justice" as unassimilable orientations is meant

Thesis

to refute this division. Justice and care each cover the entire moral domain; any institution or relation, no matter how public or private, can be judged from the perspective of justice or of care. This does not mean that there are no distinctions between more public and private domains or that some distinctions between personal and political are not useful. But these distinctions do not match up with the distinction between justice and care. Recognizing its origins within particular relationships, moral theorists have worked to extend and politicize the ethics of care. In a similar spirit, feminists should revise theories of justice originally devised with public institutions in mind, thus making it easier to bring justice home.

To this end, I review a conversation among feminists between advocates of distributive justice in families and sceptics who believe that dominant theories of distributive justice are not respectful of family relationships and moral experience. I then consider a particular wrongdoing, family assault, draw connections between assault and domination, and urge that assault be considered an injustice. Finally I offer one principle of family justice—respect for embodied willfulness.

I bypass entirely several critical issues of family justice. I do not consider the question, Who has the right to bear and raise children?[15] I am concerned primarily with families that already include children and, more generally, generations; the example of injustice I select for focus—family assault—is notoriously suffered by children as well as women, and the elderly are also frequently its victims. Nor do I consider crucial issues of social or legal intervention in families to protect vulnerable members from failure of care or justice. Rather I am concerned with justice *within* families, that is, with ideals of justice family members might adopt to regulate—and to inspire—their relationships with each other.

Finally I do not take up the difficult question of defining "families." I have in mind moderately extended families in which—at the least—some people are identified as children, parents, grandchildren, grandparents, siblings, cousins, and so forth. (Two adults living as partners without children are typically members of two or more families that, together, include frail elderly and children.) Biological connections between family relatives are highly variable culturally and among families in a culture. I have no stake in an exclusive *definition* of "families" and believe, along with many others, that heterosexist presumptions of family organization work against justice and care even within apparently exclusively heterosexual families.

Family Fairness

When theorists explicitly contrast the "private domain" of families with the public world in which justice is at stake, they usually offer three kinds of reasons for shielding families from demands of justice.[16]

Family celebrants believe that families are too good for justice. Justice negotiates between competing self-interests, whereas family members share a single interest, the good of the family and each of its members. Outside the family just individuals restrain greed and aggression in the interests of fairness; family members, bound by ties of affection and trust, require no such restraint. There are of course bad families, but they are uncaring, not unjust.

Pessimists argue, by contrast, that families are naturally, irredeemably unjust. To support their conviction that family injustice is entrenched, they point to a disturbing record of abuse and exploitation of women by men and children by parents. The source of this allegedly omnipresent injustice is a radical, incurable inequality among family members. Very young children and the elderly cannot contribute to the common good and therefore gain no leverage by withdrawing services. When they become old enough to contribute, children remain, for many years, too weak and dependent to retaliate against abuse and therefore must accept whatever terms of survival they are offered. Healthy women and men are not incurably unequal. But some pessimists argue that despite notable individual exceptions, men are by nature too violent or selfish, women "by nature" too frightened or submissive for either to abide by fair procedures for distributing the benefits and obligations of family life.[17]

Finally, some argue that even if family arrangements are often unfair and could be made fairer, efforts to impose justice are likely to disrupt family life and harm vulnerable family members. Some point to the importance of families in organizing resistance to racism, pooling scarce resources, and providing refuge from colonial and autocratic governments and from heartless bureaucratic rule. Others plead that families are more fragile than they appear and that unjust families are better than no family at all. They worry that the language of competing rights sets child against parent, children against each other, women against men, generation against generation.

Feminists, notably among them Susan Moller Okin,[18] have persuasively replied to each of these charges against family justice. However affectionate and trusting, individuals in families typically have competing interests and make conflicting demands upon numerous resources ranging from food, shared space, cash, and time for nonfamilial projects and pleasures. The fact that family members are often bound by ties of affection or depend upon each other for meeting basic needs does not make families too good for justice. On the contrary, these emotional and material bonds provide some family members with especially fertile opportunities for exploitation and domination.

Although injustice abounds in families, it is not inevitable. Families are remarkably variable social creations, some more exploitative of vulnerable members than others. Family distributions of goods and burdens can be affected by new ways of disseminating knowledge, contraceptive techniques, employment policies, economic recession or prosperity, and family law. There is no a priori reason that family organization cannot also be transformed by moral critique.

It is true that some family members are inevitably unequal to others. But even tiny children can be perceived as future contributors to a family enterprise as well as potential aggressors against other family members. Reciprocity can be presented to older children as an ideal that governs family life. In circumstances where women can control fertility in their own interests, unfair division of family labor between women and men is clearly remediable. In particular, the fact that only females bear children does not imply that women should assume a special responsibility for child care or any other disproportionate burden of household labor.

There are many causes of family disruption: natural catastrophe, the death of a family member, high rates of unemployment, or insufficient resources for minimally protective family life. When protests of *injustice within* the family threaten to disrupt family arrangements, then the suffering of disruption may be balanced by relief from the injustice. Injustices within families are painful for those directly assaulted as well as for those who watch the infliction or suffering of injustice by people they love and on whom they depend. To be sure, in families as in workplaces, ill-treated vulnerable people may fear bringing claims against aggressors because they risk losing necessary resources and connections. But the fact that protest is risky does not mean that injustice cannot be appropriately charged.

In sum, most feminists agree, families can and should be judged by strictures of justice. But many feminists also believe that traditional objections to justice within the family point to real difficulties in applying to families accounts of justice that were not devised with families in mind. It is not, these feminists argue, that families can't or shouldn't strive to be just. Rather, if one's moral reflections are inspired by the relationships and conflicts of family life, then *theories* that construe justice as impartial fairness seem seriously incomplete.

Four features of theories of justice figure prominently in feminist conversations. In theories of justice, agents are individuals; families are treated as individuals when represented by heads of families. As individuals, parties of justice may care for their families; Rawls is explicit in his assumption that just men care for future generations. But these individuals—who always sound as if they are men—are not themselves creations of relationships but rather are rational because of their detachment from them. Seyla Benhabib's account of these agents of justice is frequently cited in feminist discussion: "This is a strange world: it is one in which individuals are grown up before they have been born; in which boys are men before they have been children; a world where neither mother, nor sister, nor wife exist."[19]

Family identities, by contrast, are constructed within and by relationships. It may be difficult even to identify a *self*-interest apart from self-defining relationships. In particular, the relationships of parents with children typically involve an identification through which a parent tends to assimilate her own and her child's interests, and even identity.

Second, in theories of justice individuals are defined in terms of similar characteristics—usually some combination of rational self-interest and abilities to harm, contribute to joint enterprises, and abide by rules of fair play. Aside from these essential characteristics, individuals are "disembodied" and "disembedded"[20] from actual social relations and thus able to stand in for each other. To be sure, theories of justice only initially and hypothetically assume a "generalized other" precisely in order to formulate ideals of fairness between people with different projects, living in different circumstances. But the image of a representative man of reason, a person who might be *anybody*, is integral to justificatory strategies.

Family relationships are often constituted in terms of the differences of their members. Children differ from each other and from adults not only in size and strength but in their reasoning, emotional responses, abilities, tastes, and interests. Fairness to each typically turns upon recognizing particularities of their personality and circumstance.[21] Family ideologies are founded on images of difference, most notably on the hitherto universal fact that only females bear children. Treating male and female parents as disembodied or similarly bodied wishes away, in advance, material, psychological, and symbolic differences between women and men that *may* follow upon their different relations to birthgiving and thus leads to more general minimalization of bodily life and relationships.

Third, theorists of justice posit the fundamental equality of persons as a normative presupposition or moral ideal. To be sure, any domain that justice governs is liable to inequality. It is inequality that creates the need for justice. But the aim of distributive justice is (typically) to minimize inequality and to rationalize remaining instances in terms of a greater or another good or of benefit to the least well off.

By contrast, inequality is the stuff and rationale of family life. Theories of justice based on reciprocity find it difficult to account for justice to the indefinitely disabled. But the disabled are the principal subjects of family justice in that protection of the weak just because they are weak—young, old, ill, despairing, or otherwise especially vulnerable—is a principal point of family life. Fair relations between healthy adults, important as they are to family life, are not all of family relations; nor are these relations separable from the unequal family relations in which women and men participate.

More Kantian theorists who assume the fundamental equality of each person[22] also risk speaking aslant of fundamental conundrums of family moral life. One can—and in certain circumstances one should—insist upon the primitive equality of a healthy employed male adult and an unemployed pregnant woman already bearing primary responsibility for young children; of socially and academically integrated children and their sibling with Down's syndrome; of an aphasic eighty-four-year-old, the linguistically fluent speakers surrounding her, and a two-year-old just beginning to talk. But such equality is frankly metaphysical. In actual families stark and sometimes irreparable inequalities such as the not atypical ones I have just mentioned provide the primary materials of moral reflection. Someone who imagines herself ignorant of her place among unequals imagines herself outside much of family moral experience.

Finally, in theories of justice an allegedly unfair policy or relationship is tested for justice by determining whether rational self-interested individuals would consent to it. Consent is hypothetical, determined by rational reflection rather than actual negotiation. Nonetheless, the thought experiment has about it the air of real choice; it encourages individuals to imagine themselves freely undertaking or reassessing for fairness their relationships and attendant obligations.

By contrast, there is a given and yet paradoxically, fragile character to family obligations.[23] Although the scope of family obligation varies culturally and is subject to moral reflection, to recognize an obligation as familial is, in part, to construe it as beyond consent, a given consequence of relationship. In a daily way, children must be fed, a schizophrenic nephew housed, the ill tended, however "unfair" their demands and however disproportionate the responsibilities of those who feed. On the one hand, to "freely" refuse these obligations in the name of fairness seems tantamount to "freely" rejecting primary moral demands made by the vulnerable upon people able to respond to need. On the other hand, at least in current U.S. society, allegedly "given" obligations are often "freely" rejected. Some are negligent because they lack social or personal resources for effective response. Just as often, it is more independent and socially favored family members—especially men—who "reassess" and shun the daily work of meeting family obligations.

In sum, dominant theories of justice tend to idealize equality, transcendence of difference, and the ability to give or withhold consent. The moral dilemmas of family life tend to revolve around radical inequalities, embodied differences, and fragile obligations that seem beyond consent. The subjects of justice are rational and self-interested individuals able to cooperate with and harm each other. Family members are bound by emotional ties that foster mutual identification in contexts where some are not yet, or not now, able to cooperate or harm. Justice theorists can respond to each doubt about their understanding of family identities and relationships. But explanations, modifications, and "defense" often seem ex post facto and do not account for the cumulative effect of particular conceptual misfits.

In contrast to theories of justice, the "ethics of care" begins not with individuals but with the relationships in which individuality is created. This ethics recognizes irremediable inequalities inherent in many relationships, highlights virtues central to family well-being such as respect for difference, and acknowledges the binding power of "given" obligations. It is not surprising that family moralists turn more easily to this ethics for understanding and self-governance. Yet it is exactly this turning to care in despair of justice that threatens to render care private and familial while at the same time excusing families from the demands of justice.

Family Assault

Suppose, as Aristotle would allow us to say, we make a fresh start and begin thinking about ideals of *justice*, as many philosophers now think about care, with the moral experience of families in mind. Suppose, too, that we begin constructing ideals of justice by identifying the typical wrongs these ideals might right. What conceptions of *in*justice would emerge?

Consider, first, one common story of familial wrong. A healthy adult inflicts pain upon someone considerably smaller or weaker—a child or a frail, disabled person. The assaulter can cease or leave at will; the assaulted is "pinned down" under the blows, often by love, terror, and material dependence, as well as by force. Assault may consist primarily—and perhaps entirely—in abusive verbal or other nonphysical behavior in which, to invoke Simone Weil, the assaulted suffers "a humiliation" experienced as a "violent condition of the whole physical being, which wants to rise up against the outrage but is forced, by impotence or fear, to hold itself in check."[24] In speaking of assault, however, I want to underline the "whole *physical* being," the use of the *body* as a site of pain and fear of pain.

Scenarios of assault are particular to families and cultures. Assaulters may be enraged or deliberate; they may strike with their fists or employ familiar "arms"—a leather belt, for example; they may strike silently or entwine their blows with protestations of love or justifying excuses. But as I use the term, stark inequality, captivity, and the infliction of pain mark "assault." There are many ills wrought by family members upon each other that do not involve assault.

Assault exemplifies the features of family experience obscured by theories of justice. It typically occurs within and is usually one expression of a relationship. Assaultive relationships are marked by material inequalities between assaulter and assaulted. Assaultive episodes are frequently occasioned by attitudes and behavior that appear to the assaulter to express willful differences from family norms. The assaulted cannot withhold and the assaulter does not ask for consent to the relationship either generally or in its assaultive moments. If assault can nonetheless be seen as an injustice, then justice will be more firmly lodged within families.

Family assault appears to be a widespread practice that, at least in the United States, occurs in all cultural and economic groups.[25] In this chapter I do not contest these practices but rather assume, against widely shared understandings, that assault is wrong. My question is, What allows us to label this putative wrong an injustice? However, my longer-range project is to chip away at the widespread practice of family assault and the beliefs that justify it. I hope that counting assault as injustice and then elaborating demands of justice will provide a particular moral understanding to assaulters, and a language of redress to the assaulted.

Any family member may suffer assault, and most family members can become assaulters. But women and children, and after them the elderly, are the primary victims of assault; men and parents, the primary aggressors. In this chapter, I am especially concerned with assaultive relations between parents, especially mothers, and children. It is mothers with whom I identify and imagine myself trying to formulate nonassaultive ideals of family relations; it is children whom I am eager to protect.

Assault as Injustice

What, then, allows us to count assault as an injustice? First, within a framework that distinguishes two moral orientations, care and justice, family assault is more easily counted as injustice than as a failure of care. From the perspective of an ethics of care, exemplary wrongs involve indifference or neglect. Victims of sustained care-lessness are abandoned—left to feed themselves, physically or psychologically. An assaulter, by contrast, lacks virtues of restraint and detachment. The victims of assault can plausibly be compared to weaker states targeted in so-called *unjust* wars: "They that have odds of power exact as much as they can, and the weak yield to such conditions as they can get."[26] A child cries for care—pay attention, help me, catch me if I fall—but cries out against assault: It hurts! Get away. Stop.

Protests against assault draw easily on languages of justice, especially of "rights." "Women and children have an *absolute right* to be free from bodily harm."[27] "Rights" afford the assaulted a "protective distance";[28] children have "rights" against bodily invasion or psychological intrusion, "rights" to autonomy, bodily integrity, and self-assertion. More elusively, Simone Weil spoke of the "contact with injustice through pain" and heard in the cries of the assaulted a cry for justice: "Every time there arises from the depth of the human heart the childish cry . . . 'Why am I being hurt?' then there is certainly injustice."[29] To her cry of "hurt," we might add the childlike "It's not fair," recognizing a fairness that has little to do with distribution.

The designation of assault as injustice illuminates a disturbing phenomenon. It seems that there is little correlation between tendencies to assault and to neglect. Some mothers, for example, are indifferent, inattentive, even frankly neglectful, but do not assault their children. Other mothers are protective and attentive, yet engage in assault. Caring but assaultive mothers may be exhausted or powerless before their children's will. Or they may believe that assault is a useful or even necessary instrument of training. Or they may act out of an identification that compels them to beat out a rebellious, shameful, or socially vulnerable "self" as it is expressed in the attitudes or behavior of the assaulted. Whatever the motives of assault, there is no reason, without special knowledge, to assume that assaulters care too little for the assaulted or that in daily ways they do not fulfill the requirements of care.

None of these considerations preclude condemning assault from the perspective of care. In conventional understanding, families are caring institutions any of whose failures are failures of care. The capacity to restrain aggression can be seen as a virtue required for caring, the ability to moderate identification a condition of caring well. Assault is often experienced as a violation of care: a hurt levied within a particular caring relationship in which protection rather than abuse is called for. In my understanding, moral phenomena almost always can be seen alternatively from the perspective of care and justice. My point is not to exclude assault from judgments of care but to include it as an instance of injustice.

Assault and Domination

My final strategy for revealing assault as injustice is to disclose connections between assault and domination. Domination is typically thought to be itself unjust and is sometimes thought to be constitutive of injustice.[30] Assault is both an instrument of domination and a consequence of its failure. A principle of justice, I will also argue, effectively prohibits assault only if it also prohibits domination.[31]

Roughly, and colloquially, to dominate someone is to judge and control the conditions and the outcomes of her actions. Metaphorically, a dominator treats the dominated as if she were an "object of property."[32] Some dominators may actually believe that the dominated are property, as some parents seem to regard their children, as Kant regarded domestic workers,[33] and, in the worst case, as slave owners regard enslaved people. Many family dominators who would deny that they consider family members as property nonetheless reveal tacit assumptions of ownership in their actions, fears, and expressions of entitlement.

For example, because she construes the dominated as her property, a dominator believes herself entitled to instigate or halt projects in which the dominated participate, control the conditions of their exit from relationships and institutions, and circumscribe their parameters of choice. She may appropriate as her own her property's labor both directly and by garnishing wages or other remuneration. Or she may insist on loyalty and love while also setting herself up as the judge of the dominated's ambition. She may feel entitled to intrude upon friendships and sexual relations or to eavesdrop and spy in order to uncover evidence of disturbing willfulness.

Dominators may care deeply for those they dominate; they may believe that domination is necessary for the eventual happiness and perhaps even the survival of the dominated. When caring dominators are benevolent and even-tempered, it is possible that neither they nor those they dominate recognize the character of their relationship. Dominating aims become evident, however, if the dominated develops projects and ambitions, attachments and sexual desires, that are disturbing to dominators. Then the dominated appears "out of control" in a double sense: he is no longer under the control of the dominator, and he appears to have lost the self-control whose test and expression is submission or, more politely, obedience. When confronted with incongruous willfulness, even a benign dominator is apt to reassert ownership, to confirm the relation of owner to object.

It is in this moment of reassertion that connections between domination and assault often become clear. In a dominator's eyes compliance is normal, disobedience a disturbing abnormality that must be set right. Even benign dominators who never anticipate hurting or humiliating their "property" may be compelled to beat the willfulness out of someone they are meant to own. Deliberate dominators may also decide in advance to use assault as a means of reasserting control. Recognizing that people, especially perhaps children, fear pain and humiliation, they exploit these fears in the service of domination by threatening or inflicting pain and humiliation. Some dominators feel more casually entitled to visit pain and humiliation on their property whenever he or she is displeasing. Still other, sadistic, dominators assault without provocation or else elicit the behavior they punish. For them the willfulness of the dominated does not so much excuse assault as provide occasions for its pleasures and excitement.

I do not want to exaggerate the connections between domination and assault. There are many indirect, nonassaultive techniques of domination; assault may be episodic, each instance sufficient unto itself, explicable in terms of the assaulted's provocative behavior and the assaulter's momentary frustration and rage. But the connections between domination and assault, though neither necessary nor even invariable, are stronger than mere association. Domination tends to lead to, explain, and justify assault; conversely, assault in the service of domination is a frequent and also often an explicitly avowed practice.

Although family assault and domination are widespread and often deliberate practices, they are neither inevitable nor unchangeable. Although I have never known a parent who was not at least tempted to assault in the interests of domination, or any entirely free of more or less permanent desires to dominate, I have known many who disciplined themselves against assault and learned to resist their temptations to appropriate and intrude. Sadistic assaulters may profit from some combination of coercive control and therapy. More benign assaulters can learn to distinguish between domination and the training children require, query the belief that assault is an effective instrument of *training,* and develop alternative means of control. Since practices of assault and domination are liable to change, they are also liable to moral critique. Moral ideals of nonassaultive relationships are both instances and inspirations for change. These ideals are in my view, for reasons I have given, appropriately construed as ideals of justice.

Respect for "Embodied Willfulness"

I now propose one such ideal of justice: respect for "embodied willfulness." This ideal begins with the renunciation of assault as an instrument of domination but becomes a governing ideal only when it is extended to include a principled renunciation of projects of domination.

Under the concept of willfulness I gather, first, a cluster of capacities to move, initiate, instigate, and resist; second, capacities to choose and act. The motions of a tiny infant can be seen as reflexes but also as expressions of will and can be respected or punished accordingly. Toddlers initiate and resist. Developmentally, willfulness is transformed into capacities to act and choose. But there is no conceptual mark or developmental achievement that reliably separates desirable agency from the willfulness that appears to dominators to be out of control.

By "*embodied* willfulness" I refer to two truisms, what Wittgenstein called "very general facts of nature." First, capacities of will are expressed bodily—including, and for many adults especially, in bodily speech. Second, human bodies are subject to pain, fear, and memory. These two conditions of embodied willfulness account for the familiar fact I just emphasized: it is possible, often though not always, to affect a person's will by affecting her body and, more particularly, to undermine her will by inflicting bodily pain or credibly threatening to do so. People who assault with intention to dominate can be said to *exploit* the conditions of embodied willfulness. Conversely, a person who refuses to threaten or inflict pain although she is in a position to do so and understands the conditions that make exploitation possible exhibits a minimal respect for the embodied willfulness of others.[34]

A person who refrains from assault does not thereby relinquish projects of domination. A dominator might refrain from assault because she doubts its effectiveness. Freudian theorists[35] have confirmed what many mothers have learned: although assault is often psychologically relieving to the assaulter and affects the immediate behavior of the assaulted, it is not possible to predict or to limit its consequences. Bodily pain, terror, and pleasure are embedded in fantasies about the relationships in which they are experienced, and self-identity is constructed within those relationships. Children, in particular, interpret experiences of pain in ways unintended by its perpetrators. These interpretations are rarely susceptible to conscious articulation, but nonetheless—or really partly for this reason—have lasting qualitative as well as quantitative consequences for capacities to will. Nor can adult assaulters reliably predict the consequences for themselves of assaulting. However confident they may feel about the benefits of assault, the act of assaulting can excite sadistic desire, guilt, or other emotions that then undermine confidence or escalate assault.

A person who appreciates the complexities of assault may set out to develop more effective means of domination typically available to parents, "heads of household," and economic providers. Nonetheless, such a person's restraint, even though coupled with domination, can mark the beginning of respect for embodied willfulness. For by deferring to the complexities of the experience of pain, the dominator also tacitly acknowledges both the value and the unpredictable independence of the mental life of the dominated. A parent may give weight primarily to the future effects of a child's experience. But she might, like self-restraining caregivers of the elderly, come to respect psychological complexities for their own sake, irrespective of any long-range consequences.

With deeper recognition of the complexities of embodied willfulness, occasions and grounds for respect may multiply until they almost preclude domination.[36] But there is no substitute for repudiating domination itself, which means relinquishing the conception of a person as an object of property and renouncing the *ambition* to appropriate her affection or labor or to intrude upon her body or mental life. Control, and often coercion, are necessary to family life. Allegedly strong but baffled family members cannot remain kindly attentive spectators when children act cruelly or self-destructively, disabled family members push themselves beyond their limits, or the failing elderly struggle to maintain self-respect in ways that harm themselves or others. Moreover, the best-intentioned parents occasionally assault, intrude, and appropriate in ways that, were they habitual, would become patterns of domination. Only a commitment to abjure domination, to respect embodied willfulness on principle, affords parents and other "stronger" family members confidence in the character of ongoing relationships despite troubling episodes and exercises of control.

Once determined to create relationships as free as possible of *domination*, and therefore to respect in advance the complexities of embodied willfulness, family members can more thoughtfully assess habitual techniques of family governance and compensate for unwelcome interventions as well as for occasional unplanned assaults. Justifiable coercion can be enacted in the most limited and nonassaultive ways that a particular occasion allows. Control, coercion, and even unplanned assaults can be deliberately surrounded by acts and attitudes intended to *foster* a sense of confident willfulness.

It is important not to sentimentalize. Sometimes, with aggressive "senile" elderly, for example, or with children who are temporarily enraged or cruel without apparent compunction, compensatory encouragement of willfulness is impossible; forceful coercion and nonassaultive punishment is, at least temporarily, the only action available. Yet even in these cases, as in happier times and relationships, a self-conscious commitment not to dominate can give family members a sense of purposive agency, self-respect, and self-control.

Concluding Remarks

It is at best premature to look for one relationship or a single wrongdoing that can reveal the essence of family justice. I do not believe that principled respect for embodied willfulness and the relinquishing of domination can provide such a reassuring essential core. I have, for example, barely alluded to retributive justice. Yet it is a requirement of justice in families, as well as in the larger polity, to name wrongs and to hold individual members responsible for their harms. Although in current practices, assaulters may appeal to retributive justice to justify assault, it should be possible to articulate principles of responsibility in tandem with principles of respect for embodied willfulness.

Principles of fairness familiar from dominant theories are also integral to family justice, most evidently but not only in relations between healthy adults. Where fairness fails, women make claims against current gender arrangements within families and against men who profit from them. For children, too, fairness is no luxury. Day care centers, playgrounds, and households ring with the cry, "It's not fair!"—along with the related "My turn." It has sometimes been argued that fairness is more superficial than principles such as respect for embodied willfulness.[37] Such ranking seems to me distracting. Unfairness is destructive of families and other institutions and often experienced by those who suffer it as a painful insult.

No matter how multifaceted the rendering of family justice, it will never constitute the whole of family morality. Within the framework I adopt, justice is always seen in tandem with care. I have described respect for embodied willfulness in terms of the restraint a just person imposes on herself, the distances she allows and keeps, the unfair advantage and domineering appropriation she forgoes. But embodied willfulness surely, and equally, requires the responsiveness of care: feeding, comforting, and holding bodies; attending to and actively fostering the willfulness that emerges. Care also checks and informs justice when, paradoxically, it makes its claims in an intrusive or appropriative manner. Caregivers who are attentive to context can recognize the fragile character of family obligations, the necessity of family connection for vulnerable people, or the restorative capacities of family connection to those assaulted by racism or other injuries for which they find no redress. If in full consideration of these complex needs that families serve, moralists intervene in the name of justice to impose fairness or forbid assault, they will more likely "engage the moral agency" of those they seek to change or protect if they are governed by ideals of humility and mutuality associated with care.[38]

Once justice is brought into families, there is no reason to divide sharply various public from relatively private moral realms. Family justice is dependent upon the political context in which families are situated. Family assaults as well as larger patterns of family domination are often indirect reactions to public policies that legitimate bigotry and deny to some the resources that both justice and care require. All families, however impoverished, fortunate, culturally marginal, or ethnically dominant, create their moralities in an inescapably public milieu. Family values will ground and express only those public policies and commitments that have already shaped and fostered the family values they depend upon.

Although family and public moralities are inextricably linked, there is no easy matching up between them. As many feminists and some politicians are fond of insisting, children learn meanings of justice and care within their original families. But early childhood lessons are not as straightly read as moralists might suggest. Childhood moralities *may* inform adult commitment. Conversely, although less often noted, a sharper appreciation of public injustice or neglect *may* alter moral reasoning and action in families. But stories of childhood and adult moral development are still very sketchy, and outcomes are unpredictable. Children who suffer neglect and abuse may, as adults, become passionate advocates of care and justice; those who learn justice and care within their families may nonetheless be indifferent to or abusive of strangers and "aliens"; adults who lead just and caring public lives, out of whatever motives, may nonetheless be neglectful or abusive family members.

Whatever relationship individuals forge between their relatively early or private experiences and their public lives, family justice can inform more general theories of justice. Many public and political relations, for example, most interstate relations, are marked by radical inequality. Many forms of bigotry and violence are marked by fear of difference, especially different bodies. Political theorists might well reflect on family justice as they formulate principles that allow the stronger and weaker, the alien and stranger, to relate to each other with minimal appropriation or intrusion.

Irrespective of its public or political import, family justice is worthy of praise. Vulnerability may elicit a caring response but also may elicit contempt or aggression. Vulnerable family members require care yet are also often provocative and exhausting. Though family relations can, theoretically, be seen alternatively under the aspect of justice or the aspect of care, in practice, attempts toward attentive caring are intertwined with temptations to dominate. The complex efforts of family members simultaneously to respond and respect offer an illuminating and too-little-noticed example of moral endeavor.

Notes

I benefited greatly from early readings of this chapter by Virginia Held, William Ruddick, David Wong, and Marilyn Young. I later received very useful written comments from Nancy Hirschmann, Alison Jaggar, Diana Meyers, Elizabeth Minnich, Robin Schott, and Margaret Urban Walker. I learned—and am still learning—from numerous critiques and suggestions offered by people who heard this. I would like to thank especially Diemut Bubeck, Claudia Card, Ashok Gangadeen, Aryeh Kosman, Danielle MacBeth, and Lucius Outlaw.

1. I refer in particular to Susan Moller Okin, *Justice, Gender and the Family,* New York, Basic Books, 1989. I rely on Okin's work and bibliography throughout this chapter.

2. By dominant theories of justice, I have in mind especially John Rawls's *A Theory of Justice* and his and others' developments of the theory. Gauthier and Darwall have also figured in recent feminist discussions of justice, for example, in those of Iris Young and Virginia Held. Habermas has figured in discussions by Iris Young and Seyla Benhabib. I speak of dominant rather than liberal theories for two reasons: under certain interpretations, Rawlsian theories can be construed as radical; the failure of the dominant theories transcends politics. I recognize, however, that none of my criticisms apply directly to, for example, Marxist theories of justice. John Rawls, *A Theory of Justice,* Cambridge: Harvard University Press, 1971. Stephen Darwall, *Impartial Reason,* Ithaca: Cornell University Press, 1983. David Gauthier, *Morals by Agreement,* Oxford: Clarendon Press, 1986. Jürgen Habermas, *The Theory of Communicative Action,* Boston, Beacon Press, 1983, 1987. Seyla Benhabib, *Critique, Norm and Utopia,* New York: Columbia University Press, 1986. Virginia Held, *Feminist Morality: Transforming Culture, Society, and Politics,* Chicago: University of Chicago Press, 1993. Iris Marion Young, *Justice and the Politics of Difference,* Princeton: Princeton University Press, 1990.

3. The literature developing on the ethics of care is now vast. In my own thinking about care, I draw upon work by Annette Baier, Seyla Benhabib, Lyn Mikel Brown, Claudia Card, Patricia Hill Collins, Berenice Fisher, Beverly Harrison, Nancy Hirschmann, Sarah Lucia Hoagland, Nona Lyons, Joan Tronto, Margaret Urban Walker, Patricia Williams; the authors of *Women's Ways of Knowing;* and many others too numerous to mention. I am especially indebted to Virginia Held's work in feminist ethics, most recently extended and recapitulated in *Feminist Morality.* I am also indebted to Carol Gilligan and Nel Noddings, the theorists most directly associated with and responsible for proposing an ethics of care. For Carol Gilligan see especially *In a Different Voice,* Cambridge, Harvard University Press, 1982; and Carol Gilligan, Janie Ward, and Jill Taylor, *Mapping the Moral Domain,* Cambridge, Harvard University Press, 1988. For Nel Noddings, see especially *Caring,* Berkeley, University of California Press, 1984; and *Women and Evil,* 1990. *Feminist Ethics,* Lawrence: University Press of Kansas, 1991, edited and introduced by Claudia Card, offers several original articles that criticize and sometimes develop the ethics of care. *An Ethic of Care,* New York, Routledge, 1992, edited by Mary Jeanne Larrabee, collects several central articles in the ethics of care and provides a useful bibliography.

4. See especially Held, *Feminist Morality;* also Nel Noddings, *Women and Evil,* Berkeley, University of California Press, 1990.

5. Occasionally, I have heard feminists come close to rejecting justice—described as abstract or masculine—in favor of care. Socialist feminists criticize dominant theories of justice, of course, but usually without explicit reference to families.

6. This is largely the tactic of Susan Okin (*Justice, Gender and the Family*), who also offers—to my mind unconvincing—modifications of Rawls.

7. This is the tactic of Nel Noddings, particularly in "Impartiality and Care," unpublished manuscript.

8. Here I am closest to Iris Young and Virginia Held, whose writings I draw upon.

9. There are many ways to situate moral phenomena and reasoning other than within a justice-care framework. Within the justice-care framework, other ethics or moral principles retain their salience. Principles of liberty, to take just one example, acquire distinct significance within theories and practices of care as well as in the more familiar context of justice. Indeed, one virtue of the justice-care framework is that it gets us to think freshly about familiar principles by considering them from two, shifting, perspectives.

10. Gilligan has offered several versions of the relation of justice and care. Here I draw upon "Gender Difference and Morality: The Empirical Base," in *Women and Moral Theory*, edited by Eva Kittay and Diana Meyers, Totowa, NJ, Rowman and Littlefield, 1987.

11. Peter Winch, *Simone Weil: "The Just Balance,"* Oxford, Blackwell, 1989, p. 149. Winch is describing only Weil's account of justice, but what Winch says about Weil's view of justice I apply to both justice and care.

12. For an overview of possible relations between justice and care, see Lawrence Blum, "Gilligan and Kohlberg: Implications for Moral Theory," *Ethics,* April 1988, pp. 472–491; and Seyla Benhabib, "The Debate over Women and Moral Theory Revisited," in *Situating the Self,* New York, Routledge, 1992.

13. For a discussion of the debate about evidence for gender difference, see Larrabee, *An Ethic of Care.*

14. See especially Carol Gilligan and Grant Wiggins, "The Origins of Morality in Early Childhood Relationships," and Carol Gilligan and Jane Attanuci, "Two Moral Orientations," both in Carol Gilligan, Janie Ward, and Jill Taylor, eds., *Mapping the Moral Domain*, Cambridge, Harvard University Press, 1988. Gilligan seems to suggest that the sense of justice develops primarily from negative experiences of powerlessness and inequality—and, I might add, humiliation and abuse—that the child experiences or, I would add, witnesses. A sense of care develops primarily from positive experiences of attachment. Although a sense of justice also requires positive experiences—John Rawls's account of these still seems among the best—and a drive toward care might follow from experiencing or witnessing neglect and isolation, there is something right, I think, about Gilligan's perception. This raises one among the many complexities I resist discussing here.

15. See Will Kymlicka's "Rethinking the Family," which takes Susan Okin to task for just this omission. *Philosophy and Public Affairs,* Winter 1991, pp. 77–97.

16. Throughout this section I am drawing heavily upon Susan Okin, (*Justice, Gender and the Family*), who has set out the case against family justice made by, especially, Allan Bloom and Roberto Unger and made indirectly by Michael Sandel, Alasdair MacIntyre, and other theorists of justice. I draw on Okin equally in responding to the claim that families cannot provide or afford the "circumstances of justice."

17. George Gilder was an early proponent of the pessimist's view. Susan Okin attributes views like these to Allan Bloom. I have many times heard versions of the pessimist's view expressed by women and men.

18. Okin, *Justice, Gender and the Family.*

19. Seyla Benhabib, "The Generalized and the Concrete Other," originally in Kittay and Meyers, *Women and Moral Theory,* now in her *Situating the Self.*

20. I take these phrases from Benhabib, "Generalized and Concrete Other."

21. Especially well argued by Noddings in "Impartiality and Care."

22. See, for example, Allen Buchanan, "Justice as Reciprocity vs. Subject-Centered Justice," *Philosophy and Public Affairs,* Summer, 1990.

23. I am indebted throughout this discussion to Nancy Hirschmann, *Rethinking Obligation,* Ithaca, Cornell University Press, 1992. As Hirschmann points out, what I call family obligations are often construed as duties—especially when these are assigned to women—and therefore "natural" and beyond consent. I am not here distinguishing between duty and obligation.

24. Simone Weil, "The Love of God and Affliction," in George H. Panichas, ed., *Simone Weil Reader,* Mt. Kisco, NY, Moyer Bell, 1977, pp. 440 ff. The entire discussion is relevant to the weighting of physical and nonphysical pain.

25. Philip Greven (*Spare the Child,* New York, Alfred Knopf, 1991) offers a useful and passionate account of the pervasiveness of family assault. Colleagues, co-conferees, and students confirm the view that although some families are remarkably free of assault and domination, there is no subcultural group in the United States that does not include practices of family assault and that many families consider assault a legitimate and even necessary practice. *Beliefs* about assault are affected by racist projections of violence onto African Americans in particular as well as onto other "minority" or stigmatized groups. It is also true that parents without funds, space, and time and who themselves are socially humiliated are more likely to assault.

26. Thucidydes, quoted by Michael Walzer in *Just and Unjust Wars,* New York, Basic Books, 1977, p. 5.

27. Ann Jones, *The Next Time, She'll Be Dead,* Boston, Beacon Press 1994, p. 4. Italics in original.

28. The phrase is Patricia Williams's, in *Alchemy of Race and Rights,* Cambridge, Harvard University Press, 1991, p. 148.

29. Simone Weil, "Human Personality," in *Simone Weil Reader,* p. 315. See also "The Love of God and Affliction." Weil adds: "For if, as often happens, it is only the result of a misunderstanding, then the injustice consists in the inadequacy of the explanation." In my view there is no adequate explanation for family assault. But assaulters who do attempt to explain by offering justifications or excuses, themselves tacitly acknowledge requirements of justice. Adequate explanation is important in countering humiliating effects of nonviolent coercion—a matter I allude to later. I am indebted to Weil's thinking about justice and also deeply at odds with her insistence on and construction of the "impersonality" of justice.

30. Young, *Justice and the Politics of Difference.*

31. When domination is identified with injustice it, like injustice, is apt to be considered a characteristic of institutions. See, for example, Young, *Justice and the Politics of Difference,* p. 38. In my view, domination—and justice—can characterize relationships as well as institutions. To cite one example, white Americans' domination of black Americans is enacted in policies and practices that construct economic and political public life. This domination is also reflected in the personal relations—sexual, procreative, family, collegial—of both races and in their daily private activities such as shopping, hailing a taxi, or ordering at a restaurant. Many social activities that cannot be easily designated as public

or private—for example, a visit to a doctor or employment office, a conversation with a potential landlord, a teachers' conference, a "private" journey on "public" transportation—are typically affected by practices of racial domination. A person's earliest experiences of domination—as participant or witness—often occur within families, themselves social institutions, or between family members and subordinated or dominating "others." Accordingly, family relationships and history offer a particularly useful vantage for exploring the phenomenology of domination.

32. I am adapting a metaphor developed by Patricia Williams with particular reference to white Americans' domination of black Americans in *Alchemy of Race and Rights,* especially part 4. See also Maria Lugones, "Playfulness, 'World' Travelling, and Loving Perception," *Hypatia* 2, no. 2, Summer 1987, pp. 3–19.

33. Robin May Schott in "The Gender of Enlightenment" (unpublished manuscript by courtesy of the author) quotes Kant as writing in a letter to C. G. Schutz, dated July 10, 1797, "The right to use a man for domestic purposes is analogous to a right to an object, for which the servant is not free to terminate his connections with the household and he may therefore be caught and returned by force."

34. An assaulter, or even a nonassaultive thoroughgoing dominator, often appears to her victims as unpredictably and unremittingly willful. To resist willful assaulters, it may be necessary to violate their embodied willfulness—battered women injure their batterers, armies are said to engage in just wars. As I mentioned, when I speak of assaulters I have primarily in mind mothers, with whom I identify. My emphases would shift if I were thinking primarily of assaulted women.

35. What I take "Freudian" theories to reveal:

   1. The first ego is a bodily ego; the bodily ego is always already, from the start social. The ego is therefore constituted within and by physical-social relations such as holding, hurting, soothing, feeding, restraining, carrying, or beating. Because the ego is bodily social, embodied willfulness, an ego expression, is also social. Here I draw upon "Freudians" as diverse as D. W. Winnicott, Melanie Klein, Teresa Brennan, and, of course, Freud.

   2. The relationships within which any individual's experience of embodied willfulness is constructed turn crucially upon a need, said to be as important as food, to be "recognized" by those on whom one depends. Here, in addition to Winnicott, I draw especially upon Jessica Benjamin, *The Bonds of Love,* New York, Pantheon Books, 1988; and Nancy Chodorow, "Gender, Relation and Difference in Psychoanalytic Perspective," in *Feminism and Psychoanalytic Theory,* New Haven, CT, Yale, 1989.

   3. These physical-social relationships do not come neat but are created amid complex and developmentally entrenched fantasies. Hence bodily terror, pain, or pleasure experienced within these relationships are also embedded in fantasy. Here I draw upon varieties of "Freudians" starting with Freud, "A Child Is Being Beaten," London, Hogarth Press, 1919, Standard edition, vol. 17.

36. A respect for embodied willfulness may also lead to a deeper appreciation of injustices that are wrought less directly through bodies. Two examples: When birthgiving is recognized as a primary expression of embodied willfulness, then attempts to appropriate birthgivers' labor or deprive women of pleasures and powers because of their capacity to give birth can be seen as an assault upon embodied willfulness. Similarly, to persecute or

sabotage sexual desire is to undermine the bodily ego; to alienate a person from his sexual desires is to alienate him from his own embodied willfulness.

37. This is apparently Simone Weil's view and has been discussed by Peter Winch in *Simone Weil: "The Just Balance."*

38. I borrow here from Neda Hadjikhani, "On Humility: Engaging the Moral Agency of Non-Western Women." (unpublished manuscript courtesy of the author). Hadjikhani discusses Western women's relation to non-Western mothers who advocate female circumcision. She adapts concepts drawn from Carol Gilligan and from my *Maternal Thinking,* Boston, Beacon Press, 1989.

About the Book

When feminist philosophers first turned their attention to traditional ethical theory, its almost exclusive emphasis upon justice, rights, abstract rationality, and individual autonomy came under special criticism. Women's experiences seemed to suggest the need for a focus on care, empathetic relations, and the interdependence of persons.

The most influential readings of what has become an extremely lively and fruitful debate are reproduced here along with important new contributions by Alison Jaggar and Sara Ruddick. As this volume testifies, there is no agreement on the important questions about the relationship between justice and care, but the debate has deepened and enriched our understanding in many ways.

Justice and Care is a valuable collection of readings—an essential tool for anyone studying the state of feminist thought in particular or ethical theory in general.

About the Contributors

Annette C. Baier is Distinguished Service Professor of Philosophy at the University of Pittsburgh. She was educated at the University of Otago, New Zealand, and at Oxford University. Her books include *Postures of the Mind: Essays on Mind and Morals* (1985); *A Progress of Sentiments: Reflections on Hume's Treatise* (1991); and *Moral Prejudices: Essays on Ethics* (1994).

Claudia Card is professor of philosophy at the University of Wisconsin and faculty affiliate in women's studies and environmental studies. She is the author of *Lesbian Choices* (1995), editor of *Feminist Ethics* (1991) and of *Adventures in Lesbian Philosophy* (1994), and has published more than 50 articles and reviews.

Patricia Hill Collins is professor in the Departments of African-American Studies and Sociology at the University of Cincinnati. Her research has dealt primarily with issues of gender, race, and social class. Her book *Black Feminist Thought: Knowledge, Consciousness and the Politics of Empowerment* (1990) has won many awards. She is coeditor with Margaret Andersen of *Race, Class, and Gender: An Anthology* (2d ed. 1995).

Marilyn Friedman is associate professor of philosophy at Washington University–St. Louis. Her areas of specialization are ethics, social philosophy, and feminist theory. She is the author of *What Are Friends For?: Feminist Perspectives on Personal Relationships and Moral Theory* (1993); coauthor of *Political Correctness: For and Against* (1994); and coeditor of *Feminism and Community* (1995).

Carol Gilligan is professor in the human development and psychology program at Harvard Graduate School of Education and a founding member of the Harvard Project on Women's Psychology and Girls' Development. She is the author of *In a Different Voice: Psychological Theory and Women's Development* (1982) and coauthor with Lyn Mikel Brown of *Meeting at the Crossroads: Women's Psychology and Girls Development* (1992).

Virginia Held is professor of philosophy and of women's studies at Hunter College and the Graduate School of the City University of New York. She is the author of many articles and books on moral, political, and social theory, including *The Public Interest and Individual Interests* (1970); *Rights and Goods: Justifying Social Action* (1984); and *Feminist Morality: Transforming Culture, Society, and Politics* (1993).

Alison M. Jaggar is professor of philosophy and women studies at the University of Colorado–Boulder. Her books include *Feminist Frameworks*, coedited with Paula Rothenberg (3d ed. 1993); *Feminist Politics and Human Nature* (1983); and *Living with Contradictions: Controversies in Feminist Social Ethics* (Westview Press, Inc., 1994). She was a founding member of the Society for Women in Philosophy and is past chair of the American Philosophical Association Committee on the Status of Women.

Nel Noddings is Lee L. Jacks Professor of Child Education at Stanford University. Her area of special interest is philosophy of education and, within that, ethics, moral education, and mathematical education. The latest among her nine books is *Educating for Intelligent Belief or Unbelief* (1993).

Sara Ruddick teaches philosophy and women's studies at the New School for Social Research. She is the author of *Maternal Thinking: Toward a Philosophy of Peace* (1989) and is currently at work on a new book on the moral struggles involved in bearing and raising children.

Joan C. Tronto is a political theorist who teaches in the Political Science Department and the Women's Studies Program at Hunter College of the City University of New York. Her publications include essays on the ethic of care and *Moral Boundaries: A Political Argument for an Ethic of Care* (1993).

Margaret Urban Walker is associate professor of philosophy at Fordham University. She has written on moral agency, judgment, and responsibility, and the importance of feminist critical perspectives for ethics. She is working on a book about moral authority which pays special attention to questions of authority and representation in ethics.

Index